RÉSUMÉ WRITING

Résumé Writing
A COMPREHENSIVE HOW-TO-DO-IT GUIDE

Burdette E. Bostwick

FOURTH EDITION

WILEY

JOHN WILEY & SONS
New York • Chichester • Brisbane • Toronto • Singapore

This publication is designed to provide accurate and
authoritative information in regard to the subject
matter covered. It is sold with the understanding that
the publisher is not engaged in rendering legal, accounting,
or other professional service. If legal advice or other
expert assistance is required, the services of a competent
professional person should be sought. *From a Declaration
of Principles jointly adopted by a Committee of the
American Bar Association and a Community of Publishers.*

Library of Congress Cataloging in Publication Data:

Bostwick, Burdette E.
    Résume writing: a comprehensive how-to-do-it guide / Burdette
E. Bostwick.—4th ed.
        p.   cm.
    Includes bibliographical references.
    ISBN 0-471-51415-2.—ISBN 0-471-51416-0 (pbk.)
    1. Résumés (Employment)—Handbooks, manuals, etc.
    2. Applications
for positions—Handbooks, manuals, etc.   I. Title.
    HF5383.B57   1990
    650.14—dc20   89-37360
                                                                    CIP

Printed in the United States of America

10 9 8 7 6 5 4 3 2 1

Learning how to look for a job has become as much of a discipline as learning the skills for the job itself.

From an article on careers by Deborah Blumenthal in *The New York Times,* September 5, 1987.

In order that people may be happy in their work, these three things are needed: They must be fit for it: They must not do too much of it: And they must have a sense of success in it.

John Ruskin, *Pre-Raphaelitism* (1851).

When men are employed they are best contented; for on days they worked they were good-natured and cheerful, and, with the consciousness of having done a good day's work, they spent the evening jollily; but on our idle days they were mutinous and quarrelsome.

Benjamin Franklin, *Autobiography* (1793–1868), Chapter 1.

Executives don't need to be told they should be farmers.

Anonymous (1990).

PREFACE

Strictly speaking, this book is about how best to find the job you want. Writings of various kinds are the most efficient way of reaching that goal. The most important writing to start with is the résumé. It may be all the writing you need, or it may lead to other writing more appropriate to your particular situation. We show you how to use your résumé when you have finished it. All other writing about yourself proceeds from the résumé. The importance of writings other than résumés is stressed. Résumés and other writings will open doors for you and possibly do more.

As president of my own consulting firm, I work with corporations and with individuals. In my work with individuals, I utilize the techniques described in this book with a success rate of at least 80 percent.

This fourth edition includes new material and changes to expand the usefulness of the book. There has been a proliferation of new directories to aid the job seeker. These are named and explained. Your local library can be of inestimable benefit. Data have been revised to bring them up to date. New insights have been recognized and included. We have noted and embodied suggestions by readers and by educators who have used previous editions of this book as a basis for student job-search instruction. Some job-solicitation campaigns produce scores of replies; we provide a system for keeping track of them.

Whether you are unemployed, seek a new career, wish to test your marketability, or plan to move to greener pastures, your writing can be your magic carpet. It is the best way, and sometimes the only way, to disseminate important information about yourself. It is your personal advertising. Users of résumés are successful people. Surveys of those who hire show that résumés are the preferred basis on which to grant interviews.

Why should you read a book to learn how to write a résumé? Because the effectiveness of your writing may be worth hundreds of thousands or millions of dollars to you over the course of your career; and because you want your writing to be superior to that of the general run of job candidates. Writing about yourself is a specialized, concise, formal, and analytical art. People who write about themselves without training can usually be recognized by the inadequacy of their writing. There are prizes for writing a good résumé—higher income, greater achievement, increased happiness. (All the résumés in this book are based on actual résumés described as successful by the people who used them.)

How do companies sell their products? They advertise. You are a product, advertising yourself for employment.

Television is the medium favored by political candidates. No job seeker can afford this kind of publicity. Your primary advertising is your résumé. Your résumé must be forged into a sophisticated tool, honed to accomplish a specific objective: to present you better than your competition to your market.

BURDETTE E. BOSTWICK

Springfield, New Jersey
January 1990

CONTENTS

Illustrations, xi
Source of Data, xii
1. What Is a Résumé?, 1
2. Who Uses Résumés?, 8
3. Why Write a Résumé?, 11
4. The Nature of the Résumé, 13
5. The Need for a Superior Résumé, 14
6. Résumé Length, 19
7. Résumé Language, 22
8. The Elements of a Résumé, 25
9. The Right Résumé Is Muscular, 38
10. The Ten Résumé Styles, 41
    Basic Résumé, 42
    Chronological Résumé, 48
    Chronological Résumé with Summary Page, 53
    Functional Résumé, 68
    Functional Résumé, 68
    Functional-by-Company (Institution) Résumé, 78
    Harvard Résumé, 87
    Narrative Résumé, 92
    Professional Résumé, 99
    Accomplishment Résumé, 107
11. Getting Ready to Write Your Résumé, 111
12. Writing Your Résumé, 123
13. Typing Your Résumé, 127
14. Sales and Broadcast Letters, 131
15. Using the Calendar, 168

16. Job Campaign Record, 171
17. How to Read and Answer Newspaper Advertisements, 173
18. Creating a Mailing List, 181
19. Job Hunting in the Computer/Telecommunications Age, 185
20. Career Changes, 188
21. Relocation, Housing, and Inflation, 203
22. Job Interviews, 210
23. The Employment Application Form, 214
24. Established Services Available to the Job Seeker, 215
25. Job-Search Suggestions, 220
26. Job-Search Maxims, 223
Appendix A. Supplementary Résumé Examples, 229
Appendix B. Useful Words and Phrases, 308
Appendix C. Job Responsibilities in Major Job Classifications, 319
**Appendix D. A Definition of Employment Levels Used in This
   Volume, 328**
Résumés Index, 331
Letters Index, 332
General Index, 333

ILLUSTRATIONS

Help-Wanted Display Advertising, 7
Men and Women and Résumés, 8
Résumé Users: By Age Group, 10
Résumé Users: By Job Classification, 21
Résumé Users: Employed and Unemployed, 29
Analysis of Résumé Users: Entry Position, 39
Influence of College Education on Lifetime Earnings, 42
Analysis of Résumé Users: Finance, 52
Analysis of Résumé Users: Marketing, 91
Analysis of Résumé Users: Administration, 98
Analysis of Résumé Users: Production, 106
Analysis of Résumé Users: Retail, 122
Example of Pica Type, 129
Example of Elite Type, 130
Job Competition, 179

SOURCE OF DATA

The résumé data analyzed and reported in this book are taken from a sample of 1,000 résumés in my own files. They reflect information provided in more than 60 employment classifications. To my knowledge, such data have never before been systematized and analyzed. There may well be a bias toward upper and middle management. Those entering the job market may be underrepresented in the data reported here. The charts disclose significant and interesting facts about the persons who prepare résumés.

RÉSUMÉ WRITING

ONE

WHAT IS A RÉSUMÉ?

THE SHARPEST WEAPON IN YOUR JOB SEARCH ARSENAL

The word résumé (from the Latin *resumere,* "to take up again," and the French *résumer,* "to resume, summarize"), pronounced ray-zu-may, is defined by Webster's *Third International Dictionary* as a "short account of one's career and qualifications prepared typically by an applicant for a position." Sometimes the term *curriculum vitae,* pronounced ka-rick'-you-lum-vī-tee, is used. A résumé can also be defined in a number of other ways.

1. A résumé is an essential part of a job search at the managerial level.
2. A résumé, or the tools that derive from it, is the most effective instrument for finding work or for gaining one's desired vocational situation.
3. A résumé is a door opener to an interview.
4. A résumé is a formal document describing the qualifications of a job seeker.

5. A résumé is a self-appraisal that stresses past and present accomplishments in order to indicate future potential.

6. A résumé is a tool for self-evaluation that, when completed, may suggest new steps toward the attainment of goals.

7. A résumé is a brief business biography or vocational history that emphasizes experience, accomplishment, education, and objectives expressed in favorable terms.

A résumé is your personal advertisement. It is the most widely accepted medium of communication between a job seeker and a prospective employer. It differs from an ordinary advertisement in that it is not directed to the general public but to the employer. An employer may receive hundreds of résumés for a single position. If you wish to be one of the few selected for an interview, you must make your résumé superior to the common run.

Writing a résumé is not an easy task. The difficulty lies in organization and objectivity. It is not as natural to write about yourself as it is to write about a place, an event, or even another person. There are relatively few great autobiographies! At least 70 percent of the résumés I read are deficient in some respect. You can make yours a superior document by studying the methods of its preparation.

The résumé, crucial in obtaining an interview, may affect the final decision to hire. Its role is increasing because of more intense competition for jobs and possibly slower job growth as capital formation is restricted and corporations and institutions learn to function without less-productive and less-necessary employees.

You can use this book in two ways. Preferably, you can learn to write an effective résumé, stamped with your own hallmark. Or, possibly, you can adapt one of the résumé examples as a model for your own résumé. You need not master all of the résumé styles—they are included to show the options. Pick the one best suited to you.

The words *chronological* and *functional* occur frequently in this book. *Chronological* refers to the arrangement of data in the order of time of occurrence, but, unlike as in a biography or history, the order is reversed. That is, in a résumé the most recent experience is described first and older experiences last. (See the résumé on p. 48.)

Thus the main body of our résumé called *Chronological Résumé with Summary Page* (see Chapter 11, p. 43), starting with the second page, is chronological. The *summary page* is a brief interpretation of the *succeeding* pages. It is written last but placed first in the completed résumé.

The word *functional* refers to a style of résumé that describes activities in each area of experience without reference to the companies for which the function was performed or to the time of performance. For example:

EXPERIENCE

GENERAL
MANAGER

Held P&L responsibility for $10 million division. Reorganized production and cost accounting departments. Reduced costs. Set up new marketing strategies. Increased sales. Also consolidated two manufacturing plants for improved efficiency.

MARKETING
MANAGEMENT

Surveyed market for power tools. Established share of market goals for each territory; assigned quotas; installed new salesperson's compensation plan. Redirected advertising. Increased sales 36% within 2 years for one company, 23% for another company, and 10% for a third.

EMPLOYMENT HISTORY

A.B.C. Company, Chicago, IL
D.E.F. Company, Portland, ME
X.Y.Z. Company, Newark, NJ

These experiences (described in summary form here) might apply to one, two, or all three of the companies.

Brief descriptions of the various résumé styles, together with our recommendations, are given below. Detailed analyses appear later.

1. **Basic Résumé.** The best form for one entering the job market or having very limited experience. (See p. 44.)

2. **Chronological Résumé.** The second-best form (sometimes the best) for a middle- or upper-management executive, since it permits the sharpest delineation of accomplishments. (See p. 48.)

3. **Chronological Résumé with Summary Page.** The best form for a middle- or upper-management executive. In addition to permitting a clear listing of accomplishments it also contains a summary page. (See p. 53.)

4. **Functional Résumé.** An excellent form, especially for one with experience in several job functions, such as marketing, finance, and general management. A preferred form for educators at the administrative level. Some personnel executives profess a liking for this form. (See p. 66.)

5. **Functional-by-Company (Institution) Résumé.** Advantageously associates function with the company for which it was performed, but loses the impact of the pure *Functional Résumé.* (See p. 78.)

6. **Harvard Résumé.** Basically, a chronological résumé with a few distinguishing features. (See p. 87.)

7. **Creative Résumé.** For special uses only. Has no definite structure. (See p. 70.)

8. **Narrative Résumé.** A specialized form that may serve well in situations deviating from the norm. (See p. 92.)

9. **Professional Résumé.** For lawyers, doctors, teachers, and other professionals whose education and accreditation are of primary importance to the reader. (See p. 99.)

10. **Accomplishment Résumé.** Not generally recommended because its raison d'être is to camouflage, but has its advantages. (See p. 107.)

The definition of a résumé is important and bears repeating: it is a short account of one's career and qualifications prepared typically by an applicant for a position. The key words are "application for a position." In the conventional realm of résumé writing this has come to mean a stylized form of writing. Conventional wisdom abridges résumé to two basic forms, chronological and functional. I recognize 10 forms. One writer says the functional form "seems to be the format most frequently chosen by individuals who wish to disguise some flaw in their credentials." Yet, it is the form preferred in academic, public administration, and other areas.

A reviewer of this book said, "There is no such thing as a 'creative' résumé or an 'accomplishment' résumé." It's true; there was not until this book was published. The classifications I accept are my own and the titles are my own nomenclature. The titles are descriptive rather than memorable or elegant. Actually, I believe that even certain kinds of letters can be properly classed as résumés. The expansion of résumé forms has been dictated by my exposure to many different kinds of job applicants not ordinarily within the experience of personnel executives limited to the types of people hired within their industries. Recruiters and personnel executives do not conduct job campaigns for job candidates. It is only when one works with job seekers that one recognizes that approaches to the job market must be expanded beyond traditional paths. I refer to such candidates as attorneys, judges, public administrators, retailers, architects, bankers, educators, senior citizens, basketball coaches, and career changers, to name a few. There is no way to comprehend their needs without having worked with them.

The selection of a résumé form may also change with your career. You might start with the *Basic Résumé,* graduate after a few years to the *Chronological Résumé,* and finally proceed to the *Chronological Résumé with Summary Page* or to the *Functional Résumé.*

A *covering* letter is an essential short introduction to a résumé. Of the samples included in this book there will be one more "right" for you than any of the others, which you can then amend to fit your circumstances. A *broadcast* letter—different from a résumé and a covering letter—is also fully explained.

Look upon writing a résumé as being akin to drawing up a contract, writing a will, solving a complicated tax problem. You have all the elements you need. Analyze each one, express it suitably, and place it in logical juxtaposition to the other elements.

A survey of hundreds of companies conducted by the author shows these ways to get interviews, as specified by those companies:

1. Knowing someone who will interview you or will arrange an interview for you.
2. Answering help-wanted advertisements with a résumé or letter.
3. Sending uninvited résumés or other writing to possible employers.
4. Answering help-wanted advertisements with a telephone call, if invited to do so.
5. Making uninvited telephone calls to possible employers.
6. Making cold calls on personnel departments.
7. Attending campus interview sessions.
8. Advertising your availability through ads in the employment-wanted columns.
9. Sending your résumé to executive search firms.
10. Visiting employment agencies.
11. Job postings or promotions from within.
12. Attending employers' Open Houses.

Of these methods, 44.3 percent demand résumés and some others involve résumés; 8.2 percent require writing of some kind (letters, proposals) usually based on a résumé; 20.2 percent of interviews result from knowing the right person, often requiring a résumé during or after the interview.

Campus interviewing is important for entry-level jobs with large companies. Recruiters usually ask for a résumé.

Thus résumés are vitally important in over 50 percent of methods used to create interviews. In fact, we think a manager cannot normally complete the interviewed/hired succession without a résumé.

Help-Wanted Display Advertising

A survey of 1000 "help-wanted," "positions available" advertisements in *The New York Times* (Sunday) and *The Wall Street Journal* was conducted over a period of 5 to 6 weeks in February and March of 1987. The results were as follows:

1. Ask for résumé specifically   757
2. Ask for reply with full details (probably requiring résumé)   118
3. Ask for reply only   74
4. Ask for reply by telephone   51
                                                        Total   1,000

Items 1 and 2, involving résumés, came to 87.5 percent. Adding item 3, for which a résumé would be the most appropriate reply, we find 94.5 percent of the advertisements to be résumé related.

TWO

WHO USES RÉSUMÉS?

Almost every job seeker—whether unemployed or employed but wishing to change positions—needs a résumé. Résumés are prepared by persons at all levels of employment: judges, lawyers, cabinet members, managers, chief executive officers, administrators, bookkeepers, secretaries. In my experience and according to surveys, most résumés are prepared by those looking for management, professional, or performing arts positions. Résumés are not usually required for clerical and skilled labor jobs, though their wider use might possibly expand and upgrade job opportunities in these areas. The only individuals who do not need résumés are those whose outstanding careers make it unnecessary for them to seek jobs—rather, jobs seek them.

MEN AND WOMEN AND RÉSUMÉS

Executive search firms receive thousands of résumés each year. The reasons cited in this book for résumé use by job candidates are equally valid for both men and women. Furthermore, with some exceptions, there is no reason for the résumés of men to be different from those of women, or vice versa, at management levels. Twenty years and longer

8

ago women often occupied positions where résumé use was not a requirement. Many placements were made by employment agencies or secretarial schools. Nurses frequently came from nursing schools; visits were made directly to department store and insurance company personnel offices where female employment is heavy. And, of course, more so for women than for men, employment was sought near home base. Currently women are becoming as mobile as men and their need for résumé use is therefore expanding.

New social influences and economic forces have irrevocably reshaped the old employment patterns, bringing expanded opportunities to women while at the same time bringing them to use the job-search techniques that have always been successful for men.

RÉSUMÉ USERS: BY AGE GROUP

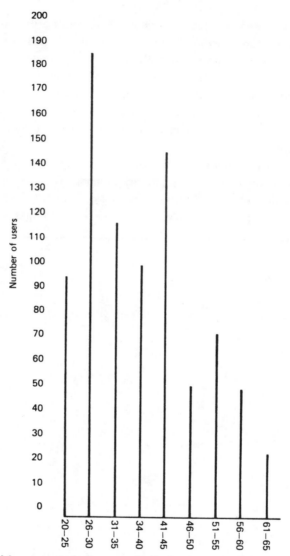

Number of users

200
190
180
170
160
150
140
130
120
110
100
90
80
70
60
50
40
30
20
10
0

20–25 26–30 31–35 34–40 41–45 46–50 51–55 56–60 61–65

As would be expected, the greatest incidence of résumé use is in the age group from 26 to 45 years (533). The most frequent users are between the ages of 26 and 30; those between 41 and 45 are next. Most of those in the age group 20 to 25 are new to the job market. (From a sample of 1000, of whom 799 gave ages.)

THREE

WHY WRITE A RÉSUMÉ?

A résumé serves to introduce you to the employer and help you gain a personal interview. You need a résumé because for most advertised *management* jobs (see p. 7) a résumé is required before an interview will be granted. Employers require résumés because they are executive time-savers. A personal interview takes hours; a résumé can be read in a few minutes.

There are other reasons for writing a résumé:

1. A résumé forms the basis for a mail campaign about yourself, using either the actual résumé or a summary of it in the form of a broadcast letter. The 50 percent or more of available jobs that are never advertised must be sought by mail.

2. A résumé can be used to test your marketability while you remain safely employed.

3. A résumé helps you to organize the facts of your accomplishments, clarifying what you can or wish to do in the future. Many advisors recommend that a résumé be updated every six months or once a year. You thus remain continuously aware of your progress, or lack of it, and of your up-to-the-minute responsibilities and achievements. What you did last year may have lost importance by reason of newer accomplishments.

4. A résumé in expanded form may help gain academic credits for "life work," an important opportunity offered by many universities.

5. A résumé may be utilized when buying a business to impart information about yourself to the seller.

6. A résumé can serve to solicit business if you are, for example, a consultant, a freelance artist or writer, or a part-time worker. A more elaborate brochure explaining your qualifications can be based on it.

7. A résumé prepares you for your job interview by forcing you to think about and express yourself in an organized way. A résumé is your personal guidance manual for speaking about yourself fluently and unhesitatingly.

FOUR

THE NATURE
OF THE RÉSUMÉ

If you do not value yourself highly, others will not value you highly. The way you feel about yourself will show through your writing. If your credentials make you the right person for the position available, the employer needs you as much as you need the employment.

A résumé is a sales presentation of yourself. It should not be a mere detailing of past job experiences. It must be alive and interesting and must present your accomplishments to the maximum degree. Make it a portrait in color, rather than a black-and-white photograph. Will it favorably differentiate you from other applicants for the position? The reader of your résumé should be able to infer from your past achievements your expected contributions in a new position. The résumé should be honest—do not inflate your abilities beyond your capacity to produce.

There are many characteristics that make people come alive as individuals—different from the crowd. Accomplishments also can be avocational and interesting to mention. In what ways you are equipping yourself for greater responsibilities in the future is of interest. Participation in scouting, your church, your community, your children's school, as an alumnus of your own school or college, successful fund raising, and other activities can be utilized to generate interest *if vocational material is inadequate.*

Your personal assets and liabilities determine how your résumé is planned and executed.

FIVE

THE NEED FOR A SUPERIOR RÉSUMÉ

To get a job, you need not be superior to other applicants; few would have jobs if only ideal applicants were hired! However, your résumé should make you appear to be superior. An employer may receive hundreds of resumes for one position. A large corporation may handle 50,000 or more résumés a year. You can improve your chance of being one of the few selected for an interview by studying how to prepare your résumé, a study relatively free of competition and likely to bring great rewards.

In actual fact, you may be superior to other applicants but no one will know it unless you get a chance to explain your qualifications. The written word is different from the spoken word. It is normal that what you say about yourself in writing seems better to you, and is better, than what you say about yourself orally. This is because in writing about yourself you have to think more clearly. The chore of writing demands clearer exposition. In a conversation you can repeat yourself or erase previous errors in a succeeding statement. What appears in writing cannot be changed. This also underscores again how important a résumé can be in helping you to express yourself properly during an interview.

Furthermore, the value of a résumé is often in the eye of the beholder: one may look for brevity (as in the case of the employment agency); another may require an ideal education and employment background (as in executive search); and another may be impressed by "buzz" words in specialized vocations. A fine résumé eclipses these restricting approaches. It overwhelms nit-picking and demands objective reading rather than subjective evaluation.

A résumé is a required job-hunting tool and can be decisive at the job award level. A good résumé can transform a nondescript applicant into a prime candidate. The techniques suggested have enjoyed immense success.

Aside from their form and style, read some of the résumés and letters for their content. They are miniature biographies of achievers, perhaps in your own specialty. It is useful to know how successful people have handled their jobs.

The résumé will create the decision whether or not to interview. The résumé will screen out 90 percent of the applicants. To be one of the 10 percent accepted for an interview, your résumé must be superior. This demands research of your mind. "Style is the dress of thoughts" (Philip Dormer Stanhope, Earl of Chesterfield, November 24, 1749).

The physical appearance of your résumé has a strong effect on its potency. Pay attention to spacing, paragráphing, headlines, underlining, upper- and lowercasing, margins, hyphenations, and centering. "Whatever is worth doing at all, is worth doing well" (Earl of Chesterfield, March 6, 1742). Your prospective employer wants to know not only what your responsibilities are or were, but what you are doing or did to meet them. List both your responsibilities and your accomplishments. Describe your accomplishments as specifically as possible; give amount, percentage, size, volume, degree of improvement.

EXAMPLE:

Responsibilities:

- Administering and mailing audits to about 400 accounts monthly.
- Test and final runs of monthly statistics report, on computer.

Accomplishments:

- Improved collections from creditors.
- Reduced monthly unresolved exceptions from 15 to 5.
- Increased cash collections from 60% to 80% of outstanding totals.
- Introduced new invoice analysis methods and increased departmental efficiency by 25%.

The reader is entitled to ask: "If a résumé will screen out 90 percent of those who send them to a prospective employer, then by using a résumé I reduce my chances of getting a job by that same percentage. If that is correct shouldn't I use some other method of seeking a job?"

There are two major reasons why a résumé will not elicit a favorable reply:

1. The résumé is poorly written. You waste your time to send out an inferior résumé.
2. The résumé is not responsive to the needs of the employer. This you cannot help.

When looking for a job, the candidate does not send a résumé to just one person. If used properly, a résumé should be sent to many prospective employers. If you answer 50 help-wanted ads and receive five answers, you are doing well. On the average, five interviews equal one job. Your résumé has accomplished what it was intended to do. Remember, 80 percent of help-wanted advertisers demand résumés. You screen yourself out of 80 percent of advertised job opportunities if you do not use one.

An even more important use for the résumé is to send it to carefully selected companies chosen according to their Industrial Classification Numbers most closely identified with your own business experience or your interest. Your affirmative responses may be even greater than those received from answering ads, because 50 percent to 70 percent of available employment is not advertised. Your most useful tools for such mailings are Dun & Bradstreet or Standard & Poor's directories. (See later discussion on creating lists.)

It is almost impossible for any job seeker to pinpoint one or two or a half dozen companies where there is a fit between you and the employer and where work is available. You might fit best in a company you never heard of and in a town or city with which you are unfamiliar.

What constitutes a good résumé?

A good résumé is one that qualifies the subject for the job sought—concisely, literately, interestingly, and honestly—and causes an interview to occur if a position is available.

For example, the ideal candidate for a high management position from the point of view of some résumé readers would have these qualifications: age 43, a successful career with broad experience, showing continuous rapid progress with two or three multidivisional companies recognized nationally for management excellence. He or she would have graduated with honors from a small Midwestern college, majored in economics, shown leadership in extracurricular activities, attended Harvard Graduate School of Business Administration (or Stanford or the University of Chicago), and earned an M.B.A. If a male, he would have an attractive wife and three children. If a female, she would be single by choice, divorced or separated, attractive, and career oriented (except in government employment).

For a recent graduate, again ideally, mix in a similar educational background, show undergraduate leadership, broad interests, motivation, well delineated career objectives, single status.

Fewer than one tenth of 1 percent of job seekers have such qualifications for any job at any level on the organizational scale.

Practiced résumé readers are noted for the ability quickly to identify the hole in the doughnut; or they read résumés subjectively rather than objectively. In any event, to the extent possible, the résumé writer must include in his document all the material and experience relevant to his or her job area and hope that "holes" will be offset by other qualities.

It is of course possible for a job applicant with poor qualifications to have a good résumé if the element of "honesty" in the definition is omitted; in this event the writing is more in the nature of a novella than a résumé and the overqualifications expressed will be discovered early in employment, leading to the job hopping that is another red flag to a résumé reader; or a well-phrased honest résumé might gain an interview even if the work background is poor.

You become qualified in your job area if, in employment, you continue the learning process to include all that any reasonable person would expect you to know and, from a résumé focus, present your qualities in appropriate language and form.

SIX

RÉSUMÉ LENGTH

There is no standard résumé length. A résumé should be as long as it needs to be to present important information concisely and interestingly. Successful résumés have been as short as one page and as long as six pages. It is conciseness, relevance, and interest that matter. A six-page résumé can be concise; a three-page résumé verbose.

For example, there are many individuals who have extensive achievements over a period of 20 or 25 years or more. Achievements follow patterns. Some résumés could almost be textbooks for others to follow in climbing the ladder to organizational success. One can hardly compress a lifetime of achievement into two pages of writing. Most employers of upper-level managers are interested in what you have done if it has been well done.

Résumés directed toward a specific job may be longer than résumés written for general distribution. One reason is that you will probably know more about a particular job in which you are closely interested and therefore can relate your special qualifications more expansively in terms of what you could or would do.

High-level administrative nonprofit positions in a governmental or educational environment may also be more extended. Managers in these areas with the power to appoint tend to want qualifications fully expressed. Where political influence is involved, it becomes very important that every ability and experience related to the function is fully delineated so that competitive influences are blunted.

If you are a Washington, a Jefferson, a Lincoln you are already advertised on Mt. Rushmore and will not need to write much; but if you are not widely known you must explain yourself. There is a happy balance between too much and too little.

The search for a perfect résumé will never end. A perfect résumé is almost impossible, but the following might be:

> To Whom It May Concern:
> Available for teaching.
> Have own course
> program.
>   Socrates

I have clocked the reading time of some two-page résumés written by professionals in the employment field. In order to conform to the widely accepted dictum upholding the two-page creed, some résumés are so densely written I am reminded of the Lord's prayer written on the head of a pin. On a closely written page, reading time is measurably greater and comprehension measurably decreased. I advocate plenty of white space.

The use of a summary at the beginning of a résumé acknowledges the importance of the reader's time and is therefore a recognizable compliment to the reader. It is also the manner in which important documents are frequently presented. It encourages the reader to study further or to read and run. It takes extra space but adds beef. There is an old saying, "The proof of the pudding is in the eating." The résumés in this volume (both long and short) have been tested in the tilt-yard, the ancient equivalent of the present-day employment arena.

Don't worry too much about length. Make your writing as strong as the arm of Thor, as beguiling as the form of Venus, as accurate as the arrow of William Tell.

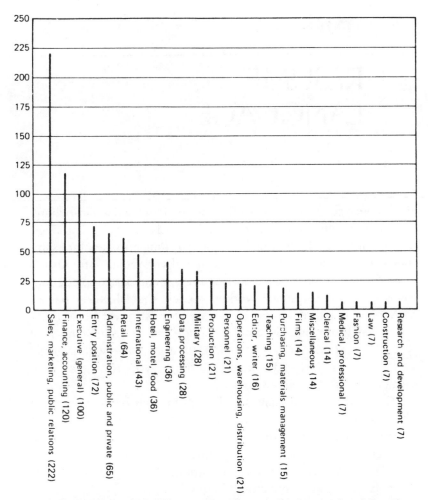

The greatest résumé use occurs in sales, marketing, and public relations. Persons employed in these areas may be more accustomed to writing, more aware of the benefits of advertising, or perhaps merely more restless than are other groups. (From a sample of 1,000.)

SEVEN

RÉSUMÉ LANGUAGE

The language of a résumé must be succinct, crisp, trenchant, expressive, interesting, and personal. Words, phrases, sentences, and paragraphs illustrating this type of writing appear later in this book (Appendix B). Use the specialized vocabulary of your job area. Scientists, data processors, lawyers, financial people, economists, engineers, social workers—each specialization has its own nomenclature. However, a résumé must never be so technical that those outside your discipline fail to understand it. If you have experience in a vocation, your language will naturally reflect it. If you have little or no experience, your misuse of technical language may give you away.

There are more languages or dialects in English than you might think. To name just a few: academic, conversational, vernacular, bureaucratic, poetic, formal, jargon, argot, Gullah. They arise from education or lack of it, from environmental exposure, from the desire to confuse, from the combined use of two or more other languages to supplement English.

The fact of a résumé language arises out of a need for clear expression in a minimum number of words to create a maximum impact. There is no time for relaxed prose. The average résumé must make its *impression* in 20 to 30 seconds. If the first impression is good, the entire résumé will be read. If the first impression is poor, it will be discarded. Average reading time is about four words per second.

There is the hope to lend excitement and create an urgency to make a decision. Most of all, there is the need of discipline to attain your objective, which dictates the "language" or mode of expression.

RÉSUMÉ READERS' CRITICISMS

The criticisms listed below are those most commonly expressed by résumé readers. You will observe that many of them are in exact opposition. There is no way to write a résumé that will appeal to every reader. Fit your résumé to the type of individual whom you expect to be reading it.

- **Too long.** The résumé is not concise, interesting, and relevant. A person required to read hundreds or thousands of résumés, however, may find any résumé that exceeds one page too long. Keep a résumé short if it is aimed at a lower-echelon personnel executive or an employment agency.
- **Too short.** The résumé does not give the reader an opportunity to make a proper evaluation.
- **Too condensed.** Paragraphs and sentences are too closely written for easy reading. It is preferable to expand spatially sentences, paragraphs, and white space rather than to try to get two pages of easy-to-read writing on one page.
- **Too wordy.** The description is verbose, with several words used for what could have been expressed in one or two.
- **Too slick.** The résumé is so well prepared as to be inappropriate for the individual presenting it and must therefore have been written by someone else. This evaluation leads the reader to suspect that the subject's qualifications are exaggerated.
- **Too amateurish.** The applicant cannot express himself or herself, which would be a liability on the job.

- **Poorly reproduced.** The résumé is carelessly reproduced, especially when duplicated on poor paper by inferior photocopier.
- **Misspellings and bad grammar abound.** Spelling and grammatical errors in a résumé show lack of the primary skills necessary for accomplishment. Poor spellers need not be low achievers, but a poor speller who does not compensate for this deficiency by having another person proofread the résumé shows bad judgment. Bad grammar is inexcusable at the executive and professional levels.
- **Reason for leaving last job omitted.** This is discussed elsewhere in this book.
- **Date of availability omitted.** If you apply for a position months ahead of the time when you can start work, include the date of your availability.
- **Geographical preference omitted.** Any geographical preferences or limitations regarding location of employment should be specified in a résumé.
- **Objective omitted.** This is discussed elsewhere.
- **Poorly expressed.** If you are unable to prepare your own résumé, have someone else write it for you.
- **Résumé is boastful.** Boastfulness is an unattractive quality. Be realistic about yourself, but do not bluster, overestimate, or exaggerate.
- **Résumé is dishonest.** You have claimed to have expertise that you do not possess.
- **Salary information lacking.** This is discussed elsewhere.
- **Résumé is "gimmicky."** It contains words, structure, decoration, or material that departs so much from the norm that it is unacceptable.
- **Sufficient data lacking.** The material is insufficient for a proper evaluation. You may have tried to condense to one page experience that requires several pages for explanation.

EIGHT

THE ELEMENTS OF A RÉSUMÉ

WHAT TO OMIT

The following information is usually best omitted from your résumé:

1. Date. Your résumé should remain current for an extended period of time. Place the date in your covering letter.

2. Race, religion, political affiliation, and the like, unless that is an essential element of your résumé. Though the law forbids discrimination for such reasons, you should not offer them as a basis for selection, which you do if you include them in the résumé. Disregard this advice if you know your prospective employer to be partial to certain kinds of people. Thus a Catholic parish would not only employ a Catholic priest rather than a Baptist minister, but might also tend to hire Catholic clerical workers—a tendency that holds equally for any religious institution.

3. Matters that are negative, detrimental, or awkward to write about.

4. Salary requirements.

- A leading reason for seeking new employment is to improve compensation. Avoid being restricted by your past salary level.

- You are entitled to the income level of the position being offered. The company should indicate what it is prepared to pay.

- Salary is negotiable—based on the nature of the position and your expected contribution to it.

- It is unwise to commit yourself to a salary level before the interview: you might underrate your potential.

- A salary that the employer finds unacceptable from a mere reading of your résumé (causing the résumé to be discarded) might become acceptable after the interview.

Some qualifications are in order, however. If an advertisement asks for salary information, you might supply it. Write it in by hand at the end of the résumé, together with bonuses and fringe benefits, if substantial, or combine all in an inclusive lump sum. I am ambivalent about this. In a very strong résumé, salary disclosure can probably be avoided even when specifically requested.

Furthermore, very significant salary growth—from $20,000 to $100,000 within a short time—shows that your employer has recognized your merits in the most important possible way, and this in turn indicates strong functional progress. In such a case, making salary data known, showing your salary growth by percentages or graphically, is another way of buttressing your accomplishments.

Finally, if your earnings are or have been at a certain level that you are confident you can match or improve in your new position, you might safely include your income expectancy in your covering letter.

5. References.

   • An employer should have no interest in your references until after he has become interested in you—after the interview.
   • A prospective employer might consult the persons given as references before interviewing you. This is undesirable because you wish to be the first one to describe yourself.
   • Persons named as references can become irritated by too many calls.
   • You will not wish to have your present employer called as a reference before employment interest in you has been indicated.

   However, any extraordinary references that you might have can be included. Extraordinary references would include famous people, individuals of stature in your area of competence, important political figures, and the like.

WHAT TO INCLUDE

The elements to be included in résumés are discussed below. The starred items are those essential to any résumé.

*1. **Your personal directory.** Name, address (with zip code), and telephone number (with area code) are obvious essentials that must appear in your résumé. The only exception is the case in which the employer is dealt with by way of an intermediary for reasons of confidentiality. The third-party approach is of course less effective than the direct approach and should not be used without good cause. Make sure that the intermediary disclaims any right to compensation from the addressee, for services rendered.

If you are employed, list your business telephone number, provided that privacy of conversation is possible. Repeated unanswered calls to an applicant's home may affect negatively the prospective employer's interest. Immediate availability can be crucial in the decision to hire.

*2. **Objective.** Your résumé should be geared to your job objective. State the objective clearly at the outset. If you know the experience and qualifications needed for a job, direct your résumé to describing, as specifically as possible, your ability to meet the criteria. Most applicants lack such information, which sometimes can be obtained from friends, acquaintances, bankers, competitors, annual company reports, and similar sources. Usually, however, a résumé is intended to meet the requirements of more than one specific job and must be written more broadly. Among the objectives toward which a résumé can be directed are the following:

- An entry position in marketing finance, or production.
- A management position in marketing, finance, or production, or in any subdivision of these functions.
- A career change—from a profession to business, from military service to business, and the like.
- An office administrative position.

There are general categories. For your résumé, choose as specific a job classification as possible from the thousands of categories in existence. A prospective employer should not have to guess what kind of a job you want.

3. **Qualifications: A brief summary, a paragraph-long summary, or an expanded full-page summary.** Having stated your job objective, you must present your qualifications for it. *For those with little or no business experience* qualifications may include courses of study, past work experience, and even character traits that can be supported:

- *Ambition* can be indicated by having worked one's way through college.
- *Motivation* can be manifested by having achieved good grades.
- *Commitment* can be shown by a long-term ambition to pursue one's objective and enrollment in training toward that end.
- *Intelligence* might be indicated by a high class standing and receipt of awards.

RÉSUMÉ USERS: EMPLOYED AND UNEMPLOYED

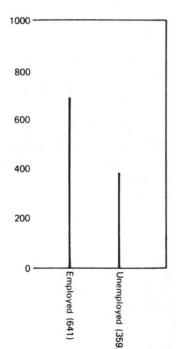

Those who are employed use résumés almost twice as much as do the unemployed. (From a sample of 1,000.)

If you have substantial work experience, a summary page is in order. The method of preparing such a page is explained later.

You can describe your qualifications either objectively or subjectively. Allowing your personality to come through will add warmth to an otherwise sterile document, especially if the résumé is short. Objective evaluations can come from official reports on personnel, such as those used by the armed forces and increasingly by many private companies that review their personnel annually, making the results available to the employee.

*4. Experience. In describing your experience give the dates on which you began and terminated the job. Use the phrase "to present" to indicate current employment. (See résumé examples.) State the name and location of the company, except when present employment must be kept confidential. "Name of Company on Request" may suffice in such cases. It is not necessary to include a company's street address. Describe briefly what the company makes, sells, or does, how large it is, and how many employees it has. Then list your responsibilities at the company. Use the company's job description of your position or create your own. A corporate job description can be a formidable and necessarily tedious document. Extract from it the highlights of your responsibilities, using key words and sentences, to avoid burdening your résumé with unneeded, though technically relevant, verbiage.

The description of responsibilities should always be followed by a statement of accomplishments. For example:

> Responsible for planning entry of Company into chain store distribution. Accomplishments: developed program, hired salesmen, implemented program, contributed new volume of $1 million first year of operation.

> Responsible for transcribing dictation from three advertising agency account executives. Accomplishments: became

expert with a word processor; increased typing speed from 50 to 75 words per minute; increased accuracy to 97%.

What you are responsible for doing takes on significance when you describe what you did about it. Ask yourself, "What needed to be done, and what did I do? What happened as a result?"

Follow methodology described for each position you have held in a company and for each company you have worked for. Describe your experience first in chronological sequence; if another style is preferred, rearrange the items later.

*5. Education. As a rule education appears near the beginning of a résumé if one has no work experience, and after experience when experience begins to outweigh education after a year or so in a job. One exception is the *Professional Résumé* for reasons explained later.

An academic degree or attendance at a college makes any mention of graduation from high school superfluous, though you might wish to list a "name" preparatory school. The high school graduate who did not go to college must mention the fact of graduation. The noncollege graduate should deemphasize education as early as possible in the résumé. Any continuation of education should be noted and described, regardless of the level.

Show your class standing if it is high; otherwise omit it. Mention the honors, awards, and scholarships you have earned. If your education or individual courses you have attended are particularly relevant to your objective, say so in your résumé (this will be self-evident in the *Professional Résumé*). Advanced degrees should be stated. At this writing a master's degree in business administration (M.B.A.) is the most valuable business degree and commands a compensation advantage of $15,000 or more annually. A doctoral degree is an advantage if related to the job objective. It is a definite asset for a researcher, teacher, scientist, writer, and public administrator.

6. **Extracurricular activities.** Listing extensive extracurricular activities can add flavor to a résumé. Omit them if they are *few,* however, and *after* you have gained substantial work experience—their significance erodes with time. If you are a newcomer to the workplace, do list teaching assistantships, tutoring, waiting on tables, elective student organization offices, sports participation, school newspaper experience, and special distinctions of any kind. They enable the employer to know you better and may strike a responsive chord that might provide an edge in selection for employment.

7. **Summer work while attending school or college.** Employers look with favor on those who have used their school or college holidays for constructive activities. Therefore, summer employment is a worthwhile addition to a résumé, and so is having partially or wholly worked one's way through college. This entry in the résumé is a character building block when experience is lacking, as it is for recent graduates.

8. **Military service.** Your service in the armed forces, with an honorable discharge, has a place in your résumé. Usually its mention should be brief. Extended description is in order, however, if military service forms a major part of your background—the young man who has been in the armed forces for two to five or more years and has no other employment experience or the career military man who seeks a new career after retirement from the service. Your service record supplies a wealth of information from which interesting, persuasive, and relevant material can be drawn as the basis for a highly effective résumé presentation. Take care to avoid an overlong discussion of your military career, no matter how extensive. Stress the factors most relevant to your civilian job objective.

9. **Professional membership.** Memberships in professional and trade associations denote an ongoing interest in expanding one's vocational experience. Some memberships are almost mandatory for certain job classifications. Any industrially, commercially, or professionally recognized membership should be listed in your résumé.

10. **Community activities.** Some companies, highly conscious of their local image, favor employee participation in fund drives, charitable board memberships, and community assistance activities. Participation in community activities may characterize you in the eyes of a potential employer as an individual with broad interests and the potential for greater managerial responsibilities.

11. **Accreditation and licenses.** Include all accreditations and licenses related to your vocation in your résumé. Examples are C.P.A., C.L.U., Licensed Engineer, Licensed Real Estate Broker, and R.N. Honorary degrees should also be listed.

12. **Patents and publications.** Patents, particularly important to the research scientist, the R&D manager or employee, and the engineer, as indicators of original thinking should always be included in a résumé. Publication carries special weight in teaching, business consulting, law, and other professions. They serve as tools in evaluating you, and as a basis for a constructive and interesting interview.

*13. **Personal data.** Personal data are date of birth, marital status, sex (if name is ambiguous), state of health (if excellent), citizenship (if potentially unclear), number of children, home ownership, willingness to relocate, geographical employment preference (if any), availability for employment (if not immediate), extensive travel experience, height, and weight.

The laws relating to equal opportunity employment make it illegal for an employer to discriminate by reason of age, color, creed, race, religion, and sex. You must judge for yourself whether to include all these data in your résumé. Give age if you are young; omit it if you are over 50. On the other hand, if no age is given, the employer may infer more years than the actual number. Approximate age can be guessed quite accurately from dates of graduation and from the length of your career. You might also consider excluding all dates from your résumé. Age is one of the greatest deterrents to employment for many reasons, such as pensions and other benefits, which become costly to employers for new employees of advanced age, and the partiality of many large companies to training their own executives.

Other personal data, we think, need not be excluded from your résumé. The employment opportunities for qualified blacks and other ethnic groups are expanding; an equal opportunity employer may be able to utilize information about your race to your advantage. Employment opportunities for qualified women are growing apace. Your height and weight will be of value only in the entertainment field. We prefer that separation or divorce be stated in a résumé, but this is a matter of personal option.

14. **Hobbies.** Mention interesting hobbies; omit commonplace ones, except golf and tennis, which engender wide rapport. Outstanding excellence in any sport or hobby should be mentioned.

15. **Languages.** A knowledge of languages other than English may be mandatory in an international business and important or helpful in many other activities. Include any language proficiency.

16. **Reason for leaving last job.** Some recruiters consider this information to be an important part of a résumé. We prefer its *omission* because the explanation can be cumbersome and disadvantageous. Furthermore, it can normally have no positive influence on gaining an interview. *The reason for leaving your last job is a matter to be discussed*

at a personal interview when you can explain it at length. However, almost everyone has had one disastrous job experience. It may even be an advantage—one story, possibly apocryphal, has it that a large employer receiving hundreds of applications for a position decided to exclude all résumés that did not show one job failure!

A résumé giving "personality conflict" as the reason for leaving a job may become discarded before a personal interview takes place; it is a reason that can give rise to complicated and unfavorable psychological reactions.

The strong trend of merger, acquisition, and restructuring activity has displaced thousands of executives who had thought they were firmly established in their jobs. Being unemployed for such reasons is understandable and carries no onus. If it is true of you, mention it. It removes a question that is always in an employer's mind.

If an employment agreement was breached, you may say so without going into details.

- The sale of a business is usually followed by changes in personnel. Mentioning this in a letter or résumé is more positive than negative.
- Divestment of a division or liquidation of a business need but a few words to make clear the reason you are looking for new employment.
- Relocation of a business to a place where you do not want to live is a good reason for you to want to leave a company, but not necessarily from an employer's point of view. The employer may think that this shows inflexibility.
- Declines in corporate earnings often mean layoffs. If your position was one that did not have an influence on earnings, you may give this reason.
- Technological changes or competition can ruin or have an adverse impact on nondiversified companies. The

U.S. garment industry has been adversely affected by competition from the Far East. Hand tailoring has declined with the advent of mass production techniques. If you were in the business of making tailors' shears, your livelihood disappeared. The ball-point pen has superseded the old ink pack pens. Pocketknives were almost universally carried at one time; now no longer. Wristwatches supplanted pocket watches. Cheap electronic manufacturing by the Japanese has replaced U.S. components in television sets and radios. Overseas auto manufacturers are increasing their share of the market with their compact, high-mileage cars. Such changes have a continuous effect on employment.

Several jobs held in a short period of time need to be explained if the period is important to the chronology of the résumé. The period can be omitted entirely if it occurs early in your career.

Employment gaps should be explained or closed as fully as possible. Gaps occurring during a recession will be understood. For those gaps difficult to justify you might consult your friends or former employers. Such terms as "consultant" and "free-lance worker" are poorly received except in areas where freelancing is common (artists and writers, for example).

17. **Security clearance.** If your past or present employment is security sensitive, specify the level of your security clearance.

18. **Aptitude and psychological tests.** Employers tend to think that most tests other than their own have little validity. In fact, such tests frequently are too generalized or diffused to be of significance. Omit test results from your résumé, unless excerpts of singular appropriateness can be used to show qualifications objectively.

19. **Photographs.** Most of the executives recruiting for business consider photographs detrimental. Photographs are

essential in the résumé of an entertainer or model and should be 8 by 10 inches or larger.

20. **Art decoration.** Simple decoration can improve a résumé. However, because "one man's meat is another man's poison," use art devices with great care.

21. **Graphs and charts.** Graphs and charts usually add little to a résumé unless they are of professional quality. A simple curve showing sales increases is not impressive. On the other hand, a 10-year bar chart of sales and profit increases or a curve of dramatic increases in your income can make valid points.

22. **Testimonials.** Testimonials can serve effectively as objective evaluations, provided you can present them without appearing to be boastful. Testimonials can be placed in any appropriate part of your résumé, particularly on a summary page or in a summary paragraph, or when discussing your handling of important responsibilities.

23. **Civil service grades.** In seeking a job with the government or in indicating the governmental level of your responsibilities to a private employer, mention of the civil service grade is useful.

NINE

THE RIGHT
RÉSUMÉ IS
MUSCULAR

Most of the individuals whose résumés appear in this book sound like achievers. In fact, some may have had disappointing careers. Others have accomplished something, but not enough, in the companies for which they worked. They might have succeeded in other companies or under other circumstances. The faults measured by the requirements of one position, or by the definition of one management, can be virtues when measured by different standards.

Your résumé should make you, too, sound like an achiever. Forget your negative aspects and stress your positive attributes. Self-analysis, aided by suggestions in this book, may reveal talents of which you have been unaware. Your chronological job history may disclose accomplishments you have underestimated. When written down, your accomplishments may sound better than you expected. They may be superior when compared to those of others doing similar jobs.

If your career has been less successful than you had hoped, it need not continue to be so. Your résumé is a means of escape from career disappointment or mediocrity to career fulfillment. It is not dishonest to have your résumé accent your most positive characteristics. No one is perfect. *You* may be just what some employer is looking for. In another position your positive attributes may bring you the degree of success that has eluded you in the past, whatever your present level of accomplishment.

Your résumé is a way to gain an interview. Make it as strong as possible to achieve that end. You cannot help yourself or anyone else with a weak résumé.

A résumé has to be written from the point of view that it is an evaluation that qualifies you for the job you want.

1. You must show that you meet the requirements of the job.
2. You must analyze your background to find those qualifications.
3. You must express yourself logically, precisely, and with individuality.

ANALYSIS OF RÉSUMÉ USERS: ENTRY POSITION

The average age is 24.5.
Females are 20 percent of sample.

REASONS FOR DIFFERENT RÉSUMÉ STYLES

One could wonder why so many résumé styles are described and recommended in this book. There are many readers and writers who believe that one basic style is suitable for almost any situation.

At the two extremes there are the recent graduate who has never had a job, and the executive of extensive experience. With a recent graduate it would be unbecoming and uninteresting to use more than a page to describe one's capabilities. His or her measurements as a desirable employee are as yet untested.

For one who has had a successful career it becomes difficult to select from among the many attributes that have been developed, and a single page becomes unnecessarily confining. But that is an easy distinction. There are other, more subtle, differences relating to one's field, such as industrial, academic, scientific, professional; or relating to one's area, such as marketing, finance, production, editorial; or relating to one's background, such as military, religious, academic, political; or relating to one's objective, such as career change (from teaching to administration, from military to business, from government to business, from a lower level to a higher level). Many of these categories are best expressed in ways different from each other. We have tried to lead the writer to the *best* way to express himself or herself under such conditions. Does this work efficiently? YES! On the basis of our experience it is the best way to approach self expression via a résumé. How do we know this to be true? We have been so informed by more than a thousand people who have used the methods described in these pages. Also, by using the methods explicated, it was possible to secure employment for 80 percent of the candidates for whom job searches were conducted by me.

TEN

THE TEN RÉSUMÉ STYLES

In this book we recognize 10 résumé styles or forms, with an infinite number of variations and combinations. The examples given should help you in choosing among them. Our recommendations appear on pages 4 and 5. The 10 styles are discussed in the sections that follow.

The word *form* is used to mean style of résumé. *Format* refers to the physical aspects of a résumé, such as its margins, headlines, underlining, and page size.

Remember that the accomplishments listed in your résumé need not be notable achievements, but achievements within the level of your responsibility only. Whether you are an office boy, a clerk, a supervisor, a manager, or a president, you can have accomplishments that are significant in relation to your job and job objective.

BASIC RÉSUMÉ

The *Basic Résumé,* best suited for those entering the job market, should contain the following items (their order may vary).

1. Name, address with zip code, and telephone number with area code.
2. Personal data (age, marital status, health, willingness to travel or relocate, date of availability).
3. Objectives.
4. Education (honors, awards, high class standing).
5. Extracurricular activities.
6. Languages other than English.
7. Summer jobs.
8. Military service.
9. Hobbies (if interesting).

This is a standard form. We recommend that job qualifications be added, if they can be properly expressed, immediately after objectives. Keep this résumé to one page. Use the *Basic Résumé* whenever work experience is very limited. Any important job experience that does exist should be described before education.

Examples of *Basic Résumés* follow.

INFLUENCE OF COLLEGE EDUCATION ON LIFETIME EARNINGS

U.S. Department of Labor statistics consistently show that a college education significantly increases lifetime earnings. The data, for example, indicate the following:

Educational Level	Increase in Lifetime Earnings
Four years of college	70%
One to three years of college	18
High school	

According to Herbert Bienstock, head of the Bureau of Labor Statistics in New York, long-term government projections show that the demand for college graduates will grow at three times the rate of demand for all workers in the United States labor force. Furthermore, jobless rates were 3 percent for college graduates and 15 percent for high school dropouts. Stephen B. Withey, author of *A Degree and What Else,* writes in a Carnegie Commission on Higher Education report that students going through college increase their interest in esthetic and cultural values and progress on the "social maturity scale," to a much greater extent than do noncollege individuals. They have a greater ability to shape their "material future," greater job security, better career prospect, and greater job satisfaction.

EXAMPLE OF BASIC RÉSUMÉ

23 Redondo Drive   (123) 456-7890
La Jolla, California 12345   R E S U M E
                                       of
                                 RICHARD SMITH

PERSONAL DATA: Born 3/10/65, single, excellent health.

OBJECTIVE:

 Association with a communications or other company in an entry position with
 opportunity for general management consistent with ability to contribute.

QUALIFICATIONS:

 Consistently high academic grades, willingness to work hard to establish
 capability; concerned with and interested in major U. S. and world problems;
 active in causes; experienced in working with general public during summer
 jobs and in retail selling since graduating from college. Volunteer work 1987
 to date. Harmonious, articulate, diligent. Senior year of high school in
 Thailand. Rudimentary knowledge of French and German.

EDUCATION:

 B. A., Government, University of Pennsylvania, Philadelphia, Pa., 1977.
 Courses in Government: U. S., South Africa, Latin America, France.
 Courses in: Principles of Management, Economics I and II, International
             Business, Business Ethics, Fundamentals of Public Speaking,
             Oral Interpretation. Dean's List, 2 years.

EXTRACURRICULAR ACTIVITIES:

 Football, lacrosse, handball; librarian assistant; mail room messenger,
 R. O. T. C.

BUSINESS EXPERIENCE:

 Nov. 22-Dec. 24, 1987   THE MAY COMPANY, Long Beach, California

 TOY SALESMAN for branch of leading department store.

SUMMER JOBS:

 1983-1986   DEPT. OF PARKS AND RECREATION, La Jolla.

 June to Nov. 1987, GATE ATTENDANT, beach area; June to Sept. 1986, POOL
 GATEMAN; June to Sept. 1985, LOCKER ROOM ATTENDANT; June to Sept. 1984,
 LOCKER ROOM ATTENDANT; June to Sept. 1983, PARK ATTENDANT. Collected
 revenues, checked residency, painted, cleaned beach.

HOBBIES: Numismatics, computer programs.

                    REFERENCES AND FURTHER DATA ON REQUEST

DISCUSSION

Basic Résumé.   What does the Smith résumé show that is of special interest to an employer?

Good scholarship leading to selection for special courses overseas. Some knowledge of foreign languages. Helped pay for education by working during summer vacations. Business-related education. Good health and superior physical coordination. Probably a conservative disposition. Employment soon after gaining degree. Intellectual hobbies. Logically organized and concisely presented résumé. An employer would grab him.

EXAMPLE OF BASIC RÉSUMÉ

MILLARD FILLMORE

1776 Patomac Ave.
New York, NY 12210
(123) 445-6789

RESUME

PERSONAL DATA:

    Age 22, single, healthy. Extensively traveled in United States, Europe, British Isles, Canada. Speak and understand some French.

OBJECTIVE:

    Position in Financial Department of Corporation, Institution.

EDUCATION:

    1982   B.S., Pace University, School of Commerce, New York, NY. Major, Banking and Finance: Corporate Finance, Management, Investment Analysis, Money Markets, Economics, Accounting.

              Admitted to Phi Alpha Kappa, Honor Finance Society, for attaining 3.5 index. Cumulative 4-year index: 3.3 of possible 4.0.

              Member of Finance Society, Pre-Law Society.

    1983--
    Present Attending New York Law School (night classes).

EXPERIENCE:

    May 1-Dec. 30, 1983 LOST COMPANY, INC.

              As ASSISTANT TO THE PRESIDENT, gained practical financial experience in helping to rescue near-bankrupt corporation. Involved in decision making and negotiations.

              Met and negotiated with substantial investors from all over the world in connection with Company plans for an underwriting.

              Participated in surveys and studies of land development project in Arizona.

              Also learned about water desalinization.

    Experience in Security Brokerage through part-time work in Uncle's business.

MILITARY SERVICE: 1979 U.S. NAVAL RESERVE, Boatswains Mate 3/c.

REFERENCES AND FURTHER DATA ON REQUEST

DISCUSSION

Basic Résumé. The Fillmore résumé utilizes the same form as the Smith résumé, with different indentation accommodating almost the identical number of words. Again, the form is a matter of choice. The fact that one has traveled extensively is usually well worth including in a résumé because travel is educational and contributes to self-development.

Fillmore's educational experience was outstanding and easily takes precedence over his business experience even though that was unique and interesting.

Although a legal education is not directly related to finance, it is nevertheless excellent training for any business career and, added to undergraduate studies in finance, will create an individual of substantial educational background that can be later utilized for professional management progress.

This résumé should be well received by executive recruiters.

CHRONOLOGICAL RÉSUMÉ

The *Chronological Résumé* is the one most frequently used by applicants who have job experience. The form offers the writer the best opportunity to highlight achievements and the reader the best opportunity to gauge the applicant's qualifications. The work experience is shown in reverse chronological order, the last or present job being given first. The various positions held at one company should also be described in reverse chronological order. This order shows the applicant's growth and development—characteristics of great interest to employers. The elements of the *Chronological Résumé* are as follows:

1. Name, address, and telephone number.
2. Objective.
3. Name of the company of most recent or present employment

    •   Brief description of the company.
    •   Responsibilities.
    •   Accomplishments (treat each level of assignment as if it were a different employer).

4. Name of the company of next most recent employment.

    •   Brief description of the company.
    •   Responsibilities.
    •   Accomplishments.

    Continue as above for each relevant employment, going back to your first job. If earlier employment is unrelated to your present objective, summarize it briefly in a catchall sentence or paragraph. Omit mention of inappropriate or undignified jobs—jobs that are unrelated to the one being sought, or jobs that poorly reflect your qualities.

5. Military service (delete this heading if inappropriate).

6. Education.
7. Extracurricular activities (including summer jobs).
8. Accreditations (C.P.A., C.L.U., Real Estate Broker, Licensed Engineer, and so forth).
9. Professional memberships.
10. Community activities.
11. Hobbies.
12. Personal data.

The *Chronological Résumé* may be two or more pages in length. Remember the rules: conciseness, relevance, and interest.

Examples of *Chronological Résumés* follow.

1676 Old Saw Street   (123) 456-7890
Boston, MA (zip)

RESUME

of

CAROLINE ALLEGARTH

Employment Objective in the Following Areas:

INVESTMENT BANKING: Municipal financial consulting; new issues; new
                        business; private placements; financial services;
                        institutional sales, research.

COMMERCIAL BANKING: Urban affairs, money market, municipal lending,
                        financial services.

Education includes:

M.B.A., B.S., superior grades, 3.7 on the 4.0 scale. Finance major.

Personal data:

Age 42, divorced, excellent health; interested in financial analysis,
riding, sports, travel, writing.

Record of Experience:

1978-Present   KUHN MARX & CO., 5 Hancock Street, Boston, MA

ANALYST, Institutional Department for investment banking company and full-
service retail and institutional brokerage. This department over the past
5-1/2 years handled approximately 35 new capital projects per year for
municipalities in Connecticut involving general obligation or revenue
bonds of about $200 million.

Responsible for:

- preparation and dissemination of information to facilitate new issue
  financings by serving as intermediary between municipality and investor.
- assistance to debt issuer to obtain best credit rating possible,
  together with lowest interest cost.
- creating environment to provide maximum marketability of bonds.
- preparation and finalization of all Official Statements including
  organization of all pertinent economic and financial data needed for
  evaluation.

The above responsibilities entailed:

- participation in all preliminary financial discussions with architects,
  bond counsels, house counsel, municipalities, solicitors, trustee banks
  and/or paying agents, syndicate members, issuers, investors and major
  banks and insurance companies, financial firms and salesmen.
- risk analysis, financing concepts and closing sales. Personally responsible for many salesmen's orders up to $2.6 million.
- examination of feasibility of capital proposals, reviewing feasibility
  reports prepared by consultants and major accounting firms, suggesting
  modifications as necessary to assure successful underwriting, inclusion
  of security provisions, rate convenants, earning tests, reserve capitalization, analysis of financial statements including balance sheets,
  breakeven points and rechecking to assure validity of risk/equity relationships.
- contacts with regulatory agencies at State and Federal levels.

50

The carrying out of these various responsibilities resulted in:

- saving issuers thousands of dollars in basis points by achieving higher ratings from rating services through personal presentations, i.e., upgrading ratings, holding marginal ratings, reversing lower ratings, sometimes getting a higher rating from one service than another and thereby mitigating the lower rating.
- ability to underwrite issues in difficult markets.
- specifically, for example, causing both Moody and Standard & Poor's to upgrade one $15.9 million Refunding School Authority Issue in 1983, which otherwise might have produced an underwriting loss.
- reduction of underwriting and other market risks.
- protection of firm against civil or criminal suits for nondisclosure with concomitant result of full profit.
- repeat business for the firm.

1974-1978   DUN AND STANDARD CORP., 27 Wall Street, New York, NY.

Member of EDITORIAL STAFF, WRITER, AND ANALYST of and for "Bond Outlook" for publisher of financial data on securities with well-known investment advisory service to clients.
- prepared weekly analysis of new bond issues.
- reviewed and evaluated municipal credit.
- analyzed economic, social, political and geographical data.
- reported on city and state general obligation, revenue and construction bonds.
- studied and evaluated annual municipal financial statements, audits, budgets, capital improvement programs.
- evaluated debt structures, histories and trends.
- reviewed and weighed qualitative factors of administration, organization, structure, efficiency and growth factors.
- utilized all types of financial data, Federal Reserve and Census Bureau publications.

Accustomed to personal interview and liaison activities with municipal officials, business managers, financial advisors and consultants and bank executives. Experience additionally included:

- training analysts.
- analysis of Standard & Poor's ratings on 8,000 issues.
- development of advertising themes.
- providing data and story lines for financial writers.
- diversified special reports, summaries and analysis.

1971-1974   WACHOVIA TRUST CO., New York, NY.

RESEARCH ASSISTANT after starting as Statistical Clerk for one of largest banks in the U.S.

- worked directly with Senior Municipal Analyst and Senior Vice President.
- prepared analytical reports on municipal securities for Officers' Investment Committees and Board of Directors.
- provided reports forming a basis for portfolio decisions.
- utilized all sources of financial and economic data as appropriate.
- maintained financial and economic charts.

<u>REFERENCES</u> <u>AND</u> <u>FURTHER</u> <u>DATA</u> <u>ON</u> <u>REQUEST</u>

51

DISCUSSION

Chronological Résumé. The Allegarth résumé is comprehensive and could have been written in several other forms, such as a *Functional Résumé* or *Chronological with Summary Page Résumé*. The chronological form was chosen because the sequence of experience shows continuous growth.

The summary page was omitted in this instance to keep the résumé short; no summary is really needed to explain the obvious high qualifications of the subject.

The résumé is written in the language of a professional expressing knowledge of her subject with literacy and compactness. Her work is specialized and complicated. Any reader will know at once that she is a highly capable individual. Despite the résumé's comprehensiveness there is still much that remains to be explored in a personal interview.

Age, education, and personal data are clearly and briefly expressed at the outset because most are highly favorable and need no extended comment.

ANALYSIS OF RÉSUMÉ USERS: FINANCE

Chief financial officer, treasurer, controller, accounting, brokerage, financial research, and intermediate positions.

The age range is 24 to 61.
The average age is 38.3.
Some 50 percent are in their thirties.
Females are 10 percent of the total.

CHRONOLOGICAL RÉSUMÉ WITH SUMMARY PAGE

The *Chronological Résumé with Summary Page* is the most effective form of résumé for middle- to upper-business management as well as in some other vocations. The summary page interprets the résumé and quickly provides the gist of the applicant's case. Remember that the summary page is always the *first* page of the résumé. It is written *last,* however, because it is based on the material appearing in the chronological part of the résumé, which must be written *first.*

A summary page establishes instant interest and creates the curiosity to learn more about the applicant's background in the subsequent pages. Psychologically it compliments the reader by recognizing that his or her time is valuable and by providing the opportunity to make a quick appraisal.

The summary page can also be used to "beef up" a weak résumé.

The summary page, however, is an extra page. If you are concerned about the length of your résumé, eliminate the summary page or reduce its content to a brief paragraph or two to be placed at the beginning of the résumé. You will find examples of résumés with full summary pages and with reduced summaries.

Because *Chronological Résumé with Summary Page* is difficult to prepare, it is explained in detail in the pages that follow. In our annotated example page 2 appears first because the summary page, page 1, is *written last.*

The summary technique is used by many writers of reports and other long or technical analyses to permit a reader to know the conclusions arrived at before studying the details.

375 Broadalban Road   (177) 377-4777
Ephrata, Va.

RESUME

of

DUNCAN SMITH

Qualified As

SENIOR MANAGEMENT EXECUTIVE

***   Record of consistent profit contributions amounting to
        millions of dollars in general management, marketing,
        production in the U.S., Canada and internationally;
        accustomed for the last ten years to autonomous multi-
        division P. & L. responsibility and responsible for at
        least eight turn-around situations involving significant
        figures.

***   Equipped to use latest management sciences utilizing
        computer programs.

***   Intimately familiar with the metal-working industry and
        with sophisticated machinery and equipment in a broad
        area of manufacturing.

***   Characterized by others as an inspiring leader, incisive
        in identifying problems, imaginative in finding and im-
        plementing solutions, strong in comprehensive, accurate
        planning leading to improved profitability.

(FOR FURTHER DATA, PLEASE SEE FOLLOWING PAGES)

54

DUNCAN SMITH

BUSINESS EXPERIENCE:

1980-Present   LEAF MACHINERY DIVISION, BRF, INC.
                            Winston-Salem, N.C.

VICE PRESIDENT, GENERAL MANAGER of $45 million tobacco machinery manufac-
turing division of $700 million leisure products conglomerate. Reported to
parent corporate Group Vice President. Supervised V.P., R. & D., Controller,
Director of Marketing, European and South American Directors.

Responsibility:

- P. & L. responsibility for U.S. division and plants in France, U.K., Brazil,
  and marketing headquarters in Switzerland.

Achievements:

- U.K. Division lost $250,000 first quarter 1980; by August Division was
  operating profitably with earnings of $80,000.
- Reduced inflated U.S. payroll by $235,000.
- Successfully introduced three new products of complex technology.
- Improved return on assets from 13.8% to 14.6%.
- Prepared, submitted and implemented five-year plan yielding compounded
  annual growth in pre-tax profits of 13.3%.

These accomplishments were engineered by the use of PERT, Critical Path Method
and other net-work techniques to improve production, eliminate bottlenecks; by
repricing; by implementing plans which had been made but not acted upon; and
by creating a new sales program.

1977-1980   THOMAS & SESSIONS, Springfield, Mo.

1979-1980, ASSISTANT to the PRESIDENT of $80 million manufacturer of meters,
electric sub-assemblies, fractional horsepower motors and other products.

1977-1979, PRESIDENT of autonomous Canadian Division with sales of $15 million.
Responsible for:

- Management of complete staff: finance, sales, manufacturing.
- Divisional profit and loss.
- Assisting the President of parent company.
- Presiding at Directors' and Stockholders' meetings.

Accomplishments:

- In 1977 losses were above $1/2 million annually; by end 1979 losses were
  eliminated and profits stood at all-time high of $1.137 million.

This was accomplished by consolidating motor operations, reducing overhead,
eliminating ineffective department in production area, re-aligning production
facilities, changing sales plans and reassigning sales responsibilities.

1972-1977   W. H. THOMPSON & CO., Harrisburg, Pa.

This company manufactures castings, wire, rod and strip, electrical wire and
cable, fractional horsepower motors and other industrial products. Volume
$300 million.

1974-1977, VICE PRESIDENT, INTERNATIONAL OPERATIONS. Reported to President.
Supervised Director of International Marketing and Managers in Canada, Mexico,
Brazil, U.K., Europe, Australia. Responsible for:

- Profit and loss responsibility for 17 international plants and all exports.

Accomplishments:

- Increased pre-tax profits from $1.07 million to $1.69 million, including
  complete amortization of start-up costs in five new plants.
- Increased volume of manufactured product from $40 million to $45.5 million.
- Restored profitability to Canadian plant operating at a loss of $52,000.
- Achieved turn-around in SARE Division from loss of $350,000 to profit of
  $120,000; similarly for Netherlands and Brazilian companies.

<u>1972-1974</u>, VICE PRESIDENT, W. H. THOMPSON & Co. of Canada, Toronto, Ontario. Supervised General Sales Manager, Controller, and three plant managers. Responsible for:

- Profit and loss for three manufacturing locations and six product lines in $12 million division.

Achievements included:

- Improvement in pre-tax profit from $396,000 to $578,000.
- Increased revenue from $13.0 million to $15.1 million.
- reversed severe loss trend at Canadian wire plant to profit over a period of three years rising from $127,000 to $374,000.
- Improved operation at Rubberoid Plant from loss of $50,000 to a profit of $400,000.

1963-1972   VANADIUM METAL WIRE WORKS
                             ALLOY DIVISION, E. H. HUMBOLT & CO.
                             Pittsburgh, Pa.

GENERAL MANAGER with supporting staff of Assistant Works Manager, Plant Superintendent, Accountant, Metallurgist, Production and Quality Control Managers and Chief Industrial Engineer.

- started as District Sales Manager and progressed successively to Regional Sales Manager, Assistant General Sales Manager, Sales Manager.

Accomplishments:

- in first year of responsibility as General Manager turned loss of $20/30 per month to profit of $300,000 with subsequent increase to $600,000.

<u>EDUCATION</u>:

<u>B.S.</u>, Engineering, 1959, University of Pittsburgh, Pittsburgh, Pa.

Graduate work in Business Management at Northwestern and Michigan State.

<u>COMMUNITY</u> <u>ACTIVITIES</u>:

Chairman, Board of Directors, National Hospital, Winston-Salem, N.C.

Chairman, Community Chest, Winston-Salem, N.C.

Member, National Presidential Committee to Study Government Options

<u>HONORS</u>:

Winston-Salem Citizen-of-the-Year Award.

<u>HOBBIES</u>:

Tennis, golf, shooting (National 12 Bore Champion).

<u>PERSONAL</u> <u>DATA</u>:

Born 3/31/38, married, two children, excellent health, willing to relocate.

REFERENCES AND FURTHER DATA ON REQUEST

DUNCAN SMITH   Page 2

BUSINESS EXPERIENCE:

1980-Present LEAF MACHINERY DIVISION, BRF, INC., Winston-Salem N.C.	Page 1 is written last. Period of employment and name of company.

VICE PRESIDENT, GENERAL MANAGER OF $45 million tobacco machinery manufacturing division of $700 million leisure products conglomerate. Reported to parent corporate Group Vice President. Supervised V.P., R. & D., Controller Director of Marketing, European and South American Directors.

Title.
Description of kind and size of company; reporting relationship; supervisory relationships. Evaluation of a candidate is improved when one knows in what areas he or she worked.

Responsibility:

- P. & L. responsibility for U.S. division and plants in France, U.K., Brazil, and marketing headquarters in Switzerland.

Nature of responsibilities.

Achievements:

- U.K. Division lost $250,000 first quarter 1970; by August Division was operating profitably with earnings of $80,000, a swing of more than $1/2 million.

Turnaround no. 1.

- Reduced inflated U.S. payroll by $250,000.
- Successfully introduced three new products of complex technology.
- Increased Division revenue 21% and pre-tax profits 13%.
- Improved return on assets from 13.8% to 14.6%.
- Prepared, submitted and implemented five-year plan yielding compounded annual growth in pre-tax profits of 13.3%.

Got rid of non-productive employees.
Managed production, marketing, finance.
Contributed profit increase.

Measured company progress in terms of financial executive.
Made plans and carried them out.

These accomplishments were engineered by the use of PERT, Critical Path Method and other net-work techniques to improve production, eliminate bottlenecks; by re-pricing; by implementing plans which had been made but not acted upon; and by creating a new sales program.

Although this man does not have a graduate degree, the tools he used show a continuing study of management techniques. Potential employees can gauge an applicant better if a brief description of the methods used to gain the results described is provided.

1977-1980   THOMAS & SESSIONS
                 Springfield, Mo.

1979-1980, ASSISTANT to the PRESIDENT of $80 million manufacturer of meters, electric sub-assemblies, fractional horsepower motors and other products.

The same sequence and method are used for each separate employment.

1977-1979, PRESIDENT of autonomous Canadian Division with sales of $15 million. Responsible for:

- Management of complete staff: finance sales, manufacturing.
- Divisional profit and loss.
- Assisting the President of parent company.
- Presiding at Director's and Stockholders' meetings.

Administered Chief Executive Officer responsibilities.

Accomplishments:

- In 1977 losses were above $1/2 million   Turnaround no. 2.
  annually; by end 1969 losses were
  eliminated and profits stood at all-
  time high of $1.137 million.

  This was accomplished by consolidating   Methods used in accomplishing.
  motor operations, reducing overhead, elimi-
  nating ineffective department in production
  area, realigning production facilities,
  changing sales plans and reassigning sales
  responsibilities.

1963-1977   W. H. THOMPSON & CO.
                   Harrisburg, Pa.

This company manufactures castings, wire   Description of what Company
rod and strip, electrical wire and cable,   made and its volume.
fractional horsepower motors and other
industrial products. Volume $300 million.

1974-1977, VICE PRESIDENT, INTERNATIONAL
OPERATIONS. Reported to President.

Supervised Director of International Marketing and Managers in Canada, Mexico, Brazil,
U.K., Europe, Australia. Responsible for:

- Profit and loss responsibility for 17   Multi-division responsibility
  international plants and all exports.

Accomplishments:

- Increased pre-tax profits from $1.07   Increased profits.
  million to $1.69 million, including
  complete amortization of start-up costs
  in five new plants.
- Increase volume of manufactured product   Improved production.
  from $40 million to $45.5 million.
- Restored profitability to Canadian plant   Turnaround no. 3.
  operating at a loss of $52,000.
- Achieved turn-around in SARE Division   Turnaround no. 4.
  from loss of $350,000 to profit of
  $120,000; similarly for Netherlands and   Turnaround no. 5.
  Brazilian companies.

1972-1974, VICE PRESIDENT, W. H. Thompson
& Co. of Canada, Toronto, Ontario. Supervised General Sales Manager, Controller,
and three plant managers. Responsible for:

- Profit and loss for three manufacturing
  locations and six product lines in $12
  million division.

Achievements included:

- Improvement in pre-tax profit from   Increased profits.
  $396,000 to $578,000
- Increased revenue from $13.0 million   Increased sales.
  to $15.0 million.
- Reversed severe loss trend at American   Turnaround no. 6.
  wire plant to profit over a period of
  three years rising from $127,000 to
  $374,000.
- Improved operation at Rubberoid Plant   Turnaround no. 7.
  from loss of $50,000 to a profit of
  $400,000.

1963-1972   VANADIUM METAL WIRE WORKS,
                   ALLOY DIVISION, E. H.
                   HUMBOLT & CO., Pittsburgh,
                   Pa.

GENERAL MANAGER with supporting staff of
Assistant Works Manager, Plant Superintendent, Accountant, Metallurgist, Production
and Quality Control Managers and Chief Industrial Engineer.

- started as District Sales Manager and   Sales experience.
  progressed successively to Regional Sales
  Manager, Assistant General Sales Manager,
  Sales Manager.

Accomplishments:

- in first year of responsibility as Gen-   Turnaround no. 8.
  eral Manager turned loss of $20/30,000
  per month to profit of $300,000 annually
  with subsequent increase to $600,000.

Offered and accepted position with Vanadium
(as described).

EDUCATION:

B. S., Engineering, 1959, University of
Pittsburgh, Pittsburgh, Pa.

Graduate work in Business Management at
Northwestern and University of Michigan.

COMMUNITY ACTIVITIES:

Chairman, Board of Directors, National   Took leading role in community
Hospital, Winston-Salem, N. C.   activities adding to image of
                                                 corporation among employees
Chairman, Community Chest, Winston-   and others.
Salem, N. C.

Member, National Presidential Committee to
Study Government Options.

HONORS:

Winston-Salem Citizen-of-the-Year Award.   Recognized for community activities.

HOBBIES:

Tennis, golf, shooting (National 12 Bore   The hobbies are interesting and
Champion).   well worth including.

PERSONAL DATA:
Born 3/31/38, married, two children,   REFERENCES and FURTHER
excellent health, willing to relocate.   DATA on REQUEST

address   telephone

RESUME

of

DUNCAN SMITH

qualified as

SENIOR MANAGEMENT EXECUTIVE

THIS IS WRITTEN <u>LAST</u> BUT
WHEN COMPLETED BECOMES PAGE
ONE OF THE RESUME.

*** Record of consistent profit con-
tributions amounting to millions
of dollars in general management,
marketing, production in the U.S.,
Canada and internationally; accustomed for the last ten years
to autonomous multi-division
P. & L. responsibility and responsible for at least eight
turnaround situations involving
significant figures.

This is a concise statement of
the accomplishments described
in the body of the resume and of
the nature of this man's responsibilities which were at the highest
level (P. & L.) and covering the
major divisions of a business:
marketing, production, finance.

*** Equipped to use latest manage-
ment sciences including PERT,
CPM and other network techniques
to accomplish company goals.

This is evidence of professional
management.

*** Intimately familiar with the metal-
working industry and with sophisticated machinery and equipment
in a broad area of manufacturing.

This statement identified the
general area in which management
has been exercised.

*** Characterized by others as an in-
spiring leader, incisive in identifying problems, imaginative in
finding and implementing solutions,
strong in comprehensive, accurate
planning leading to improved profitability.

An <u>objective</u> evaluation of the
subjects most important qualities.

60

DISCUSSION

Chronological Résumé with Summary Page. The Duncan Smith résumé is a good example of an executive's résumé. It is longer than most because the subject has a long history of accomplishments. Those who hire executives want a comprehensive picture of the subject before expending, and perhaps wasting, time on an interview of several hours. The form of résumé was selected because there is nothing to hide in his chronology, with achievements increasing in each successive position. Furthermore, the *Chronological* form permits maximum capitalization on accomplishments. A résumé of this kind could be written only by a man who is supremely confident that there is no area of management in which he does not have experience and knowledge to support his claims.

Evidence of continuing formal management study is indicated by the use of network techniques to reach decisions. Experience in all the elements of management is shown: marketing, finance, production, general management. Used to being known for qualities of leadership and imagination, he does not hesitate to state them in his résumé, because he knows that the readers of his résumé will not learn about these qualities unless he tells them.

Mr. Smith's résumé creates a favorable attitude. If his interview techniques and his actual experience as brought out in an interview are as good as his writing, he is assured of employment.

The summary page is used in this instance to highlight some areas in his career and some material that contributes to his total image. It should make the reader want to read the body of the résumé.

The résumé provides a strong basis for selection for an interview and for an interesting interview discussion.

275 John Brown's Crossing   Home (212) 321-7654
New York, NY 10012   Office (212) 456-0987

R E S U M E

of

VINCENT BENET

an experienced

EXECUTIVE SALESMAN

* * *   Approximately 20 years of experience with leading company
         in personal sales, marketing and regional sales management.

* * *   Record of success in achieving national recognition for
         type, quality and volume of sales produced; received
         bonuses and awards; more important - produced outstanding
         profits.

* * *   Experienced in hiring and training salesmen, developing
         quotas and objectives, formulating and implementing market-
         ing and sales strategies and techniques.

* * *   A record as hardworking winner with reputation of being
         the man "least wanted to be in competition with."

* * *   Enjoy excellent contacts among key personnel of major
         companies. Adept at establishing and maintaining
         productive relationships and experience in customer/public
         relations; an exceptional and exciting platform public
         speaker.

* * *   37 years old. Bachelor of Arts Degree with honors and
         considerable graduate work in Psychology.

* * *   In short, achieved all quotas seven times out of ten
         years; in three of these years, quotas had been raised
         out of all proportion to previous historical sales - in-
         creased sales by 400% - boosted profits.

FOR FURTHER DATA PLEASE SEE FOLLOWING PAGES

* Record of success in achieving a 400% increase in sales as a
   result of effective sales management:

<u>1972-Present</u>   BRIDGE CO., Freeport, NY

       This is a major producer of business machines and data
       processing equipment.

       As SALES MANAGER, Office Products Sales and Data Entry
       Sales, in the Brooklyn and Queens area, have been respon-
       sibile for:

       - Supervision and training of six salesmen.
       - Development of schedules, strategies and techniques to
          develop leads and increase sales. Brooklyn and Queens
          are unique in that they have relatively few very large
          customers. It was, therefore, necessary to tap the
          potential smaller market. This was done and the
          region generated 10% of nationwide sales.
       - Achieved heavy personal sales and won sales bonuses
          year after year; became one of the highest producers
          in the company.
       - Participated in the establishment of sales quotas and
          product mix and developed promotional programs.
       - Systematically and effectively converted "low grade
          sales" to become high-grade sales involving increased
          profitabilities.
       - Instituted a regional policy to require cash deposits
          on orders and substantially decreased cancellations. So
          dramatic were the results that this became standard
          company policy.
       - Maintained a "get tough" collection policy without
          sacrifice of good will or cordial public relations.

* Other experience in maximizing sales through modern sales management
   techniques:

<u>1964-1972</u>   BRIDGE CO., Boston, MA

       As SALES MANAGER, supervised a group of salesmen and achieved
       sales quotas seven out of eight years.

       - Maintained continuing market surveys to determine customer
          needs.
       - Worked closely with key personnel of customers and potential
          customers to maintain sales of accessories and supplies,
          upgrade equipment and provide corporate technical and
          maintenance services.
       - Nearly tripled personal earnings.
       - Designed retail accounting equipment that ultimately
          resulted in multimillion-dollar sales.

* Demonstrated talent for industrial and consumer sales; achieved countrywide leadership:

<u>1962-1964</u>   IBM CORP., New York, NY

As ACCOUNT MANAGER/SALES REPRESENTATIVE achieved sales quota each year and was responsible for:

- Development of an outstanding sales record; substantially contributed to my division's becoming the leader on a country-wide performance record.
- Successfully penetrated accounts such as Railway Express, Texaco, American Can and others.

<u>1959</u>   GROLIER CORPORATION

Sold encyclopedias door-to-door throughout New York, New Jersey, Massachusetts, Connecticut, Rhode Island, Vermont, etc. part-time while attending college.

Finished seventh out of 1,000 salespeople in national 20-week contest.

* <u>MILITARY SERVICE</u>

<u>1957-1959</u> UNITED STATES NAVY

Served as Instructor at the U.S. Naval Academy at Annapolis. Received special commendation for class overall proficiency, then the highest in Academy history.

* <u>EDUCATION</u>

<u>1962</u> UNIVERSITY OF GEORGIA

Received a Bachelor of Arts degree and attained the Dean's List in the senior year.

<u>1973-1977</u>   NEW SCHOOL FOR SOCIAL RESEARCH

Completed several courses in Psychology which contributed to my understanding of human relations and markedly influenced the success of sales activities.

At college, played varsity football, lacrosse, was Sports Editor, worked summers during college.

* <u>PERSONAL DATA</u>

37 years old, married, one child, excellent health.

<u>REFERENCES AND FURTHER DATA ON REQUEST</u>

DISCUSSION

Chronological Résumé with Summary Page with Variation. The variations from the norm in the Benet résumé are a final paragraph summarizing his most important assets and headlines emphasizing the outstanding factor in each chronologically listed position. Either variation or both can be used. Headlines can serve to unify the items in a résumé if they are informative, relevant, and important.

This résumé reflects the personality of the subject in the use of punctuation, quoted phrases, and relatively informal language imbued with a sense of excitement.

The summary page serves an effective purpose in giving a special dimension to the subject apart from the material in the résumé.

This is a salesman who sounds like a salesman and would undoubtedly receive invitations for interviews upon submitting this résumé.

A summary page can often be used to incorporate material that does not fit gracefully into the body of a résumé.

90 Divine Towpath   (000) 456-7890
Stage, CT 12345

RESUME

LILY LANGTRY

MAGAZINE EDITORIAL DIRECTOR - EDITOR

Qualifications: Twenty years of successful experience as Managing
                 Editor with unusually broad responsibilities embracing
                 three successful magazines with a largely female reader-
                 ship; and as Executive Editor, Managing Editor, Fea-
                 tures Editor, Assistant Editor in reverse chronology;
                 with three different publishers.

                     Publishers Weekly said: "The most knowledgeable
                     woman's editor in the field." (June 1984)

                     Magazine Writer's Digest said: "Miss Langtry has
                     helped more aspiring writers than anyone I know."
                     (Jan. 1983)

                     Magazine Guild said: "Miss Langtry has identified her
                     markets and hit them in the bull's-eye'; without ques-
                     tion one of the most talented editors in her field."
                     (Nov. 1980)

Objective   COMPETENT in all areas of manuscript selection and pur-
evaluation by   chase, production, control, organization and administra-
Corporate   tion, wide author contacts and excellent reputation for
Manpower   judgment, decisiveness and creativity.
Development
Committee   Possesses in high degree ability to lead, supervise,
on Executive   train and gain loyalty and dedication of staff.
Evaluation: Oriented to profitable operations.

                 SENSITIVE to editorial and reader needs; capable of
                 bringing them together to gain optimum circulation and
                 to make changes quickly as need appears. (Dec. 1975)

Employment   1971-1985 - National Publications, New York, NY
history:
                 1965-1971 - Hillside Publishing Company, New York, NY

                 1964-1965 - Rex Magazine Company, New York, NY

Education: B.S., Journalism, University of Syracuse, Syracuse, NY,
                 1963.

Personal data: Single, excellent health, no dependents, willing to
                 relocate.

REFERENCES **AND FURTHER DATA** ON REQUEST

DISCUSSION

Creative Résumé. Ms. Langtry's résumé is an excellent example of much relevant and attractive material condensed for presentation on one page. Ms. Langtry, a successful writer, was able to describe 20 years of experience in about 200 words while expressing a competence that might easily have required several pages. She has effectively made use of the words of others, permitting discussions of talents that would be ill-received if expressed subjectively.

The résumé does not follow a formal pattern and is therefore a *Creative Résumé.*

Objective statements can often be obtained from such sources as references, personal evaluations, military evaluations, and press clippings. If well expressed, they can be used as shown in this résumé.

FUNCTIONAL RÉSUMÉ

The *Functional Résumé* organizes work experience by function, such as general marketing, management, production, finance, or their subfunctions. Chronology is disregarded. To facilitate comparison, we have refashioned one of our *Chronological Résumé* examples into functional form.

The *Functional Résumé* stresses the scope of experience, much as does a summary page. It has the disadvantage of not relating accomplishments to the pertinent company or companies. Most employers are familiar with other companies, especially in the same industry, and take company affiliations into account when judging accomplishments. The same experience is more impressive if gained at a widely known company than at an unknown company.

The writer of a *Functional Résumé,* not being hampered by chronology, can easily change emphasis or camouflage past experience. This is advantageous in cases in which past job experience is best explained in a personal interview, rather than in writing. We reiterate that the main purpose of a résumé is to gain an interview; it is not a substitute for an interview.

The *Functional Résumé* tends to be shorter than the *Chronological Résumé.* The example that follows has been further shortened to avoid monotonous repetition. Both the *Functional Résumé* and the *Functional-by-Company (Institution) Résumé* are well regarded by institutional recruiters.

CONSTANTINE BISHKO
375 Broadalban Road
Ephrata, PA 12345
(177) 377-4777

SENIOR EXECUTIVE experienced in all areas of General Management

SUMMARY OF QUALIFICATIONS

Record of consistent profit contributions amounting to millions of dollars in general management, marketing and production in the U.S. and internationally; accustomed to autonomous multidivision responsibility. Equipped to use all management techniques to accomplish company objectives.

GENERAL MANAGEMENT	Accomplished seven divisional turnarounds leading these divisions from high five-figure losses to six-figure profits in periods ranging from three months to two years.
PRODUCTION	Successfully engineered and produced four new products of complex technology supervising Manufacturing Manager, Controller, various engineering disciplines and marketing development.
MARKETING	Conceived and implemented new marketing plan which broadened distribution and increased volume 27%; increased profits 9%.
FINANCE	Instituted new financial controls and procedures; increased cash flow 19%; improved R.O.I. 13%; set objectives and achieved financial ratios which became envy of the industry.
TECHNICAL BACKGROUND	Intimately familiar with the metalworking industry and with sophisticated machinery and equipment in a broad area of manufacturing.

FOR FURTHER DATA PLEASE SEE FOLLOWING PAGE

EMPLOYMENT HISTORY

1975-Present   LEAF MANUFACTURING DIVISION, BRF, INC., Winston-Salem,
                NC.
1972-1975   THOMAS & SESSIONS, Springfield, MO.
1967-1972   W. H. THOMPSON & CO, Harrisburg, PA.
1958-1967   VANADIUM METAL WIRE WORKS, Pittsburgh, PA.

EDUCATION

B.S., Engineering, University of Pittsburgh, Pittsburgh, PA.

Graduate work in Business Administration and Management at Northwestern
and Michigan State Universities.

COMMUNITY ACTIVITIES

Chairman, Board of Directors, National Hospital, Winston-Salem, NC.

Chairman, Community Chest, Winston-Salem, NC.

Member, National Presidential Committee to Study Government Options.

HONORS

Winston-Salem Citizen-of-the-Year Award.

HOBBIES

Tennis, golf, shooting (National 12-Bore Champion)

PERSONAL DATA

Born 3/31/33, married, two children, excellent health. Willing to
relocate.

REFERENCES AND FURTHER DATA ON REQUEST

Functional Résumé.   Mr. Bishko has experience in all four major facets of management—marketing, finance, production, and general management. The *Functional Résumé* is particularly suitable for expressing such experience. It is also suitable for one who has had the following experience:

IN MARKETING

   Territory selling
   Regional management
   Sales or product management
   Sales management

IN FINANCE

   Accounting
   Controller
   Treasurer

IN PRODUCTION

   Foreman
   Superintendent
   Plant manager
   Director of R&D
   General manager

IN EDUCATIONAL ADMINISTRATION

   Teaching
   Curriculum planning
   Administration

The subject areas can be further expanded to include, for example, network techniques in production planning, other important financial ratios, and the most important markets.

11 East 81st Street
New York, NY 10000

Home (212) 000-0000
Office (212) 000-0000
X37

R E S U M E

ELOISE LE BEQUE SANTINI

OBJECTIVE: Editor or Assistant Editor, domestic or international.

EXPERIENCE

EDITOR: 1983-Present McGRAW-HILL CO., New York, NY.
                Editor of trade magazine, Main Floor Merchandising, with
                A.B.C. verified circulation of 90,000; changed format, im-
                proved editorial content, organized and balanced advertis-
                ing space with resulting increase in advertising revenue
                of 23%.

TRANSLATOR &   1980-1983 ARCHITECTURAL DIGEST, Boulder, CO.
EDITOR: Translated French and Italian editorial material into
                English, selected photographs, and edited for publication
                (New York office).

ASSISTANT   1980-1983 NATIONAL GEOGRAPHIC, Washington, DC.
EDITOR: (concurrently) Full- and part-time editor of new geograph-
                ical reference book (New York office).

ANNOTATIONS   1982 CONSORTIUM OF UNITED MUSEUMS, New York, NY.
EDITOR: (concurrently) Edited computer-generated data, including
                annotations to 30,000 films; for verification of names
                and addresses for producer's directory; editing for con-
                sistency of information.

TRANSLATOR: 1979-1980 MAINSTREAM PUBLISHING CO., New York, NY.
                Translated from English into French for all outgoing ma-
                terial to launch international information service. Trans-
                lated from Italian to English, Source book on Italian
                Renaissance structures with photographs and titles, 12,000
                entries; for new book.

EDITORIAL   1978 JOVANOVICH & SPEAR, New York, NY.
CONSULTANT: Consultant in preparation of books on conversational French
                and Italian.

PUBLICATIONS: A comparative study of Dante's narrative and dramatic modes.

(continued)

EDUCATION: B.A., Bryn Mawr College, Bryn Mawr, PA, 1977.
                Columbia University, New York, NY, doctoral candidate.
                La Sorbonne, Paris, France, Certificat Supérieur de Langue
                    Française.

LANGUAGES: Fluent in French, Italian and Spanish.

PERSONAL DATA: Age 29, single, excellent health.

REFERENCES: Available on request.

DISCUSSION

Functional Résumé.   The Santini résumé resulted in a position, whereas two previous résumés of a different style had failed. The young woman found the job market difficult because she had spent too much time in academia, had never had a full-time job of any importance, and left the impression of being overintellectualized for the give and take of commercial enterprise. Upon analysis, however, a listing of her activities showed an amazing breadth of experience and willingness to handle detail that would unquestionably have value to a publisher, if her scope could be properly expressed. Lack of consistent work experience was glossed over. Only positive elements were stated. There was once a popular song with a title applicable to résumés: "Accentuate the Positive."

This format is sometimes recommended by public library advisors, among others, but in a different way, for example, using character elements—motivated, leader, multilingual, educated, disciplined, experienced, accomplished, and so on—where Miss Santini headlined her work functions. We think that such an adaptation (character elements) of the *Functional* style would be useless, except possibly for one with no work experience, such as a recent graduate. Should that be your status, try this variation and compare it with a more traditional format. We do not recommend the listing of character attributes in this style because it is or can easily become showy, boastful, subjective, aggrandizing.

78 Whitney Road   (789) 123-7654
Gastonia, NC 77777

R E S U M E

of

<u>JOHN KAY</u>

<u>TEXTILE EXECUTIVE</u>

Progressive career in textile industry beginning with textile education
and graduation with honors, continuing with important assignments for
major textile manufacturers, culminating in part ownership of speciality
knitting company growing from inception at zero to $7 million in three
years. Recently sold interest in this profitable enterprise to partners;
now available for employment in the industry as Director of Marketing
or Manufacturing or both.

EXPERIENCE

As General Manager: Created company, starting with zero sales, climbing
                      to $7 million in three years, operating profitably.
                      Directed building of dye house. Started new depart-
                      ment for giant textile manufacturer ($800 million
                      plus) aimed at Men's Wear market for single and
                      double knits.

                      Purchased complete equipment needed for new depart-
                      ment (reaching $30 million volume). Established new
                      basis for profitable pricing.

                      Set up R.&D. program to promote growth.

As Director of   Departmentalized each phase of manufacturing assign-
Manufacturing: ing efficiency and capacity ratings; established
                      basis for dependable delivery schedules. Imple-
                      mented new procedures for determining true costs as
                      basis for profitable pricing.

                      Initiated improved quality control. Utilized (DKJ/36
                      and other) double knit pattern lock, nonjacquard and
                      interlock machines, rib transfer machines, single
                      knit equipment 18 to 26 cut, tuck bars, wheels, rale-
                      ways, plain jerseys, finishing, dyeing and bulking
                      equipment; with continuous upgrading.

                                                        over please

As Marketing   Developed seasonal lines by market end-use and fiber
Manager: mix.

                      Developed special programs for key customers, pre-
                      sented new programs and lines.

                      Created new sales programs and new advertising. In-
                      troduced "coordinated look" in Men's Wear, achieved
                      dominant market position for new Division of giant
                      textile producer.

                      Maintained close "intelligence" liaison with sales-
                      men and customers.

EMPLOYMENT RECORD

1980-1983   NEW WEAVE COMPANY, New York, NY
                      VICE PRESIDENT AND GENERAL MANAGER

1970-1980   INTERNATIONAL FABRICS, INC., New York, NY
                      GENERAL MANAGER, $60 million Men's Wear Division

1967-1970   TERJAVIAN ET CIE, Brussels, Belgium
                      DIRECTOR OF MANUFACTURING for North Carolina mill of
                      $1 billion international knitter after earlier sub-
                      ordinate experience.

MILITARY SERVICE: U.S. NAVY, 1965-1967. Served as Flight Lieutenant
                      aboard Aircraft Carrier in South China Sea.

EDUCATION: B.S., New York Institute of Textile Technology and
                      Merchandising, Hamilton, NY, 1964. Graduated Cum
                      Laude.

                      Graduate work at Bennett University, New York, NY, 196
                      Scholarship Award from International Institute of Tex-
                      tile Design.

LANGUAGES: French and Spanish (fluent).

HOBBIES: Platform tennis (ranked in first 10), skeet.

PERSONAL DATA: Age 42, married, three children, excellent health.
                      Willing to relocate.

REFERENCES AND FURTHER DATA ON REQUEST

76

DISCUSSION

Functional Résumé. The Kay résumé utilizes language appropriate to the industry. By naming the types of knitwear and knitting machinery the applicant illustrates his mastery of production techniques as well as an understanding and implementation of objectives. The marketing section shows imagination in theme development to create an important share of market.

Like all other résumés in this book, this résumé shows what a successful person has done to improve job performance and how such improvement invariably contributes to the profitability and well-being of a company or institution.

The experiences related in this résumé could have been equally well expressed in other résumé styles. The *Functional* form was selected because of some inconsistencies in the chronology of employment and achievements, which would have been disadvantageously disclosed in the *Chronological* form but could easily be explained during an interview.

FUNCTIONAL-BY-COMPANY
(INSTITUTION) RÉSUMÉ

The *Functional-by-Company (Institution) Résumé* lists functions for each employer. In this respect it is superior to the *Functional Résumé*. However, the listing of functions performed for a company need not be chronological, which, though a bit misleading to the reader, may be of advantage to you. Keep in mind that a résumé is an evaluation of you. In taking "poetic license" with your chronology you may improve your résumé and gain an interview, during which discrepancies can be explained.

Preceding comments aside, the *Functional-by-Company (Institution) Résumé* is well suited for teachers and professors and is well received by academic recruiters. Two examples follow, including one for the educational area.

EXAMPLE OF FUNCTIONAL-BY-COMPANY (INSTITUTION) RÉSUMÉ

100 Accomplishment Way   Home (123) 456-7890
Erewhon, MN 12345   Office (098) 765-4321

R E S U M E

HORATIO ALGER

EXECUTIVE

SUMMARY OF QUALIFICATIONS

Experienced in all areas of management: Marketing, Production, Finance
and multidivision operations. Record of consistent profit contributions
in identifying and developing new markets, in creating more effective
advertising themes, in reducing manufacturing costs and lead times, in
reducing inventories, increasing cash flow and doubling price of common
stock in a period of 12 months under adverse market conditions.

EXPERIENCE

1975-Present   GENERAL LEISURE PRODUCTS COMPANY, INC., Winona, MN

                1982-Present, PRESIDENT and GENERAL MANAGER with P.&L.
                responsibility for $100 million leisure products manu-
                facturing division of $600 million conglomerate. Report
                to parent company President. Supervise Vice Presidents of
                Marketing, Manufacturing, Human Resources, Planning,
                Finance, and R.&D.

R.&D.   - led Research & Development team in development of new
                  concept in grass-mowing equipment.

MARKETING   - made innovation in merchandising and advertising home
                  snow removal machine.
                - utilized technology developed in mowing machinery to
                  manufacture snowmobile; captured first place in Alaska
                  race test.

MANUFACTURING   - selected new wholesale organization to concentrate on
                  Company (with partial financing by Company).
                - increased volume from $60 million to $100 million in
                  four years.

FINANCE   - increased value of AMEX-listed stock from six to 12-1/2
                  in 1985, based on earnings multiplication.
                - reduced inventory by one-third, leading to increase in
                  ROI.

                                          over please

1980-1982, VICE PRESIDENT, MANUFACTURING

MANUFACTURING   - consolidated manufacture of motors in one plant here-
                  tofore distributed among four plants around the U.S.
                - closed least efficient manufacturing plant; utilized
                  space for needed new warehouse.
                - reorganized flow of production for motors, building own
                  specialized automated equipment; reduced lead time from
                  six to three months and manufacturing cycle from two
                  months to two weeks.
                - restyled mowers, snow removers, electric garden tools;
                  developed, with R.&D., new concept in electric grass
                  shears which became nationwide best sellers and con-
                  tributed $6 million of profitable new volume.

1978-1980, GENERAL MANAGER, Caracas, Venezuela

MANUFACTURING   - recognized application of new technology to manufacture
                  of small horsepower motors; increased plant productivity
                  by 30%; technology adopted in three U.S. plants with
                  similar results.
GENERAL   - met with government officials to gain "favored manu-
MANAGEMENT   facturer" status in Venezuela, leading to lower export
                  duties.
                - expanded distribution to Colombia and Brazil with
                  consequent doubling of volume.
FINANCE   - reorganized accounting procedures; speeded corporate
                  monthly reports by ten days each month, leading to
                  quicker identification of problem areas and increase in
                  profits from 6% to 15% before taxes.
MARKETING   - conducted market research leading to distribution of
                  wider group of U.S. manufactured products in South
                  America, with only minor changes in styling.

1975-1978, SALES MANAGER for U.S. and South America

MARKETING   - studied marketing procedures in the U.S. and South
                  America.
                - studied company potential for new products in areas of
                  competence.
                - increased U.S. sales 25% through new system of regional
                  profit centers and improved training methods.
SALES   - switched main distribution efforts from traditional
                  outlets to newer forms of distribution.
                - increased sales in South America by 15% and recom-
                  mended change in product mix which led to accomplish-
                  ments previously mentioned.

1966-1970   AVERILL & HARRIMAN COMPANY, INC., Dellmore, IL

            VICE PRESIDENT, MANUFACTURING for small ($40 million)
            manufacturer of marine motors. Responsible for:

            - complete manufacturing operations and R.&D. Department.

Accomplishments:

MANUFACTURING - set up new production line using new automatic equip-
                 ment.
               - cleared out accumulated inventory of excessive parts
                 and raw material, improved turnover from three to four
                 times annually.
               - reorganized engineering department, breaking up
                 authority into Quality Control, Production Control,
                 Production Engineering, Methods Engineering.
               - conducted cost studies leading to 11% reduction in
                 costs.
               - conducted value studies; made decision to purchase
                 fasteners and other components at a saving of 16% in
                 raw material costs.
               - accelerated manufacturing cycle time by 17%, leading
                 to a further cost reduction of 12%.

Invited by executive search firm to consider position with General
Leisure Products; accepted.

1958-1961 AUTOMOTIVE PARTS, INC., Jackson, MI

           ASSISTANT PLANT MANAGER (one of seven) for $100 million
           manufacturer of small parts for the BIG-3 auto manu-
           facturers.

           Learned automatic and automated production methods with
           one of the most advanced companies in the industry.

MILITARY SERVICE: U.S. ARMY AIR FORCE, 1961-1966. Captain. Served in
                  Vietnam.

EDUCATION: B.S., Engineering, California Institute of Technol-
                  ogy, Pasadena, CA, 1962. Graduate work in Business
                  Management, 1956 Stanford University, Stanford, CA.

COMMUNITY   Chairman, Board of Directors, National Hospital,
ACTIVITIES: Winona, MN.

                  Chairman, Community Chest, Winona, MN.

HONORS: Winona Citizen-of-the-Year Award.

HOBBIES: Tobogganing (National Two-Man Champion), skeet, trap,
                  crosscountry skiing.

PERSONAL DATA: Born 3/31/32, married, three children, excellent
                  health.

REFERENCES AND FURTHER DATA ON REQUEST

DISCUSSION

Functional-by-Company (Institution) Résumé. The Alger résumé illustrates how career progression can be effectively expressed using a combination of the *Functional* and the *Chronological* styles.

This applicant started in production, moved quickly to another company utilizing the production skills learned earlier, and became head of manufacturing for a medium-sized company. Here he demonstrated good management skills in all areas of production. He moved again to a position involving marketing to round his experience and immediately showed talent in this field, advancing quickly to general management of the company's South American division and two years later to the vice-presidency of the headquarters plant. By this time his ability in each position gave such strong indications of the highest qualities of leadership that he was appointed president of the company with results that made a strongly favorable impact on the company and its stockholders.

This is a capsule illustration not only of excellent management but also of career planning, in which the subject determined to make himself knowledgeable in all areas of management.

One First Avenue   Home (212) 332-4455
Brentwood, NY 54321   Office (212) 432-6688

CURRICULUM VITAE

OF

SAMUEL JOHNSON

OBJECTIVE

Administrative Position with a Foundation, Educational or other
nonprofit organization.

EDUCATION

M.S., Education, Columbia University, New York, NY, 1966.

B.S., History, University of Pennsylvania, Philadelphia, PA, 1967.
Cum Laude.

Doctoral studies in Philosophy of Education.

SUMMARY OF QUALIFICATIONS

Eleven years of experience in the development of sound educational
systems, administration and teaching.

HONORS

Cited in "The Last 20 Years of Education in the United States," 1st
ed. (1975-1984), Langston and Rhodes, 1985.

Named in Who's Who in Colleges and Universities, 1964, 1965, 1966.

Bronz Star in Vietnam, 1967. Silver Star, Vietnam, 1968. Captain,
U.S. Army.

over please

83

PUBLICATIONS

The Influence of Experimentation on Basic Learning Skills, Barnes and
Dunlop, 1980, 342pp.

Basic Education in a Changing Society, Noble and Morrow, 1979, 307pp.

Paper: A Comparison of Test Scores in Reading and Writing.   Columbia
         University Review, 1976

ACCREDITATIONS

Boston Board of Education, License No. 123456.

New York State Regents License No 987654.

ADMINISTRATIVE EXPERIENCE

1977-Present: OLIVER W. HOLMES UNIVERSITY, Brentwood, NY

UNIVERSITY PLANNING OFFICER for University with student body of 2500
projected to rise to 3600 by 1987, faculty of 350 projected to 500
by 1987.
- Established plans for operation of University with student body expansion 1977-1987 including organization, functional responsibilities,
  philosophy.
- Provided plans for space needs, faculty expansion, additional
  courses of study, new doctoral program, budgets, sources of income.
- Recommended enlarged emphasis on teaching skills vs. publication and
  outside consulting activities.

1975-1977:   GOVERNOR WHEELOCK ACADEMY, West Falls, MA

ASSISTANT HEADMASTER for small (400 pupils) preparatory school in rural
setting.

-Upgraded teaching staff.
-Supervised construction of new gymnasium
-Participated in fund-raising activities.
-Coached football and lacrosse.
-Worked with Headmaster and Board of Trustees on ten-year plan for
 Academy.

EDUCATIONAL SYSTEMS EXPERIENCE

1973-1975:   NEW YORK STATE REGENTS COMMITTEE ON CURRICULUM REVISION

Invited as one of a committee of seven to study, evaluate and recommend
changes in existing methods of teaching at the grade levels 7 to 12.

                                                    over please

- Instituted study of comparative reading and writing tests among 400 high schools chosen by lot in New York State; evaluated data; recommended revision in reading and remedial reading to encompass, as appropriate, individual student teaching, group teaching by skill levels, and reemphasis on phonetics for nonhandicapped students.

- Instituted study of methods of teaching mathematics; recommended that study of "New Math" be taught in grade 12 instead of grade 9. Recommended additional emphasis on computer mathematics.

- Recommended expanded use of E.D.P. recordkeeping, marking, teacher evaluation, Beta system development utilizing minicomputers in specialized areas.

TEACHING EXPERIENCE

<u>1971-1973</u>: BENJAMIN FRANKLIN HIGH SCHOOL, New York, NY

<u>History</u>, <u>History of Western Civilization, History as a Guide to the Future</u>. Developed and selected materials that were highly motivating, varied, skill-directed, individualized. Rated in annual Board of Education review, "Thorough knowledge of subject." "Superior in instructional approach." "Effective in discipline."

Appointed by Principal to Policy Committee which participated in making decisions related to instruction, administration, overall school evaluations.

Helped write Federal Government proposal for creation of a teacher corps in New York City in conjuction with school district personnel, university department heads, principals and teachers.

VITAL STATISTICS

Born 3/31/46, married, three children, excellent health.

REFERENCES AND FURTHER DATA ON REQUEST

DISCUSSION

Functional-by-Company (Institution) Résumé—Nonprofit Objective.   In an educational or scientific career the pertinent credentials should be given at the beginning. Though essentially *Functional-by-Company (Institution),* the Johnson résumé starts with education and lists honors, publications, and accreditations immediately thereafter.

The career begins with teaching, proceeds to curriculum planning and to administration, and culminates in a presently held responsible position at a large university.

The job history is progressive, it has led to the formulation of an educational philosophy, and it embraces the kinds of experience most useful in performing the operating functions within the job objectives named at the outset.

Academic degrees, continuing study, an understanding of the student mind, and research in experimental and orthodox teaching methods project an individual who can contribute much to the growth and development of a nonprofit institution, particularly in academe.

HARVARD RÉSUMÉ

The *Harvard Résumé* is widely used because of its appearance and its immediate association by sophisticated readers with the Harvard Graduate School of Business Administration. It has narrow margins and long, rather informal paragraphs. The density of writing often makes it difficult to read.

Accomplishments are less sharply delineated in the *Harvard Résumé* than in other types of résumés. An unusually large amount of personal data might be given. The form usually is *Chronological,* sometimes *Functional-Chronological.*

An example of the *Harvard Résumé* follows.

R E S U M E

Tyne E. Tym
3 Dickens Lane
Grosvenor, MN
(123) 456-7890

OBJECTIVE

A general management or marketing opportunity where broad experience in
mechanical products would be valuable. Major emphasis in background includes:

- P.&L. responsibility.

- General Management, sales management and field sales experience.

- Extensive experience with wide range of markets and new product development.

EXPERIENCE

Jan. 1983   LIMITED CO., INC. Harrison, MO
   to
Present   Residential division of Keeping Co., Inc, an independent
            sheet metal contractor, with annual volume in the range of
            $12 million, serving residential, commercial and industrial
            markets.

Vice-President

Formed and autonomously manage a new division concentrating on the residential market. Sales were increased by 100% in first two years while
getting new division started; earned profit from beginning amounting to
12% before taxes in second year.

Accomplishments also include:

- Developing and implementing an overall business plan; market analysis;
  order forecasting; production plan; manpower needs and recruiting plan;
  training; P.&L. forecast; facilities and equipment; capital expenditure and operating capital requirements.

- Recruited and trained over 300 people.

- Developing product changes, standardized, production and standard costs
  to achieve 16% reduction in product cost.

- Developing consumer financing plans with St. Louis and Kansas City
  banks to support expanded sales activities.

- Taking the organization into new product areas to expand markets and
  eliminate seasonal weaknesses.

1980   COMPANY HALT, INC, Joliet, MO
to
1983   A_$5 million manufacturer of mechanical equipment for commercial
        and industrial use.

General Sales Manager

Responsible for all sales through 23 independent U.S. dealers and 35
overseas distributors; with a staff of five.

Orders were increased by 20% in weakening markets which had shown a de-
cline.

Earnings were increased through:

- price increases.

- reducing expenses through strict budget applications.

- implementing product cost reduction programs to obtain lower costs in
  a period of rising prices.

Also made changes in representation; set up new dealers; instituted new
training program for all dealers retained; redirected advertising.

1966   UNINVITED COMPANY, INC., Middletown, MO
to
1980   A $100 million manufacturer of plumbing equipment for resi-
        dential, commercial and industrial use.

Manager, Dealer Development, March 1979 to April 1980

Responsible for all Crane dealer activities to sell commercial and residential plumbing supplies. New dealers were established through company
financing and long-range plans for growth. This involved management of
internal staff, regional staff and local offices in recruiting and training qualified personnel to own and operate dealerships. It also involved
development of management skills to support business start-up at a profit.

The organization grew from 30 to 60 dealers and the sale of products from
$40 to $50 million.

Manager, Dealer Distribution, March 1977 to March 1979

Responsible for managing three sales districts in the development of a
dealer organization. This involved market analysis, recruiting and training.

Sales were increased from $2 million to $3 million.

Manager, Market Research, 1974-1977

Headed a marketing group to promote and sell all types of plumbing products in the industrial and wholesale markets. Supervised marketing
departments and research department. New marketing strategies and sales
opportunities were created through new product and system ideas.

Sales Engineer, 1973-1974

Given responsibility to increase market share, profitability and new porduct development. Developed marketing program, coordinated sales and bidding strategies and trained field sales personnel.

Field Sales Engineer, 1966-1973

Sold all types of plumbing products to apartment owners, architects, contractors, industrials, wholesalers and dealers. Increased sales 230% during this period.

1959   U.S. NAVY
 to
1966   Assigned to Destroyer, South China Sea, Lt. Commander.

EDUCATION

University of Missouri, Columbia, MO

B.S. degree, Business Management, 1965

PERSONAL

Age 43. Born in the small town of Hackett, Arkansas, where father owned and operated a retail hardware store for more than 40 years. Married childhood sweetheart who attended University of Missouri during two of my undergraduate years. We have five lovely children, including two sets of twins. I am 6'4" in height, weigh 230 lbs. and played varsity football during my last three years at the University. Remain in excellent health.

REFERENCES AND FURTHER DATA ON REQUEST

DISCUSSION

Harvard Résumé. The Tym résumé features continuing career development from field sales to general management. You will note that achievement started with increases in territory sales. Management was impressed and gave the subject the opportunity to get similar results in a more responsible position. Success here led to market research management and finally to management of all dealer activities. Opportunities apparently did not come fast enough, and Mr. Tym moved to another company. Soon he changed employment again to obtain general management experience, so that now he is equipped for P & L responsibilities in addition to those in marketing. The business biographies of successful people are replete with illustrations of the desire to learn leading to employment changes—sometimes at a temporary financial sacrifice but usually to one's ultimate benefit in terms of greater success.

The *Harvard* form of résumé expresses this career exceptionally well. Note the expanded comments under personal data.

Analysis of Résumé Users: Marketing

Sales management, advertising, public relations, product manager, salesman, market research. Titles range from vice-president to salesman.

The age range is 23 to 56.
The average age is 36.
Some 46 percent are in their thirties.
Females are 2.6 percent of the total.

NARRATIVE RÉSUMÉ

The *Narative Résumé* can be a pleasing variation from formal presentations. You might use this format if you write well, including about the difficult topic of yourself, or if your background is unusual, with perhaps a strong academic foundation. The *Narrative Résumé*, because of its relative rarity, can have extra impact. Remember, however, that it will appeal to some résumé readers only.

Examples of situations in which the *Narrative Résumé* might be effective appear in this book. The form is exceptionally suitable for the *vita brevis* ("short life") type of description of one's lifework. Personal statistics and information about education, military service, hobbies, and the like can be woven into the narrative or given in a separate section.

The disadvantages of the *Narrative* form could be lack of unity, coherence, and compactness. There is also the ever-present difficulty of narrating one's personal and professional life history sufficiently objectively.

EXAMPLE OF NARRATIVE RÉSUMÉ

V I T A

of

HENRY GEORGE DITMARS

10 Torrid Avenue
Hot Springs, Mo.

For 20 years I have been associated in various capacities with
such institutions as Newark Museum (Newark, N. J.), Metropolitan Museum of Art, New York, N. Y., Mellon Museum of Natural
History, Pittsburgh, Pa., Yates Museum, London, England, as follows:

Director, Curator of Fine Arts, Curator of Ancient Ceramics, Direct-
or of Special Services, Program Planner, Assistant to the Director.

I have traveled extensively in South America, Europe, The Balkans,
the Mediterranean and Aegean Islands individually and leading
groups in archeological exploration funded by the National Geographic Society. Five years ago I was President of the Explorers
Club.

I have been responsible for the following, some with national attention:

> Showing of French Impressionists at the Metropolitan Museum
> of Art drawing the largest public attendance ever experienced
> at this museum.

> Purchase, at auction for $9 million, the famed painting by
> Buardicio, Venice Beneath the Sea.

> Arrangements with the French Government and the Louvre for
> the traveling exhibition to 27 museums around the U. S. of
> roman bronzes and statuary of the first millennium A. D.

> Supervised the razing, shipping and reconstruction and res-
> toration of the Temple of Zeus from Piraeus (Greece) to its
> present home in the Mellon Museum requiring two years of
> study and planning.

I am currently Director of the new Museum of Fine Arts in Kansas
City, Mo. where I aided in raising $37 million for construction and
purchase. I am responsible for assembling all of the works currently on display. The new Museum has received wide publicity in the
media and has been acclaimed for purity of design and discrimination
and elegance in content attracting visitors from all over the world.

I have told my Board that for the immediate future the direction of
the Museum will be more administrative than creative and I am looking for a new post where my particular combinations of experience
and talents can be used in a culminating effort of achievement in the
public interest.

I am a graduate of the New England School of Fine Arts, B.A. and
attended the Harvard Graduate School of Business Administration,
M.B.A. graduating with distinction and majoring in Museum Administration.

My age is 45. I am married to a lovely wife and am proud of our
three children, two of whom are now attending college.

Publications include:

Museum and Public Participation, Lippencott Press, 1980.

Heavenly Taste, Scribner's, 1978.

Greek Exploration: Story of a Dig, University Press, 1974.

Your suggestions as to any suitable activities for me within your knowledge will be appreciated. I have notified the Kansas City Museum of my planned departure in six months from this date.

DISCUSSION

Narrative Résumé. Mr. Ditmars is a scholar and has published widely and successfully in the world of art. He therefore chose the *Narrative Résumé,* which is well suited to the individual with an unusual background. In fact, it is difficult to see how this kind of career could have been expressed suitably within the formal strictures of another résumé style.

As would be expected, Mr. Ditmars starts by describing his background and career progression. He mentions his travel, which plays an important part in his career. He gives examples of some of his achievements to let the reader know the scope and size of his responsibilities. The credentials of education and publications are provided. The résumé may be used as a letter by the addition of the complimentary close.

Mr. Ditmars is of course a composite of many different people. There could hardly be one real person such as Mr. Ditmars.

1 Saladin Way   (890) 123-4567
London, UT 12345

RESUME

WILLIAM LYON HEART

PERSONNEL DIRECTOR/MANPOWER DEVELOPER

Born September 30, 1953, single, excellent health. Residence and travel
in Belgium, France, Tanzania, Kenya, Holland, Germany, Switzerland, Italy,
Tunisia, Morocco, Ivory Coast, Uganda.

Educated as follows:

M. Divinity, M.R.E., 1979. St. Christopher's Seminary, Becton, NY.

B.A., 1974, University of Notre Dame, South Bend, IN.

Postgraduate:

1981, 10 months, Sociology, Louvain University, Belgium.
1980, 12 months, Sociology, Anthropology, Social Research, Princeton Uni-
    versity, Princeton, NJ.
1978 (summer), Social Change, Social Psychology, Princeton University.
1977 (summer), Anthropology, Cross Cultural Research, Loyola University,
    Baltimore, MD.
Languages include: French, Spanish, Kisukuma, Kiswahili.

Hobbies include: SCUBA diving, mountain climbing, any racquets game.

Employment experience:

1981-1985: INTERNATIONAL CATHOLIC CHARITIES, New York, NY.

1976-1981: Extracurricular activities while studying included: art ex-
hibits, community relations and marriage counseling, labor negotiation,
consulting, initiation of dramatized TV programs on human relations nationally televised on Channel 3, New York City.

I give the preceding statements first because they are the raw data forming the platform for my life to the present and can be tied up in a neat
little package and set aside.

In 1981, acting as Program Developer, Sociologist and Personnel Director
for the Overseas Division of the International Catholic Charities, I conceived the idea of researching two African church organizations of 7000
members to ascertain the level of their functional efficiency. I was
authorized to carry out such research and as a result suggested a program utilizing sociological techniques to provide job enrichment and
stronger support of the Division by the organizations studied. My report
was read with some skepticism but nevertheless the thesis was finally
accepted and I was appointed to implement the suggestions made.

Essentially my suggestions involved a program of personnel reformation and membership education to serve as a model for other branches which would ultimately involve as many as 75 organizations with 60,000 members and 500 supervisory personnel. I spent seven years in Africa on this project in the following activities:

- clarifying the objectives and roles of leaders through reexpression in communications and seminars.
- developing a personnel policy embodying employee relationships.
- conducting role-playing sessions and strategy meetings to help bring solutions to administrative problems and improve interpersonal relationships.
- periodic evaluation of activities to assess their effectiveness.

I published the following articles during this period:

Restructuring Pastoral Programs
Catechetical Program
Youth Study Program
Attitudes in Marriage
Aspects of Communication Between Church and People
Attitudes of Youth Toward Christianity and Marriage
Attitudes of Adults Toward Christianity and Marriage
Training Manual for U.S. and African Organization Personnel

These publications appeared in English and appropriate African languages.

As a result of these and related activities we enjoyed a 50% increase in membership, the program was implemented in 35 additional organizations, relationships between local and overseas personnel were improved, tensions among U.S. workers in Africa were alleviated, medical care was bettered and a library for school children was established.

I am not sure what you may think my education and experience fit me for but I wish to leave Church work to embark upon a career in business.

I think my best contributions would be made in the area of personnel, although I would be willing to take any position that would be effective for you while giving me the opportunity to establish a new career.

My qualities include an understanding of and liking for people, some creativity, practical experience in working with people, a good education and an abilty to conceive and implement progressive plans.

REFERENCES AND FURTHER DATA ON REQUEST

DISCUSSION

Narrative Résumé. William Lyon Heart spent about 30 years of his life in study and service contributing greatly to the expanded usefulness of his organization. At the end of that period he made a reappraisal and, deciding that such service need not be a lifelong commitment, chose to try employment in the private sector. This career change required an evaluation of his past to determine the areas in which he might be most effective. His experience in dealing with people logically suggested the areas of personnel or manpower development.

Being a competent, well-educated writer, but lacking business experience, Mr. Heart selected the *Narrative* form, thus notifying the reader that his was an unusual situation calling for a different approach to the job market.

As expected, the subject's obvious interpersonal communications skills, combined with an innovative mind, resulted in a successful résumé that appealed strongly to selected readers. Though without the discipline present in more formal résumés, it has the coherence, unity, logical sequence, and interest needed to make it a compelling document.

ANALYSIS OF RÉSUMÉ USERS: ADMINISTRATION

Supervision, college and school administration, public administration, foundation executives, and hospital executives.

Age is 21 to 56.
Average age is 35.
Females are 25 percent of the total.

PROFESSIONAL RÉSUMÉ

The traditional "learned professions" are law, medicine, and theology. More broadly, a professional is one who has special knowledge enabling him to advise, guide, or instruct others. Teaching is a profession, as is any vocation requiring extensive specialized educational preparation, such as accounting, engineering, or science.

A *Professional Résumé* therefore places initial emphasis on academic qualifications for the profession. Any other form can serve to present the balance of the information, except the *Narrative*. The most appropriate forms are the *Chronological Résumé with Summary Page* and the *Functional Résumé*.

134 East 34th Street   (212) 323-5454
New York, N. Y. 10017

R E S U M E

of

EPHRAIM TUTT

ATTORNEY

OBJECTIVE: Association with law firm in general corporate and
                 securities areas, including litigation.

SUMMARY OF   Awareness of legal needs of business with ability
QUALIFICATIONS: to provide clear answers and effective remedies for
                 corporate legal problems, including litigation when
                 necessary. Intimate knowledge of the Securities
                 Act of 1933 and Exchange Act of 1934; the rules of
                 the major stock exchanges; private placements, lost
                 securities, arbitrations. Fully familiar with tax and
                 securities laws and accounting procedures. Effective
                 in client relationships.

                 Admitted to practice in New York State and New
                 Jersey.

EDUCATION: J. D., University of Michigan School of Law, Ann Arbor,
                 Mich., 1977.

                 B. A. degree, Princeton University, Princeton, N. J., 1973

PERSONAL DATA: Age 30, married, two children, excellent health.

PROFESSIONAL EXPERIENCE:

1983-Present   WILD, SPENCER AND KING, INC., New York, N. Y.

    ASSOCIATE with law firm.

    Provide services to clients with wide range of problems but with particular
    concentration on broker-dealer and specialist problems, controversies involving
    securities laws, sometimes leading to litigation, registrations of public
    offerings with S. E. C.

    - personally and successfully represented clients before N. Y. Stock Exchange,
      American Stock Exchange and S. E. C. involving disciplinary matters.

    - successfully completed and closed a public offering for a corporation
      formerly privately owned.

    - prepared broker-dealer applications for N. Y. S. E. membership.

FOR FURTHER DATA PLEASE SEE FOLLOWING PAGE

<u>1979-1983</u>   HORNBLOWER, BIDDLE CO., New York, N. Y.

ASSOCIATE HOUSE COUNSEL for major Wall Street Investment Firm.

- won arbitration involving large client of firm.

- approved many Rule 144 sales.

- successfully prosecuted or defended Firm position in connection with customer claims.

- aided in drafting a compliance manual for firm; completed compliance inspection of branch offices.

<u>1977-1979</u>   MIDWEST STOCK EXCHANGE, Chicago, Ill.

INVESTIGATIVE ATTORNEY

- investigated violations of member firms and their personnel of Exchange
  rules and regulations and of other regulatory agencies.

- prepared charge memoranda for prosecutions which led to disciplinary action
  by the Exchange.

- reviewed law suits and arbitrations to find if any violations existed.

<u>REFERENCES AND FURTHER DATA ON REQUEST</u>

101

DISCUSSION

Professional Résumé. In a *Professional Résumé,* different approaches must be used for different objectives. For example, a doctor wishing to be considered for a state, municipal, or federal position, or a hospital administrative position must describe administrative capacities in addition to medical competence. A thorough background search may be necessary to find a platform for administrative excellence in an otherwise purely professional (specialist) career.

Attorney Tutt's problem was to make a dignified presentation that would at the same time support his objective. Some of his more interesting activities were described to give the reader a chance to evaluate his experience level and potential.

Legal cases are often highly complex and legal language is exact. A résumé in the legal profession must therefore avoid too much detail. Competence must be suggested rather than explicated. Emphasis is on results rather than responsibilities and methods.

Litigation Lane   (203) 100-1111
Cos Cob, CT 12345

R E S U M E

of

HENRY L. ADAMS

ATTORNEY

OBJECTIVE:

"Of Counsel" relationship and general association taking advantage of
Federal Tax expertise.

SUMMARY OF QUALIFICATIONS:

Awareness of legal needs of business and ability to provide clear
answers and effective remedies for corporate legal problems.

Broad background in acquisitions and joint ventures for major
corporations with record of application of fresh and sophisticated
approaches to problems, and successful negotiations.

Extensive experience in general corporate work and general practice;
formerly Special Attorney for I.R.S. Expertise in resolution of
complex tax problems.

VITAL STATISTICS:

Age 50, married, three children.

EDUCATION:

L.L.M., 1966, Harvard University, Cambridge MA
J.D., 1959, University of Michigan, Ann Arbor, MI
    Article: "Chancery Practice and Procedure"
    77 New Jersey Law Review 162
B.A., 1957, Brown University, Providence, RI

FOR FURTHER DATA SEE FOLLOWING PAGES

PROFESSIONAL EXPERIENCE:

1966-Present   ALEXANDER, BOTTS & CAREY, New York, N.Y.
                 RUSKIN & GREENWOOD, New York, N.Y.

SENIOR ASSOCIATE

Experienced, both as Senior Associate with present firm and as outside
General Counsel to a subsidiary of Loew's Corp., in the successful
implementation of acquisition and joint venture projects, requiring
legal and business sophistication, skillful negotiation and careful,
often innovative restructuring and drafting. Tax planning and
imaginative project revision have been routine elements of this process.
Acquisition work has included "all cash" deals, stock for stock deals, and
stock for assets with deferred payments.

Sound working relationships were established with senior executives
and counsel for such corporations as Remington-Rand, American Home
Products, Standard and Poor, Gimbel Bros. in implementing joint ventures
and acquisitions from letter of intent to final closing.

Experienced in corporate tax problems, including accumulated earnings
tax, sales of assets, income and asset problems of REIT'S, pension
and profit-sharing plans, deferred compensation contracts, accounting
methods, stock options, liquidations, exempt organizations, net
operating loss carryovers, reallocation of income, stock valuations,
state and local tax problems.

In these matters, engaged in research, planning and counseling
involving the preparation of legal memoranda, opinion letters, protests
and ruling requests; negotiated with IRS at district, regional and
national levels.

Experienced in general corporate work, including planning, negotiating and drafting for incorporations, stockholders' agreements, buy-
sell agreements, employment contracts, liquidations and related minutes
and resolutions. Corporate real estate work involved purchases and
sales, shopping center joint ventures, tax shelter partnership deals,
options, mortgages, guarantees, etc.

Experienced in general practice matters, including wills, trusts,
estate plans, general contracts, trade name and trademark agreements,
franchises and matrimonial settlements.

1962-1966   INTERNAL REVENUE SERVICE, Washington, DC

SPECIAL ATTORNEY, Office of General Counsel. Primary responsibility
involved representing the Government in tax disputes:

- Settlement negotiations with corporate and individual taxpayers
  and determination of whether to settle or litigate.
- Preparation of pleadings, motions, subpoenas, stipulations, briefs
  and other documents for cases pending before Tax Court.
- Conducting trial cases in Tax Court.

COMMENDATIONS:

"The Lawyer's Lawyer gratefully acknowledges the contribution of Henry L. Adams to continuing legal education in the U.S. by reason of his authorship of the article, 'Syndications: Federal Tax Aspects,' published in The Lawyer's Lawyer, April 1976."

Chief Counsel, U.S. Treasury Department, IRS:
"I would like to take this opportunity to express my appreciation for the splendid work you have performed for this office. . ."

Judge of the Circuit Court of the U.S.:
"I can say without reservation that Mr. Adams has been an effective advocate for the Commissioner in extremely complex cases where the petitioners are represented by highly skilled attorneys . . ."

ADDITIONAL PROFESSIONAL ACTIVITIES:

Books:

Federal Tax Manual: three-volume set of tax-annotated form books, approximately 3,000 pages.

Successful Underwriting for New Companies, 550 pages.
Connecticut Law Journal: ". . . an excellent working tool for the legal practitioner in acquainting himself with all aspects affecting the public issue and sale of securities of a business enterprise . . ."

New Jersey Law Journal: "This work is recommended particularly for the day-to-day practical workings of the business lawyer who needs a quick, good, reliable reference . . ."

Revision Editor of Moody on Wills.

Articles:
On various corporate tax problems, published in 1961, 1962 and 1967.

MEMBERSHIPS:

American Bar Association
New York Bar Association

REFERENCES AND FURTHER DATA ON REQUEST

DISCUSSION

Professional Résumés.   The two preceding résumés give objective first and a summary of qualifications second, with education and personal data following thereafter. In the Tutt résumé, experience is more limited than in the Adams's résumé, in which more detail was therefore incorporated. Both attorneys illustrate their backgrounds with excellent examples that are, as could be expected, consistent with their objectives. Considerable research was needed to select the most relevant and significant cases from scores or hundreds of them.

Both résumés show individuals of considerable expertise, capable of bringing exceptional abilities to any firm.

Note the inclusion of objective commendations and a listing of publications where applicable.

ANALYSIS OF RÉSUMÉ USERS: PRODUCTION

Plant manager, production manager, inventory control, quality control, and the various engineering disciplines.

The age range is 31 to 58.
The average age is 45.
Age in percentages
    35 percent are in their forties.
    37 percent are in their fifties.
    16 percent are in their thirties.
There are no females in the survey.

ACCOMPLISHMENT RÉSUMÉ

The *Accomplishment Résumé* lists accomplishments without reference to dates and companies and without regard for a chronological order. It is often used by individuals who wish to disguise age, length of experience, employment gaps, lack of progress in recent jobs, job-hopping, and other matters that are easier to explain in person during an interview than in writing. Do not let these reasons dissuade you from using this form if you like it, however. Some nonprofit executive employment services favor this style.

The elements of the *Accomplishment Résumé* are the following:

1. Name, address, and telephone number.
2. Summary of qualifications.
3. List of accomplishments (the most important is given first).
4. List of companies by whom employed (no dates).
5. Military service (no dates).
6. Education (no dates).
7. Hobbies, professional memberships, community activities, and honors (no dates).
8. Personal data (omit age).

An example of the *Accomplishment Résumé* follows.

58 Orchid Avenue
Nemesis, NV 12345   (123)   456-7890

NERO WOLFE

OPERATIONS EXECUTIVE

* * *   Experienced manager with proven record of accom-
          plishments in creating profits and often innovative
          solutions to corporate problems, representing tens
          of millions of dollars.

* * *   Record of progress to increasingly important respon-
          sibilities in every employment. Accustomed to work-
          ing with and leading staffs in improving systems and
          procedures, in developing harmonious labor relations,
          in organizing projects for most efficient completion.

* * *   Excellent in written and oral communication with
          wealth of experience in construction, maintenance,
          site selection, leasing, facilities planning, display,
          floor layout, contract negotiation, organization of
          diverse departments involving multimillion-dollar
          programs.

* * *   Experience in the activities enumerated has been
          worldwide.

FOR FURTHER DATA PLEASE SEE FOLLOWING PAGE

108

ACHIEVEMENTS:

Cost saving of %1 million in one year using reduced level of personnel
and no loss of efficiency.

Completed $50 million construction project in five months with four
general contractors saving Company from financial difficulty.

Saved $35,000 annually by devising new method of inventory control.

Set up central purchasing for ten units, saving 13% on annual purchases
of $12 million.

Planned, coordinated and supervised a multimillion-dollar construction
project with cost saving of $183,000 and bonus to contractor for beating
deadline by two weeks.

Planned new housewares department (100,000 sq. ft.) for increased traffic
and improved merchandise visibility without loss of business during re-
construction.

Saved 12% in electricity and fuel in group of 37 nationally known department stores, saving more than $3 million in annual costs.

Reduced cost of new two million sq ft. warehouse 25% by creating flexible
storage locations, making changes in rack specifications and other
creative planning.

Reduced insurance costs for a three million sq. ft. building by a program
of continuous maintenance.

Consolidated insurance on a national basis at a cost saving of $10 million
over a period of two years.

Devised new security methods that reduced shoplifting and other causes of
loss by 75% with a resultant saving of $13 million. And more.

The preceding accomplishments were achieved for the followign companies:
    Great Atlantic and Caribbean Coffee Company, Vice President.
    The International Insurance Companies, Vice President Operations.
    Allied Retailers, Incorporated, Buildings Manager
    Hughes Construction Company, Field Engineer.

EDUCATION: B.S., Rice University, Houston, TX

PERSONAL DATA: Married, 3 children, excellent health. Willing to relocate.

REFERENCES AND FURTHER DATA ON REQUEST

109

DISCUSSION

Accomplishment Résumé. The material in the Wolfe résumé was condensed from another résumé of about four pages to two for purposes of illustration. It suffers from a lack of relationship between achievements and employers and lack of explanation of work methods (such as determining the flow of information from the point of sale to the computer, making time studies of jobs, and so forth), which would have added greatly to an understanding of this man's value and the reasons for some of his assignments. Nevertheless, it is effective in presenting a man whose every assignment has been so successful that an employer in need of such skills would be inclined to interview him.

Actually, the original résumé, written in *Chronological* form, was very impressive. A broadcast letter summary elicited replies from 70 percent of the companies approached—an unusually high percentage. Not all replies, largely from the top officers, resulted in interviews, but they provided a base for aggressive follow-ups, leading to personal interviews.

ELEVEN

GETTING READY TO WRITE YOUR RÉSUMÉ

PREPARING FOR THE JOB SEARCH—LEARN YOUR JOB

Proper preparation can reduce the time spent on the job search itself by at least 50 percent, or perhaps by as much as three to six months. Preparation time will consist of the following:

- Analyzing your background and preparing its presentation: a half hour to an hour for each year of experience.
- Writing and polishing your résumé: six to eight hours.
- Preparing a general letter: one hour.
- Researching companies (a minimum of 200) to which you wish to present yourself: eight hours.
- Addressing envelopes, inserting letters, stamping, and mailing: two to three hours.
- Studying and practicing interview techniques: eight hours.

- Traveling, waiting, indecision, and similar items: add a half hour to each hour listed above (as a safety factor).

For example, if you have had 10 years of experience, you will need the following preparation time:

- Five to ten hours of self-analysis writing about yourself.
- Six to eight hours for résumé preparation.
- One hour for appropriate covering letters.
- Eight hours for name research (200 companies).
- Two to three hours for mechanics of mailing.
- Eight hours to sharpen interview techniques.
- Eight hours as a safety factor.

Thus 45 to 57 hours are required to prepare for a job search. It will be time well spent. Take time in the beginning; it saves time in the end.

All the preceding sections in this book have been preparing you to write your résumé. The key to this task is the analysis and orderly listing of your job responsibilities and achievements. You must know yourself: what you were or are expected to do, what you actually did or are doing, and how your action affected your job, your section, your department, your division, or your company or organization.

To help you organize these facts, we have prepared an analytical questionnaire. We suggest that you use it. It has been carefully set up to make you think about yourself, recall forgotten activities, and focus on actions instrumental in your vocational life. You must first recall events, and then describe your recollections. The second task is made easier if you do it after you have performed the first. Jot down the things that you have accomplished in the form of informal notes, using single words, phrases, and sentence fragments. These notes will serve as the basis for the actual résumé.

SIX BASIC STEPS

Follow these six basic steps in writing your résumé:

1. Assemble the raw data (from your answers to our analytical questionnaire).
2. Refine the data (initial draft).
3. Select the most relevant data.
4. Translate the data into suitable language. Your sentences and paragraphs are the building blocks that you can move around to fit your chosen résumé form.
5. Select your résumé format.
6. Write your résumé.

YOUR ANALYTICAL QUESTIONNAIRE

Before starting your résumé, gather the data for it by answering the analytical questionnaire that follows. Your answers will serve to give your résumé focus, direction, and the proper "slant." If you have difficulty in answering a question, skip it for now and return to it later. Take plenty of time to think about yourself and to make a thoughtful self-analysis. Depending on your background, completing the questionnaire will require a half hour to several hours.

Write down:

1. Your name, address, and home office telephone numbers.
2. Titles of jobs desired, if possible. If you cannot supply them at this time, briefly *describe* the job you want. Identify several jobs by assigning to them the letters A, B, C, and so on, using the same code in Question 3 below.
   Turn to Question 11 and answer it before answering the questions that follow.

3. Qualifications that you believe you should have for the jobs A, B, C, and so on, listed in Question 2. (Most data should be in answer to Question 11). *For example,* if your answer to Question 2 is "sales manager," you might answer the question as follows:
    a. Appraise pricing and distribution policies.
    b. Recruit and train sales staff.
    c. Maintain distributor liaison.
    d. And so on.

    Now *underline* the qualifications you have *and* list any other qualifications you feel you should have for the jobs you desire.

4. Your age, marital status, number of children, home ownership, car ownership, and so on.

5. Military service.
    a. Dates, branch of service, rank.
    b. Special training, courses, responsibilities.

6. Education—dates, schools, academic degrees, and proficiency in languages.

7. Major and minor courses. List courses relevant to the jobs desired. State your class standing if possible. Describe scholarships, awards, and honors.

8. Extracurricular activities at school (sports, jobs, social activities, etc.).

9. Hobbies and your degree of proficiency in them, travel (if extensive), memberships in societies and community activities.

10. A summary of your employment history. *Work backwards,* giving the last job first. Use three columns to assemble the following information:

Dates of beginning job and leaving job (years only); titles	Company and address	Job

11. For each job just listed, starting with the *last* job, give the following data. Treat each position or important assignment with the same company, or with important clients of your employer, as though it were a separate and distinct job. Answer *each* question carefully.
    a. Job title.
    b. Dates of beginning and leaving job (by transfer to another company or by promotion or change within the company).
    c. Beginning and ending salaries or earnings.
    d. Name of company and division or department within company.
    e. Description of what the company makes, sells, or does.
    f. An indication of size of company—by sales volume, number of employees, number of plants, and number of branches or stores, for example.
    g. The title of the person for whom you worked (president, foreman, sales manager, etc.).
    h. The number of persons you supervised (if any).
    i. The kinds of employees you supervised (engineers, clerks, etc.).
    j. The types of equipment you used (or that was used under your supervision) and for what purpose. This will be relevant for such jobs as production manager and computer executive, but irrelevant for others.
    k. Your responsibilities. Describe them briefly but fully; give facts, rather than abstract generalities. Consult Chapter 9 under "Experience" before answering this questions.
    l. Your accomplishments. Describe them briefly but specifically.

       • The problem you were faced with.
       • What you did about them.
       • What you achieved and how.

That is, what did you see that needed to be done, what did you do about it, and what happened as a result? Do not list mere claims, such as "I increased sales." Give facts: "I found that sales were only $150,000. I made a market survey and determined that the market needed a 'widget.' I introduced a new line of widgets. I trained salesmen by doing X Y Z. Sales increased in six months by $50,000." Such an analysis is important. You need it in your résumé if you are to stand out from other job applicants. It will also reassure you that you are qualified for the job you want, in addition to refreshing your memory and providing valuable *rehearsal and training* for your job interviews.

12. References: name, title, company, address, and telephone number (and extension). Do not include references in your résumé; assemble them for use at interviews.

GUIDANCE IN ANSWERING THE QUESTIONNAIRE

Two sample answers to this questionnaire illustrate what you should *not* do. Here is how one man answered Question 11:

> 1972-present (name of company). AREA SUPERVISOR. Began February 1972 as restaurant manager in failing unit. The unit started to show profit after four weeks. I was promoted to supervisor of two units after three months. In the following months I was given the entire Maryland area to supervise (five units). A new type of concept was developed, and I was picked to bring it into a profitable operation. At that point the larger-volume (Philadelphia) units were given to me to supervise. At my request, I was moved to the New York area as supervisor in July 1973. Since that time I have opened three large-volume units for the chain, both in New York and in Pennsylvania. All of the six units now under my supervision gross $1 to $1.5 million per year.

This very successful man needed prodding before supplying additional information vital to his case. In the final résumé (following), the portions with data initially not disclosed are underlined.

1972-present (name of company)

AREA SUPERVISOR for a rapidly growing, limited menu, full service, $30 million AMEX-listed restaurant chain with 30 locations; earlier single unit manager responsible for New York and Pennsylvania area supervising six $1 to $1½ million units each with a staff of 60 to 90 people.

–Indoctrinated company with new cost concepts which have contributed significantly to rapid growth from nine units in 1971 to 30 units currently.
–Reduced food cost from 40% to 35%.
–Opened three large-volume units: hired, trained complete staffs, installed systems.
–Accustomed to exercising controls through analysis of computer printouts daily on food, liquor, payroll. Trained managers in use of cost analyses.

Earlier managed failing unit; turned it from loss to profit in four weeks by exercise of proper controls, by establishing incentive system, and by gaining cooperation of employees. Personally contributed to success of 15 of existing 30 units and set standards for entire operation.

Prod yourself for the type of detail that, as just demonstrated, can turn a poor résumé into an effective one. What did you see that needed to be done? In this case the corporation was in need of profitability. What did you do about it? In this case the man created better cost concepts. What happened as a result? In this case the units became profitable.

In our second example of how *not* to answer the analytical questionnaire the subject took a shortcut. The result again was the omission of vital information.

1. John Abrams, 367 Couture Avenue, Pasadena, CA 12345. Home (123) 456-7890. Office (432) 654-0987.
2. Sales manager.

3. a. Styling of line.
    b. In charge of all shipping.
    c. Distribution of goods to the factory—what goes into work at the machines.
    d. Production.
4. 36—married—3 children—own home and car.
5. U.S. Naval Reserve 1965–1973—2 years active—6 years reserve.
6. High school graduate—4 years—with some college.
7. Academic.
8. Worked in specialty shop—worked in bowling alley. Sports—bowling, football, baseball, horesback riding.
9. Horseback riding, photography.
10. Seventeen years in the employ of Toni Co., 1967–1984.
11. a. Sales manager.
    b. 1967–1984.
    c. $45 week to $560 week.
    d. Sales department.
    e. Ladies' ready-to-wear.
    f. 35 employees—$4,500,000.00.
    g. President.
    h. Supervised up to 10 employees.
    i. Salesmen, shipping clerks, production workers.
    j. Sewing machines, cutting machines, taping machines.
    k. Making sure all machines were running in proper order. Responsible for putting them in proper order if not working. Selling, getting orders by phone out of town. Getting merchandise from the factory in time to ship goods. Getting piece goods in on time as per delivery order. Consistently, I had to be after these people to get the goods I needed to run the business in a proper manner.
    l. In the 17 years I was with the company, I worked up from delivery boy to sales manager. The achievement of being able to book $1.0 to $1.21 million a year.

The man omitted the following important information.

1. Business increased from $2 million to $4.5 million during his tenure.

2. The business was discontinued because of the owners' retirement.

3. The company had a sales showroom in conjunction with the factory, where he accomplished a lot of selling to out-of-town buyers.

4. He was in charge of purchasing, inventory control, and sales forecasting and was production manager in addition of being sales manager.

5. He supervised seven salesmen operating nationally and reported to the president.

6. His association with buyers was such that he could book large orders by telephone.

7. He was an excellent salesman himself, in addition to successfully managing a sales organization.

8. He personally sold to most of the major Los Angeles and other West Coast stores and was responsible for getting business from such national accounts as Sears, Ward, and Penney.

The final résumé, with all information included, follows.

367 Couture Avenue
Pasadena, CA 12345

Home (123) 456-7890
Office (432) 654-0987

R E S U M E

of

JOHN ABRAMS

SALES MANAGER - APPAREL

*** Seventeen years of experience in apparel field with
one company, for last ten years as Sales Manager,
responsible for increasing multimillion-dollar business
by 75%. Owners retired and business was terminated.

*** Close associations with leading buyers of women's
dresses and pants suits all over the United States,
experienced in selling to department and specialty
stores, chains, giant national retailers and in maintaining productive contacts with major buying offices.

*** Effective trainer and leader accustomed to managing
national sales organization. Management versatility
led to expanded responsibilities including production,
purchasing, shipping, and assistance in styling and
pricing in addition to marketing.

*** Excellent personal salesman with ability to get and
retain customer loyalty and write business either by
personal calls or by telephone, with hundreds of leading buyers across the country.

*** Capable of bringing additional volume and profit to
any women's wear manufacturer.

FOR FURTHER DATA PLEASE SEE FOLLOWING PAGE

120

BUSINESS EXPERIENCE:

1967-1984   TOO MUCH CO., INC. Los Angeles, CA

SALES MANAGER for $4.5 million manufacturer of Women's Apparel with showroom and factory in California; sold nationally to department and specialty stores, chains and such giant retailers as Sears, Ward and Penney. Supervised staff of seven salesmen and Production Manager. Reported to President. Owners decided to retire and business was terminated. Responsible for:

- developing increased sales through leadership and training of seven salesmen, and personal selling.
- sales forecasting, inventory control, purchase of piece goods and trimmings.
- aiding in pricing and styling.
- expediting production as necessary to achieve prompt shipments.

Accomplishments:
- rose from delivery boy to Sales Manager with earnings increases to 12 times starting salary.

- increased volume 87%; opened scores of new customers; developed existing customers.

- personally accounted for sales of $1.0 million to $1.25 million annually to leading accounts around the country.
- improved turnover by rigid inventory controls.
- curtailed price increases by creative piece goods purchasing.

MILITARY SERVICE:

1965-1973 U.S. NAVAL RESERVE. Two years active duty; Airman 3rd Class.

EDUCATION:

Three years at University of California in Los Angeles.

EXTRACURRICULAR ACTIVITIES:

Worked while attending high school and college; participated in football, lacrosse, bowling, riding.

HOBBIES:

Riding, photography.

PERSONAL DATA:

Age 36, divorced, two children

REFERENCES AND FURTHER DATA ON REQUEST

Assistant buyers, buyers, merchandise managers, store owners, retail advertising, display executives, and store managers.

Average age is 40.5
Females are 11 percent of the total.

TWELVE

WRITING
YOUR RÉSUMÉ

To begin with, turn to *your* answers to Question 11 in the analytical questionnaire. Write your résumé first in the *Chronological* form. Write dates of employment (beginning and ending) for the most recent position. Write name of company for which you work (or worked).

Write your title and describe briefly what the company does. Write in the first person, but avoid the use of "I." Describe each responsibility concisely, in a brief, almost terse, sentence or phrase. Omit responsibilities that are unimportant or negative with respect to your objective. For example, if clerical chores are part of your job as an office manager, make no mention of them if your job objective is "office manager." Now briefly and clearly write your achievements. Emphasize contributions to profit, cost savings, new techniques or methods you introduced, mechanical or product improvements, training programs, departmental reorganizations, accuracy, and anything else about you that is positive.

What did you do and what happened as a result? To answer these questions, use the words that are best understood in your field, but avoid overly technical language (study the résumé examples included in this book, as well as the vocabulary section in Appendix B). Use simple words wherever possible if they say exactly what you mean. For example, the employment of a computer programmer, recommended by the department head, may require the approval of a higher-level executive. The chances are that the executive is unfamiliar with computer jargon, but he *will* wish to know whether you can communicate your special expertise to nonspecialists. Such terms as FORTRAN, COBOL, and second-, third-, and fourth-generation identification numbers are all fine, but use them sparingly, except in answering advertisements that are themselves highly technical.

Follow this procedure for each position that you have held. The most recent jobs are usually the most important ones. "Most recent" may mean the past year for a young person or the preceding 10 to 15 years for an older person. Give most space to the areas of your greatest accomplishments. Account for time back to your earliest jobs, unless they are completely irrelevant. For example, if you have been a city administrator for several years, it is unimportant that you were a waiter or a porter at some previous time. Several years can be bunched together as "1974–1979, various unrelated positions as bookkeeper, cost analyst, station agent, prizefighter."

After your business, professional, or other vocational experience, list military service. An outstanding military career would require a detailed description; dates, service arm, and rank will suffice for an average one.

Education, extracurricular activities, community activities, awards, personal data, and others follow, as discussed elsewhere and as exemplified in the many résumé samples in this book.

As a final sentence add "References and further data on request."

If you wish to add a summary paragraph or page describing your accomplishments in functional terms, first review the accomplishments sections of your résumé and your answers to Questions 3 in the analytical questionnaire. Suppose that you have described your accomplishments as follows:

a. Promoted to manage larger office which was operating at a loss.

    b. Increased sales from $5.0 million to $7.8 million.
    c. Reduced staff of sales managers from 8 to 2.
    d. Brought operation from loss to profit.
    e. Assigned to another losing office to attempt similar recovery.

Your front page summary might then read like this:

Assigned successively to branches operating at a loss. Consistently successful in creating profitability in every position, increasing sales and revenues variously from 60% to more than 100%, and reducing costs by streamlining management.

Or you might have made the following listing of accomplishments.

    a. Assigned to manage new venture; set up new corporation.
    b. Went from ground-breaking to start-up in five months, one month ahead of schedule.
    c. Worked within forecasted capital and expense budgets.
    d. Wrote off all start-up expenses and put company in a profit position within five months of start-up and three months ahead of schedule.
    e. Increased profit from 35% to 40%.
    f. Developed cost-reducing shift schedules, fringe benefit packages; improved productivity.
    g. Program influenced the establishment of a second profitable subsidiary.

This front page summary might then be in order:

Experience as general manager includes all areas of responsibility from original incorporation, site selection, building design, and construction, and hiring and training to start-up and operations; all work consistently ahead of schedules.

Record of profitability improvement from increased revenues. Cost savings by innovative planning in connection with work scheduling and worker incentive packages. Set viable precedent for further profitable corporate expansion.

Review the *Chronological Résumé with Summary Page* annotated for additional explanation of résumé layout and the preparation of a summary page or paragraph. Under this setup you are essentially turning specific accomplishments into a more generalized description of what you did. That is, you are using specific accomplishments as the basis for an expressive summary—if you increased profits from 35% to 40% (specific) you are a manager who can add profitability to a corporate activity (functional).

A correctly written résumé should flow, one action or achievement leading to the next. You had certain responsibilities. As a result you took certain actions. The actions were of such and such a nature. They culminated in the results described. The results saved time and money. Additional profits were created, morale was improved. Each assignment for a company or a succession of companies brought increased responsibilities. Results were progressive or foward moving.

This evolutionary development of a career is best shown in the *Chronological Résumé with Summary Page*.

THIRTEEN

TYPING YOUR RÉSUMÉ

Type your résumé on good quality (16- to 24-pound weight) 25 percent rag paper 8½ by 11 inches in size. Reproduce your résumé by offset printing to retain its good appearance. The sheet can be folded in various ways to obtain a "different look." We prefer standard size and format, using *content* and *language* to create an exceptional résumé.

White, unembellished paper is best, though a blue legal backing or simple colored borders can be attactive. Whether you are an artist, writer, graphics specialist, or government administrator, the person reading your résumé most wants to know what you can contribute to the company or organization in profit, leadership, initiative, reliability, and the like. As an artist or designer you might best expend your effort in preparing a superior work portfolio rather than in embellishing your résumé. Keep the résumé neat, but informal in a nonprofessional format.

Use short sentences. Observe grammatical rules and conventions. Punctuate for readability rather than by strict rules. Use underlining and uppercase letters for emphasis.

Keep paragraphs short. Double or triple space between paragraphs. It is easier to read a properly spaced résumé of three or four pages than one page of closely written, overcrowded copy.

The physical appearance (format) of your résumé matters very

127

much. Typing, layout, margins, headlines, centering, paragraph-
ing, spacing, spelling, punctuation—all have bearing on the
effectiveness of your résumé. Poorly done, they wreck a good
résumé. Well done, they enhance a poor one.

Choose the format that you consider to be the most appealing
from the many résumé examples in this book. Some specific
guidelines for typing your résumé and your summary page are
given.

COMPARISION OF PICA AND ELITE TYPES

Pica type requires about 18 percent more space, double spaced,
than does elite type. A typewritten page with 1-inch margins at
top and bottom would show a difference of 2 inches between
the two type sizes. Three inches take in about eight lines of pica
type and nine lines of elite type in double-spaced copy. Three
more lines of elite type than of pica type would fit into a 9-inch
space. Single spacing doubles the number of lines. The size of
paragraph indentations will affect these estimates.

Almost all successful corporations use advertising as one of their basic techniques for building business and improving profitability. A resume is an individual's method of advertising himself or herself; perhaps the only method of advertising for the great majority. Some people hire public relations firms to gain an image; some have important or newsworthy accomplishments that place their names in the news media. Most rely on a resume to circulate information about their talents or expertise.

In writing about oneself it is best to be dignified and professional. The modern resume has evolved as a rather formal document. At its best it is concise, informative, and literate. Unlike a novel it cannot use the devices of plot, humor, imagination, and length to create and resolve situations. It is real and subject to the

Almost all successful corporations use advertising as one of their basic techniques for building business and improving profitablity. A resume is an individual's method of advertising himself or herself; perhaps the only method of advertising for the great majority. Some people hire public relations firms to gain an image; some have important or newsworthy accomplishments that place their names in the news media.

In writing about oneself it is best to be dignified and professional. The modern resume has evolved as a rather formal document. At its best it is concise, informative, and literate. Unlike a novel it cannot use the devices of plot, humor, imagination, and length to create and resolve situations. It is real and subject to the infirmities that each of us has and to the limitations of time, space, and honesty. These limitations require the discipline of formality. Add to this the difficulty of self-expression and you find another reason to have and follow rules of procedure. That is what this book is all about.

FOURTEEN

SALES AND BROADCAST LETTERS

Sales and broadcast letters are the equal partners of the résumé. They are easier to write after the résumé has been prepared because they epitomize the résumé. They have a special place in the job campaign. The word "broadcast" is widely used to describe one way in which a sales letter can be used. Your sales letter is a "broadcast" letter generalized for mailing to many companies; it is a "sales" letter when you tailor it for sending to a specific company as a solicitation for a position or in answer to an advertisement.

The broadcast letter is a special type of employment application that is widely circulated to top company executives, rather than the personnel department. Its role derives from the fact that 50 to 75 percent of available jobs are never advertised and must be tracked down by mail.

When using the broadcast technique, whether for résumés or for letters, you judge the effectiveness of your mailing by the percentage of response, as would be the case with any mail order product. A response (inviting you to an interview) of 2 percent is fair; 15 percent is excellent.

Broadcasting is one of the quickest and most effective ways of finding a position. Send out at least 100 and preferably as many as 300 broadcast letters. The broadcast letter is used in such cases as the following:

1. Your career level makes it appropriate to bypass the personnel department.

2. Your talents and experience may have special appeal to a company executive.

3. Your special abilities may cause an executive to employ you now for a position that will actually become available only later.

4. Your qualifications might exactly meet the requirements for a position that the company has been unsuccessfully trying to fill for some time.

5. Your unusual qualifications may be particularly appreciated by a particular executive.

6. You might be well and favorably known at the top executive level of many companies.

7. Your qualifications might lead to an executive reorganization, making a place for you that did not exist until your letter acted as the catalyst to initiate such action.

8. Many top executives, including chief executive officers, like to be made aware of the availability of certain kinds of people.

9. Recruiting an executive by way of a broadcast letter can save a company thousands of dollars in search fees.

The use of a résumé in these conditions would nullify your objective—résumés are almost automatically routed to personnel departments. Your broadcast letter might lead to requests for your résumé, which, sent at this point, serves the positive function of satisfying the company's affirmative interest in you.

By using the broadcast letter approach you are not deprecating the personnel department. Many personnel departments do not handle the employment of personnel at higher levels where the subtleties of character and required expertise are difficult to gauge. Employment ideas, amorphous at first, often may be formed only after an interview. Many corporations do not even list employment directors by name in the standard directories.

The rules for writing a good sales or broadcast letter are these:

1. Start with either (a) a point that you think will be interesting to the addressee or (b) your reason for writing. If you use the first alternative, follow with the second; if you begin with the second alternative, follow with the first.

2. Give examples of other qualifications that show how specially qualified you are to provide superior services in your area of expertise. Give four or five carefully chosen examples. Highlight them in short sentences and paragraphs. Leave white space between each point.

3. Follow with a general statement that sums up your qualifications.

4. Provide personal data if favorable—age, marital status, number of children, education.

5. Ask for a personal meeting.

6. Ask for a reply.

You will write a better letter if you have already completed a résumé. Select the material for your letter from your résumé. Your sales letter is a summary of your résumé.

Start the letter by identifying yourself and your field of specialization.

I have 15 years of successful, progressive experience in marketing management in the pharmaceutical and health care fields with a $100 million company.

State your objective:

> I want to become associated with a medium-size company or a division of a large company in the Southwest or Midwest where I will have complete marketing responsibility and opportunity for growth.

List some of your accomplishments:

> In six years I increased regional sales of pharmaceutical and health care products from $9 million to more than $30 million while maintaining or improving profitability.
>
> Recruited, trained, and led a sales force of 60 salesmen, 3 field assistants, and 7 district managers.
>
> Three of the 7 district managers under my leadership were awarded "Manager of the Year" recognition.

Indicate special qualities:

> I have been a successful salesman. I have trained scores of salesmen and managers to sell and manage effectively. I am innovative, motivated, and dedicated and possess the quality of leadership to a degree that has made my region first among all company regions in four of the last seven years. I am experienced in budgeting, forecasting, advertising, promotion, and compensation administration.

Give favorable statistics:

> M.B.A.; B.A. in marketing; age 35; married.

Ask for an answer.

> I would like a personal interview to discuss my potential for contributing to your company and opportunities for me to grow within your company. I look forward to your reply.

Broadcast letters may take up too much of the page to leave room for a full heading (name and address). To personalize them, use the salutation only, such as "Dear Mr. Jones."

Preferably use one or two pages of Monarch-size stationery (7½ by 10 inches).

Examples of broadcast/sales letters follow. One broadcast letter similar to those shown produced an unprecedented response of 75 percent, a significant number of which suggested interviews or left the way open for later follow-up.

In the examples following, salutations, have been omitted in most letters. In practice, salutations must, of course, be included.

WILLIAM J.K. POLK
1795 Mecklenburg Avenue
Maury, TN 00039

1. For most of my career (10 years) I was associated with one company, the last two years as president and general manager and before that as senior vice president.

2. I left that company to enter another as executive vice president, on the assurance that I could acquire it within three years. I reorganized the production and marketing, reducing costs over 20% and expanding sales by more than 100% within a year and a half, resulting in unprecedented profits. The owner has declined to sell at any reasonable price, and I am now seeking another position with a small-to-medium-size company offering growth and compensation consistent with my abilities.

3. Here are some examples of my record:

4. - as president of $50 million company, developed a new division from zero to more than $10 million over a period of four years, with a pretax profit of 20.3%.

5. - doubled the sales of a second division $10 million (now grown to $20 million) by stimulating technical progress and introducing new products.

6. - reorganized marketing strategies of a third division, introduced installment sales, increased volume 63%, reduced overhead 15%, expanded computer facility, and designed a plan to reduce the impact of fluctuating currency exchange.

7. - adapted a product, developed for internal use, to meet market needs and added a fourth division to the company which, within two years, produced $3 million of sales at pretax profit of 35%.

8. These and other achievements may suggest that I am an innovative manager who could be useful to a company seeking management and growth.

9. I am married, have three children, attended Cornell University (B.S. Administrative Engineering), received my M.B.A. from Columbia. Honors include Phi Beta Kappa and Tau Delta Pi.

10. If there is interest on your part, I would enjoy a personal meeting. I look forward to the pleasure of hearing from you.

11. Very truly yours,

12. William J. K. Polk
Home (201) 000-0000
Office (201) 111-2222

DISCUSSION

---

1. Mr. Polk starts with his occupational level to help the reader understand immediately who he is. The length of his career suggests his age.

2. He relates an interesting set of circumstances that differentiates him from the usual and at the same time indicates his executive ability; announces his objective; and recommends a compensation level that is readily understood.

3. Leads into examples of his effectiveness.

4, 5, 6, 7. Examples.

8. Makes general statement.

9. Provides personal data.

10. Asks for personal meeting.

11. Asks for reply.

12. Gives telephone numbers.

This writer will gain executive attention. His level of responsibility establishes a rapport with the reader. After a successful career with one company he did what most people would secretly like to do—made plans to have his own business; but it didn't work out. Writer explains concisely what else he had done. He suggests how one with his background could be useful to the reader. He can afford to understate, rather than belabor, his excellent educational background.

What does this letter convey?

- General management ability of a high order.
- Experience in all facets of general management, and contributions to each.
- Innovativeness.

- A strong sense of profit motivation.
- A record that suggests value to any company in need of management strength.
- Abilities that showed themselves as early as the undergraduate period.
- An age between 36 and 38 inasmuch as "most" of his career is 10 years: graduation with master's degree at 23; 2 or 3 years in employment not disclosed; 10 years in one company; 1½ to 2 years in present company.
- He chose to write this letter to the CEOs of selected companies.

This is an actual letter. It resulted in satisfactory employment.

WILLIAM Z. TAYLOR
1784 Rough & Ready Way
Orange, NJ 12468

1. Currently, I am Director of Marketing and board member for a small ($50 million) chemical company.

2. I am looking to upgrade my career in a new position offering broader opportunity either in marketing or general management.

3. Based on my record of effectiveness I can bring dynamic marketing performance and decisive management skills to any company with a need in these areas.

   To illustrate:

4. - for present company, in a period of less than four years, increased volume 150% and provided the earnings base for further expansion and plant modernization; I now participate in all corporate financial, production and marketing planning.

5. - the growth was achieved by means of market analysis, planning, raising plant productivity, setting objectives and creating new strategies; and getting out into the field with customers and salesmen to explain the new programs, resulting in individual orders of as much as $2 million.

6. - in earlier employment with giant international chemical company, progressed from salesman to senior management; tripled regional sales in five years to more than $40 million; achieved rank as No. 1 region in sales and profitability in three successive years.

7. - trained and recommended 15 individuals for promotion to enlarged responsibilities, some of whom are now at top management levels in the company.

8. These are but a few highlights. I have made significant contributions in all marketing areas: advertising, sales, promotion, administration; in financial areas; investment and acquisitions; and in production with cost-cutting innovations, for two employers during my career.

9. I am 41 years of age, married, have three children, earned an M.B.A. at the Wharton School, University of Pennsylvania, and continue my education in new techniques and technologies regularly.

10. If my qualifications meet a need in your company, I'd enjoy a personal meeting.

11. I look forward to your reply.

    Very truly yours,

    William Z. Taylor
12. (234) 000-0000 Home
    (234) 000-1111 Office

DISCUSSION

1. Mr. Taylor says who he is to set the tone of his letter.
2. Explains what kind of a job he is looking for, to let the addressee know at once the reason for the letter.
3. Makes a general statement about his accomplishments, which are then supported with examples.
4. Examples of a very major contribution resulting in the assignment of broader responsibilities.
5. Describes methods used to achieve the results mentioned, which give credence to his marketing abilities and suggest general management caliber.
6. Example of experience in much larger company to give added breadth to his background.
7. Example of his leadership ability by his salutary influence on those who worked for him.
8. Lists the specific areas in which he had had important experience, showing in more detail his areas of particular competence.
9. Provides essential personal data.
10. Asks for a personal interview.
11. Asks for a reply.
12. Provides both home and office telephone numbers for the convenience of his addressee.

These are the elements of a good letter. Such a letter will gain favorable responses from companies that have an opening. The preparation of this letter required several hours of close analysis of this executive's background. The true nature of what he had done for his employers did not immediately surface. When the data supporting point 4 finally emerged, they changed the whole concept of this executive's approach to a new career.

There are many forms. Here are others: Start your letter with a strong statement about an accomplishment or a capability as shown below:

> I made contributions to sales, production, and financial management leading to expansion, lower costs, and better profitability while the chief operating officer of a $50 million corporation.
>
> If you are in need of a senior executive who is accustomed to achieving outstanding results, you may be interested in the specifics of the above and additional highlights in my background.

or

> With an earlier background as a statistician/data analyst (B.A. and M.B.A. degrees) I have used this ability, now as a manager, to reduce costs $2 million and add sales of $12 million within a period of two years, for a $200 million division of a giant company.
>
> If you are in need of a creative marketer who can use data as tools for developing strong forward progress, you may be interested in some of my other accomplishments.

or

> I am experienced in securing a 2000 mile smuggler-infested coastline along a foreign shore; and in maintaining security for 27 manned outposts in the same area.
>
> If you have need for a security officer, I have had training with one of the best educators (U.S.M.C.) and experience under the most rigorous conditions (wartime).

This form is also ideal for a consultant seeking assignments. For letters addressed to top corporate officials I consider it a little abrupt.

Examples of additional sales/broadcast letters follow.

Dear Mr. Roosevelt,

I was called upon to work with a reasonably successful pocketknife manufacturer, as a consultant. A study of the business showed a number of things to be wrong:

- sales confined to a geographical section
- outmoded displays and packaging
- a sales force that was nonproductive 40% of the year
- lack of accurate cost data
- no budget for sales, advertising, or administration
- a line of great breadth, of which sales of many items were only a few hundred a year
- product emphasis on numbers that had ceased to be popular 50 years ago.
- a completely frustrated sales department
- many employees just hanging on until retirement

In two years' time, devoting one day a week to these and other problems I was able to achieve.

- national distribution
- a reduction in number of items manufactured of 33%
- a sales increase of 50% with a 25% increase in profit
- a new and popular line of knives
- a new concept of a pocketknife (with patent) of which over 100,000 were sold on the first calls of the salesmen on their customers with the new product
- the automation of certain production activities
- budgets for sales, manufacturing, and administration

Not many companies are in such bad shape. But these achievements illustrate the breadth of my skills.

If your company could use a "total approach" to your problems with the promise of innovative suggestions to produce higher sales and profits, perhaps I could be useful.

A personal exploratory meeting without obligation would be very welcome.

Your reply is keenly anticipated.

Very truly yours,

Dear Sir:

Your investment in the creative mind of an experienced executive can produce greater returns in the next 15 years than almost any other investment you can make.

I am such an executive. You may be interested in a man competent in Corporate Planning and Economic Development. Here are some of my accomplishments:

- As a negotiator, represented an aircraft company for contracts involving over $50,000,000 in sales. I am skilled in management and government agency interface, verbally and in writing.

- As an aerospace engineer, I was among the first to introduce and implement Systems Engineering Management procedures. I am familiar with the important methods of profitability management; management by objective, management by exception, PERT, and others.

- As C.E.O. of a company, I developed programs to assist economic development in the Caribbean through use of Systems Management in accomplishing industrial breakthroughs.

I have a record of adding $100 million in extra profits to three companies by whom I have been employed.

Age 50, married, three children, excellent health, B.A., Economics.

Can you use an executive with these qualifications in your business? If you can, let's discuss it. I'd like to work for you.

Your reply will be appreciated.

                        Sincerely,

                                                    143

BROADCAST LETTER FROM AN EXECUTIVE SEARCH FIRM
WORKING ON SPECULATION

CANDIDATE NO. 1087

In the course of our work for Fortune 500 clients we have met a young, personable, effective, creative, experienced marketing vice-president who had had a career of 10 years with two leading consumer goods companies.

He has been instrumental in a major way in increasing sales over 50 percent for each, at the same time lowering the percentage cost of sales. He earned his M.B.A. at the Harvard Graduate School of Business Administration.

His present company has been absorbed by a giant conglomerate and he expects that the new owners will restaff with their own people. He is willing to relocate.

We do not have an assignment at this moment for this executive, but his qualifications are so good that we think you might be interested. If so, please write for complete details without obligation. Refer to client number 1087. Salary requirements in the eighties, plus incentives.

If you use this method of seeking interviews, it will be at your own expense unless the search firm working on speculation is willing to absorb the costs.

A comprehensive national list of executive recruiters, including those who work on speculation, is available for $10 from Consultants News in Fitzwilliam, New Hampshire.

Dear Sir:

I have 15 years of successful experience in financial areas: six years as bond analyst for a leading underwriter; six years as editor, writer and analyst for a large investment advisory service; three years as a research analyst for a major Boston bank.

My competence includes the ability to make effective underwriting presentations to achieve better bond ratings through restructured analyses, understanding of legal requirements in connection with, and effectiveness in, accomplishing sales closings.

I am accustomed to the orderly presentation of complex financial and economic data, the preparation and finalization of all official statements, and have a complete understanding of money and capital markets and exchanges. I am also familiar with and experienced in regional specialization, and have an excellent knowledge of marketing techniques.

I would like a personal interview to discuss the possibility of joining your company.

My educational background includes M.B.A. and B.S. degrees in finance. Personal data: age 36, married, excellent health, prefer Boston location.

Your response will be appreciated.

                                    Sincerely,

BROADCAST LETTER: CORPORATION COUNSEL

WILLIAM FILLMORE
1800 Cayuga Road
Buffalo, NY 123456

I am a broadly knowledgeable general counsel and administrative executive seeking association with a corporation that can use strong management and skillful and innovative leadership in these areas.

My current position is Vice President and General Counsel of a major
$500 million textile company. Because of a pending merger with a
larger company, I wish to make a change in employment. Somewhat iron-
ically, during my tenure I have had major involvement in acquisitions
and divestitures amounting to more than $80 million.

I would like to highlight some of the kinds of activities in which I
have participated effectively:

- managed domestic and international litigation of diverse
  matters exceeding $200 million in claims; all cases won or
  favorably settled.

- saved company $12 million in plant expenditures by seeking
  and obtaining revised environmental permits.

- held legal responsibility for more than $100 million of
  real estate transactions.

- operated the international division of West Point Cannon,
  turning a losing operation into profitability within two
  years.

- personally negotiated profitable agreements in 16 countries
  around the world; identified and worked with top legal
  specialists in 28 countries altogether.

Some other categories in which I have competence are these:
corporate strategies, budgeting, antitrust, contracts; secured
selling arrangements and security agreements under the U.C.C.; environmental compliance; EEOC and OSHA problems; joint ventures, licensing,
profit-making, and avoiding excessive legal spending by doing work
in-house. My references are of the highest order.

If this background suggests a personal meeting with you or your
designate I would look forward to it.

With kindest regards,

William Fillmore

Gentlemen:

With 15 years of successful experience in marketing management for major companies largely involving power tools and a record of consistent progress from salesman to manager of a $30 million region, I am a qualified marketing executive.

Among my accomplishments:

- over a period of six years increased regional sales from $9 million to nearly $30 million while staying well within profitability guidelines.
- recruited, trained and led a sales force of 60 salesmen with two field assistants and seven district managers.
- of seven district managers under my leadership, two ranked first and second nationally with the first awarded recognition as Manager of the Year.
- planned effective promotions and advertising on the way to achieving sales increases described.
- successfully promoted 25 of my salesmen into corporate positions in various areas: Product Planning, Marketing, Regional and District Management.
- upon assignment to important Atlanta District brought it from fifth to first place in sales and earnings and won Manager of the Year Award.
- earlier developed District, which ranked last in sales, to fourth position nationally.
- as salesman was routinely among top salesmen in the U.S., winning sales contest and earning numerous awards.

I am an effective innovator, sales leader and trainer, with a solid background in modern management techniques and concepts, banking and finance. B.S., Business Administration, age 40, married, two children, own home, excellent health.

I seek a position as Director of Marketing or General Sales Manager for a medium-size corporation in the tool industry.

If my qualifications are of interest to you, I would like an opportunity for a personal meeting.

                    Sincerely,

Dear Sir:

I am 35 years old, well educated, motivated, with successful experience in sales, office management, PR/client relations and advertising. I am currently employed with a national temporary employment organization in a management capacity.

I seek a position that provides opportunity for growth to management, preferably in a people-oriented environment where I can utilize abilities in persuasion, communications, and leadership, such as sales promotion, PR, communications, advertising, film production; willing to travel.

Some of my achievements:

- increased business 100% for present employer by selling services to new accounts.

- worked with PR firm in organizing and producing successful fashion shows, obtaining talent, choosing garments, accessorizing, photography and writing, including press releases.

- supplied effective help in writing copy, production of sales films, scripts, story boards; and market research for major consumer goods client of well-known advertising agency.

I have extensive training and experience in the performing arts under nationally known teachers; was a National Honor Student; have won State awards in writing and mathematics.

I look forward to hearing from you.

Sincerely,

Dear Sir:

I am seeking to associate with a medium-size company or a division of a large company in the Southwest where I will have complete marketing autonomy with senior general management opportunity.

I am accustomed to multimillion dollar marketing responsibilities for corporations in the office equipment industry.

My current responsibility is Marketing Development for Smith & Company, Inc., known worldwide for management excellence.

The following indicate my capabilities:

- increased Company's revenues in the Eastern Region by 53% in three years by identification of new markets and new applications for existing products.

- headed marketing team in the analysis of a new market and its requirements to the development of a new multimillion dollar market.

- created complete marketing plan for these new products.

- learned basic selling in door-to-door canvassing on a commission basis for leading manufacturer of photocopiers after earning M.B.A.

I am thoroughly indoctrinated with advanced marketing and management techniques; have received company awards for outstanding contributions; believe that I bring significant profitability and management advantages to a company in the consumer products area.

Age 35, married, excellent health. Undergraduate degree in Economics; Dean's List; Honor Roll; graduated in top 10% of class.

If my qualifications are of interest, I would like to have a personal interview.

I look forward with great interest to hearing from you.

Sincerely,

BROADCAST LETTER FROM AN INTERNATIONAL MARKETING EXECUTIVE

Dear Sir:

My background is 10 years in intensive training and successful administration in marketing a wide range of consumer products, including
major appliances, in South America with profit-center responsibility
for $22 to $36 million operations for a billion-dollar international
corporation.

- In 1984 I made a profit study which led to the discontinuance
  of unprofitable operations and a saving of $1 million annually
  in G. & A. expenses.
- In 1983 I established a new dealer structure and introduced 6 new
  products recommended by me which added over a million dollars to
  annual volume.
- From 1981 to 1983 I increased sales with another group of new
  products from $50,000 to $1 million.
- In 1979-1980 as a retail store manager, I increased sales from
  $400,000 to $600,000.

I have successfully trained hundreds of sales managers and salesmen.
I am experienced in budgeting, sales forecasting, market research,
advertising, product analysis. I have a strong profit motivation
and have demonstrated high leadership qualities.

Age 33, married, excellent health, B.S. Accounting, fluent in
Portuguese, Spanish and French.

May I have an interview to discuss my potential contributions to
your Company?

I look forward to your reply.

                                    Sincerely,

WILLIAM PIERCE
1804 Congress Street
Hillsboro, NH 10543

Dear Ms. Jones:

I have been employed by two multibillion dollar companies in progressively more important duties over the past 11 years, involving marketing and economics research encompassing the creative interpretation and extrapolation of data resulting in new marketing strategies, sales increases and cost savings amounting to millions of dollars.

My experience includes projections, financial analysis, cost studies, territory analysis, product and line studies, advertising effectiveness, analysis, feasibility studies, computer utilization and systems and long-term (25-year) economic planning.

Because my work has been effective for major companies, I would like now to have expanded responsibilities and new challenges in a multinational company - my reason for writing to you.

Here are some specific examples:

- after conducting a marketing analysis, I recommended a new sales approach to drugstores, which has resulted in a 20% increase in retailer inventory turns and a $15 million increase in volume.

- developed a marketing strategy for selected items based on extrapolations of model territories resulting in raising share of market by 10%.

- studied trade promotions, couponing, and test market results and made other evaluations leading to a rescheduling of promotional activities and an annual increase in one line of products of $13 million a year over the past three years.

- recommended a capital improvement program (accepted) improving return on investment by 7%.

- restructured forecasting technique to accomplish an $18 million reduction in inventory with improved product availabilities.

I have been extensively commended for these achievements, but the present organization does not provide room for the expansion of my responsibilitie in the near future.

I am 34 years of age, married, with two children, possess an M.B.A. from the Tuck School at Dartmouth and am multilingual in German, French, Spanish, Romanian and Hungarian.

If my qualifications suggest that I might have interest to you, I would enjoy a personal meeting.

Your reply will be appreciated.

Sincerely,

Mr. James Eastland, V.P. Finance,
Equitable Prudential Co.
1000 Third Avenue
Chicago, IL 10020

Dear Mr. Eastland:

In my present position I have become expert in restructuring all the
components of a real estate income statement to estimate the market
value of income-producing properties for the purposes of investment,
divestment, or use.

I have been able to identify opportunities which have been put to use,
with considerable success, by such companies and institutions as General Motors, A.T.&T., I.T.&T., Koger Properties, Prudential Insurance
Co., Yale University, Texaco, 245 Park Avenue, Loew's, and many
others.

My methods include the following studies:

- physical description, underlying fees, air and subsurface rights
- lease analyses (terms, tax and escalation liabilities; caps)
- debt structure, costs, discounted cash flow analyses (I do my
  own computer programming for this purpose), yields
- demographics, trends, projections, comparisons.

In addition to the careful and precise exposure of value for all kinds
of real estate, I have had special experience in the analysis of regional
shopping centers.

My value would relate to companies with large pension or other funds to
invest for whom I could provide reliable analysis and creativity in the
identification of real estate investment opportunities to produce optimum yields.

One of the greatest opportunities existing today for the enhancement of
return on investment (and capital gains) lies in real estate.

I have both J.D. and B.A. degrees. Age 34, married.

If this background is of interest to your company, I would enjoy a
personal meeting.

Sincerely,

152

Dear Sir:

For fifteen years I have been successful and innovative for a multi-million-dollar company as Manager of Research and Development in the consumer products field.

My general assignment is to provide my Company with a continuing and timely supply of new designs and competitively superior product relating to all aspects of development of mechanical and electrical consumer products.

I have advanced consistently through the organization to increasing responsibilities starting as Project Engineer and successively as Chief Development Engineer, Development Manager, Project Manager to present position as Assistant Manager, Research and Development.

My accomplishments include:

- Design and development leadership in creating famous product now marketed internationally.

  Cost reduction projects that saved Company millions of dollars and resulted in the revitalized marketing of established products with a substantial contribution to corporate volume.

- Patents involving new art.

- A new approach to research and development evaluation procedures providing full performance functioning not before available and contributing both to better product and to improved customer relations.

- Consistent operation within budget and for 1984 a budget saving of $765,000, while maintaining full and effective services.

My experience includes management and leadership of large technical groups, technical writing, product evaluation procedures, project programming, budget administration, computerization of data and primarily the exercise of pragmatic creativity in the approach to successful product development.

Hold B.S. and M.S. degrees in Engineering. Age 48, married, three children, own home, excellent health.

Sincerely,

(000) 123-4567

Thomas Watson
90 Numbers Way
Easton, Pennsylvania 00000

Dear Sir:

With ten years of progressive experience in data processing, currently department manager, I am qualified for similar responsibilities in a larger company.

My experience includes systems planning, systems analysis and programming. For the last five years I have supervised a staff of 20 in preparing a management information system that has given management new and more timely data leading to substantial growth and improved efficiency. Experience includes NCR 390 and IBM advanced third generation equipment.

Some accomplishments include:

- epitomization of massive reports to a brief document providing top management with all data in a relatively few pages; total profit, profit by division, sales, inventory finished and in process, forecast, accounts receivable, accounts payable, all compared with five preceding years.

- reduction of payment time from 60 days to 15 days through more rapid invoicing.

- production control records that have helped reduce inventories by more than $1 million annually with a goal of $2 million now in reach.

- analysis of sales by customer by product leading to new corporate objectives.

I have been given a series of problems to solve, by management, and commended for providing expeditious answers while reducing machine time by 20%.

My education includes M.B.A. in Computer Science from New York University School of Business Administration and a B. S. in Business Administration from Dartmouth's Tuck School.

My age is 32, I am married, we have three children. I am in excellent health. Relocation would present no problem.

If you have a suitable opening with opportunity for general management I would appreciate an interview.

Sincerely,

BROADCAST LETTER FROM OIL COMPANY EXECUTIVE

---

350 Riverside Drive   Home (212) 123-4567
New York, N. Y. 10075   Office (212) 321-1000

                            John D. Oyler

Gentlemen:

I have had twenty years of experience with large international oil companies in
the following areas:

- estimating exploration and drilling costs.

- organizing equipment, people and materials for new exploration and drilling and forecasting capital needs.

- budgeting operations and projecting cash flow; monitoring progress.

- evaluating drilling results; changing procedures if needed.

- controlling wild wells.

- presenting programs to prospective investors.

During this period I have made profit contributions running to millions of dollars
resulting from correct equipment selection, cost economics, risk/reward
calculations, recruiting and training, contractor supervisor and onsite controls.

My experience has been worldwide from drilling rig operator to managing engineer.

I have been responsible for budgets up to $600,000 per day.

I have a reputation for innovation, sound planning, safety, harmony in working relationships at all levels and with foreign governments; accurate hydrocarbon
assessments.

The experience related has been with Gulf and Mobile.

My education consists of the following:

M.E.A., Engineering Administration, Cornell University, Ithaca, N. Y., 1960.

B.S., School of Mines, Oklahoma City, Okla., 1955.

Additional graduate work in Automation and Electrified Lease Operations and
in Computer Systems.

Age 42, married, three children, excellent health. Willing to relocate.

References and further data are available upon request.
May I discuss employment with you?

Very truly yours,

ALFRED MANSUR
Cup and Lip Drive
Bartlett, NJ 07000

Dear Mr. Jones,

I have been employed by two multibillion dollar companies
in progressively more important duties over the past 11
years, involving marketing and economics research encompassing the creative interpretation and extrapolation of data
resulting in new marketing strategies, sales increases and
cost savings amounting to millions of dollars.

My experience includes projections, financial analysis,
cost studies, territory analysis, product and line studies,
advertising effectiveness, analysis, feasibility studies,
computer utilization and systems and long-term (25 year)
economic planning.

Because my work has been effective for major companies I
would like now to have expanded responsibilities and new
challenges in a multinational company, my reason for writing to you.

Here are some specific examples:

- after conducting a marketing analysis I recommended
  a new sales approach to drug stores which has resulted
  in a 20% increase in retailer inventory turns and a
  volume increase of $15 million

- developed a marketing strategy for selected items based
  on extrapolations of model territories resulting in
  raising share of market by 10%

- studied trade promotions, couponing, test market results
  and made other evaluations leading to a rescheduling of
  promotional activities and an annual increase in one
  line of products of $13 million a year over the past
  three years

- recommended a capital improvement program (accepted)
  improving return on investment by 7%

- restructed forecasting technique to accomplish an $18
  million reduction in inventory with improved product
  availabilities

156

I have been extensively commended for these achievements, but the present organization structure does not provide room for the expansion of my responsibilities in the near future.

On a personal basis I am 34 years of age, married, with two children, possess an M.B.A. from the Tuck School at Dartmouth and am multi-lingual in German, French, Spanish, Romanian and Hungarian.

If my qualifications suggest that I might have interest to you, I would enjoy a personal meeting.

Your reply will be appreciated.

Sincerely,

I have just completed a survey of 27 hardware (or department, drug, supermarket) stores in suburban North Jersey
and I find that of the 36 sealing compounds you manufacture,
only one was generally displayed, while there were many
packages of your biggest competitor generously displayed.
Furthermore I did not find a single one of the displays you
feature in the trade magazines in any store. Your new line
was completely absent. I shall be glad to show you my
survey if you would like to see it.

My purpose in writing you is that I am looking for a position
in a senior executive capacity in marketing or general management and I think my background would be especially valuable to your company.

To give you an example of what I have accomplished for my
present company, also in the same industry as you:

--I have brought my company to the premier position throughout the U.S. in such markets as hardware, department
   stores, chains and mass merchandisers (distribution with
   over 95% of the best hardware wholesalers, industrial
   distributors, and department stores)

--achieved 55% of the total snips business in the U.S.;
   70% of the quality scissors business; 25% of the hand
   cutting garden tool business (the latter against larger
   and intrenched competition)

--multiplied total volume 13 times (developed a campaign
   that sold a year's normal production in six months)

--redesigned lagging existing products to make them best
   sellers against all competition

--doubled Christmas sales volume by changes in packaging

--positioned company for worldwide dominance by devising
   new method of production

158

My company has not had a single year in 10 years when
profits did not increase at least 20% after taxes.

My work has encompassed and contributed to every area of
general management.

If this kind of background would be of interest to you I
would welcome a personal exploratory meeting at any time
or place you designate.

I look forward to your reply.

Yours very truly,

Sherlock Holmes

Mr. John W. Mason, Chairman
General Auto Corporation
Feneral Power Park
Detroit, MI

Dear Mr. Mason:

I am a businessman and a writer, a graduate economist, and a student of
government with experience as follows:

1985-Present, Executive Assistant to Senior Vice-President, Automobile
Oil Corp., where I am partly responsible for the widely acclaimed
institutional advertising campaign directed toward a better understanding
of the energy industry and U.S. and world economies.

1980-1985, Chief Executive Officer of a small durable goods company,
which I built from $2 million annual sales to $10 million. I retain a 20%
stock interest.

1975-1980, Deputy Assistant to the Chief of Government Regulations,
Department of Energy and Transportation, Washington, D.C.

1973-1975, Research Analyst, Ford Foundation.

My education is as follows:
Ph.D., Government, Stanford University, 1974
M.B.A., Harvard Graduate School of Business Administration, 1972
B.A., Economics, University of Chicago, 1970
   Phi Beta Kappa, Magna cum laude

My experience has made me an enthusiastic advocate of free private
enterprise. I believe that major American businesses must be even more
forceful in presenting themselves understandably to the public and to
the government. I am convinced that business can not only retain but
expand its influence on the U.S. economy with salutary long- and
short-term results on the living standards of the American people and,
by extension, to the living standards of the world. In other words, I believe
in the expansion of the quality of life through the resources of American
business.

I want to be a part of and a leader in this progress. My position with
Automobile Oil Co. is safe and interesting. However, I want to expand my
area of influence with a more diversified company, or a group of such
companies. My company knows of my plans. My work is not academic; it
multiplies profits.

I'd welcome a chance to discuss this with you.

160

THIRD PARTY ENDORSEMENT: SAMPLE LETTER

Mr. J. Russell Stout, Vice President
Colgate Cyanamid Co., Inc
Colgate Park
Bright Bond, NY 08967

Dear Mr. Stout:

I retired last year as Vice President of the Empire Bank, but continue my association as a consultant to the bank and as a member of the Board of Directors. One of my assignments has been upgrading our manpower development department. In this capacity I have had an opportunity to meet a large number of promising executives both in and out of this company.

I have also become aware of your own change in marketing strategy from product to market departmentalization with which, incidentally, I agree.

The purpose of this letter is to tell you about a young man who has had substantial success in his own company but now faces an uncertain future because of his company's acquisition by a much larger one.

He has had a ten-year career since gaining his M.B.A. degree at Stanford and is widely recognized in his industry (chemicals). In the last couple of years he has been credited with increasing share of market for his company's major line of proprietaries by more than 50%, and at a increased R.O.I. He also introduced the same marketing moves in which you are currently involved.

It occurred to me that such a man might be of interest to you. If so, call me or drop me a line and I'll set up a meeting. Needless to say, I have no personal or financial involvement in this other than an interest in seeing a highly talented individual find the right spot for his career development.

Kindest regards,

William Van Buren

PROPOSAL LETTER

Here is an example of a letter that might have been written following a meeting initiated as a informal discussion of mutual interests, rather than as a job interview.

Dear Mr. Buchanon,

Thank you for the opportunity to sit down with you two weeks ago and explore interesting aspects of the hand tools business. I have been interested in this area for many years, for special reasons, although my experience has been in consumer soft goods. It was good of you to give me your sales figures broken down by territory and states.

Just as an exercise for my own edification, I have used Department of Commerce figures on sales in the hand tools classification, expressed in percentages by states. Using your figures for New Jersey, your best state, as 100%, I have extrapolated what each state would do in sales if it were as well handled as New Jersey. Calculating your potential sales in this way and allowing for certain distributional aberrations of which I am aware, I find that *you have a potential national market 327% greater than your present sales.* I know you sense this, but these figures prove it.

Furthermore, using Florida as an example, where your sales of circular saws are greater than all the rest of the United States together because of special circumstances (a retiree with an encyclopedic knowledge of saws, selling direct to retailers), an opportunity of huge dimensions is uncovered.

You might be interested in studying these figures. I have also noted some of the steps that would need to be taken to move toward such objectives. My experience in marketing tells me that this would not be an easy accomplishment, but very possible in, for example, a dedicated five-year program.

I have had personal experience in implementing programs of this kind, and know that their achievement is possible.

I will 'phone you in a few days. I will be glad to find the time for an in-depth discussion of these findings if you are interested.

Again, thank you for the opportunity to learn more about your business. My hobby is business analysis.

Kindest personal regards.

There are many small businesses, such as this one (sales about $1.8 million) that reward their owners and a few others with substantial incomes. I know of one company president, operating a business of only $750,000 annual sales, who paid himself $125,000 a year 15 years ago. The comforts of operating in a small niche often settle into inertia and becloud substantial opportunities well within reach. These smaller company executives are often easier to meet than those in the upper echelons of giant companies.

This letter resulted in a job offer.

100 Petticoat Lane
Far Hills, NJ 07100

Mr. Hamilton Beach, Chairman
Bankers Holding Company
100 Wall Street
New York, N.Y. 10001

Dear Sir:

From time to time some of your larger customers, clients or friends
may ask you if you know of an available, competent executive to guide
a corporation effectively.

On the possibility that you have or may have such a request, I am
enclosing my resume which describes a successful, contributory
career.

I shall appreciate your referring to me any opportunities which may
come to your notice, or passing this along to someone else who might
have interest.

Sincerely,

WT
Encl.

William Tyler
(201) 321-7654

A GENERAL COVERING LETTER

Lewis Carroll
57 Mirror Road
Denver, CO (zip)
(123) 456-7890

Mr. Henry Gladstone, Pres.
Senator Playing Card Co.
30 Mosswood Avenue
New Orleans, LA (zip)

Dear Sir:

I have a consistent record of profit contributions arising from competence in general management, marketing and production for major companies in the U.S. and overseas; accustomed to P.&L. responsibility.

I am widely experienced in power tools and sophisticated machinery My resume is enclosed.

May I discuss mutual opportunities in your company with you?

Your reply will be appreciated.

Sincerely yours,

LC   Lewis Carroll

RESULTS OF A TYPICAL JOB CAMPAIGN UTILIZING A BROADCAST LETTER

CANDIDATE PROFILE

Functional area:	Marketing
Age:	50
Geographical employment limitation:	Eastern half of U.S.
Employment history:	
Early career:	18 years very successful
Recent career:	12 years 4–5 job changes; effective executive, but work not attended by recent success

NATURE OF CAMPAIGN

Number of letters sent:	191
Selection of addresses:	Careful selection of companies suitable to subject's background, ranging in size from $40 million annual sales to large conglomerates over $1 billion

(Note: for smaller companies, subject wrote to President or Chairman. For larger companies, he wrote to Vice President, Marketing. For giant companies, he wrote to Vice President of Marketing or Vice President of Personnel. All letters were addressed to selected individuals by name.)

TECHNICAL DETAILS

Stationery used:	24 lb bond, Monarch size
Color of stationery:	White

Method of reproduction:	Offset
Heading on letter:	Letterhead typed
Method of addressee fill-in:	Same typeface as body of letter
Length of letter:	1½ pages
Signature:	Personally signed
Replies:	Sent to third party to avoid residence disclosure

RESPONSES

Number of replies:	101, with 43 different titles grouped as follows:
	15 Chairmen and Presidents
	18 Vice Presidents
	25 Directors of Personnel, variously titled
	14 Managers of professional staffing (and various titles)
	29 Miscellaneous
Number of interviews:	6*
Number of job offers:	3

RESULT

Accepted job offer as head of marketing for division of multibillion-dollar company.

*The number of invitations to interview was reduced by the extreme caution of this candidate in protecting his identity; nevertheless, his campaign worked. The author's personal experience shows that mail campaigns are successful in eliciting job offers at least 75 percent of the time.

FIFTEEN

USING THE CALENDAR

The time to look for a job is when you need it, whether it is summer, Christmas week, or any other time. However, to *optimize a job campaign that includes mailings,* use the calendar to identify the best time of the year for attention to you.

The business calendar is shrinking. Out of 365 days only 189 are usually productive in the context of a job search, and this number is probably overstated. It does not include Jewish holidays, Wednesday closings in New England, fishing and hunting days in the Midwest, week-day golf in the South, or holidays like Election Day, Veterans Day, Flag Day, Washington's and Lincoln's birthdays, or the disruptions that occur when the individual states and the federal government fail to concur on the proper date for a given holiday.

Furthermore, traditional two-week vacations have given way to four to six weeks for executives and long-service employers.

The calendar year is an arbitrary measurement. The more typical business year is October 1 to September 30. One works eight months, until May 31, slows down in June, rests part of July and August, whirls through Labor Day, and recovers from rest and whirling in September, to start October with fresh vigor. It is no accident that the automotive industry model year begins in October.

168

There is another shorter hiatus in January and February for two weeks, for trips to Florida or skiing country, or for cruises. The business year is further interrupted by conventions, other business travel, directors' meetings, government meetings, and miscellaneous days off. It is no wonder that employment decisions are notoriously slow in the making. The 189 days have probably shrunk by now to 150 days.

In your job search, in using the mails you should avoid July and August, Christmas week, and Thanksgiving week. Aim at the first five months of the year, the last three weeks of September, the month of October, and the first half of the months of November and December. More specifically, try to have your mail delivered on Monday, or better still, Tuesday of the most useful weeks. After a Monday holiday, however, Wednesday

		JANUARY							FEBRUARY							MARCH				
S	M	T	W	T	F	S	S	M	T	W	T	F	S	S	M	T	W	T	F	S
	1	2	3	4	5	6					1	2	3					1	2	3
7	8	9	10	11	12	13	4	5	6	7	8	9	10	4	5	6	7	8	9	10
14	15	16	17	18	19	20	11	12	13	14	15	16	17	11	12	13	14	15	16	17
21	22	23	24	25	26	27	18	19	20	21	22	23	24	18	19	20	21	22	23	24
28	29	30	31				25	26	27	28				25	26	27	28	29	30	31

		APRIL							MAY							JUNE				
S	M	T	W	T	F	S	S	M	T	W	T	F	S	S	M	T	W	T	F	S
1	2	3	4	5	6	7			1	2	3	4	5						1	2
8	9	10	11	12	13	14	6	7	8	9	10	11	12	3	4	5	6	7	8	9
15	16	17	18	19	20	21	13	14	15	16	17	18	19	10	11	12	13	14	15	16
22	23	24	25	26	27	28	20	21	22	23	24	25	26	17	18	19	20	21	22	23
29	30						27	28	29	30	31			24	25	26	27	28	29	30

		JULY							AUGUST							SEPTEMBER				
S	M	T	W	T	F	S	S	M	T	W	T	F	S	S	M	T	W	T	F	S
1	2	3	4	5	6	7				1	2	3	4							1
8	9	10	11	12	13	14	5	6	7	8	9	10	11	2	3	4	5	6	7	8
15	16	17	18	19	20	21	12	13	14	15	16	17	18	9	10	11	12	13	14	15
22	23	24	25	26	27	28	19	20	21	22	23	24	25	16	17	18	19	20	21	22
29	30	31					26	27	28	29	30	31		23	24	25	26	27	28	29
														30						

		OCTOBER							NOVEMBER							DECEMBER				
S	M	T	W	T	F	S	S	M	T	W	T	F	S	S	M	T	W	T	F	S
	1	2	3	4	5	6					1	2	3							1
7	8	9	10	11	12	13	4	5	6	7	8	9	10	2	3	4	5	6	7	8
14	15	16	17	18	19	20	11	12	13	14	15	16	17	9	10	11	12	13	14	15
21	22	23	24	25	26	27	18	19	20	21	22	23	24	16	17	18	19	20	21	22
28	29	30	31				25	26	27	28	29	30		23	24	25	26	27	28	29
														30	31					

and Thursday become the preferred days. Avoid having mail delivered on Friday. Monday is a busy day for diving into accumulated decisions, Tuesday is more relaxed, Friday (TGIF) is a tapering off day when new decisions are seldom made.

Some people are even superstitious about Friday; for example, it is supposed to be a bad day to move into a new home, and of course Friday the 13th is the worst day to do anything! None of this is absolute, of course. It is just giving yourself the edge when it is possible to bend the calendar to your uses.

In correspondence, avoid the shaded days, weeks, and months on the calendar on page 169.

SIXTEEN

JOB CAMPAIGN RECORD

If you conduct a well-presented job campaign, by mail or otherwise, you will need to keep a record of what happened. A mail campaign, for example, might well produce scores of replies that need to be followed up. Here is a suggested record form.

Company name
Company address and tele. no.
Name and title of responder
Type of response: (form letter) (personal letter)
Nature of response: (pos.) (neg.) (maybe)
Follow up required:
  More info. ( )
  Call for app't. ( )
  Other ( )
Size of company
Type of business
Position available

SUGGESTIONS

Look up company in a directory.

Get copy of its annual report.

Assess geographic location.

Keep careful record of oral or written communications.

If possible, talk with someone who is familiar with the business or institution.

If company products are on sale in your area, call on the merchant and ascertain his or her attitude toward the company.

Make a personal assessment of the company people you meet.

SEVENTEEN

HOW TO READ AND ANSWER NEWSPAPER ADVERTISEMENTS

Advertisement for Senior Systems Programmer

Major job functions will require you to support communications software in a TCS/VS/CICS environment, and analyze and resolve technical problems. Your background should exhibit a detailed and complete comprehension of VS operating systems, TCAM knowledge, 3–5 years systems programming experience in an OS/VS shop, specific knowledge of CICS internals and SMP, good verbal skills, and a willingness to perform goal maintenance skills.

Forward your résumé and salary history in confidence to (name of company and individual follow—a brokerage company).

This ad means:

1. You must have substantial experience in programming and systems packages.
2. Your experience should have been with IBM software.
3. The symbols are all within the communications area, not in applications programming.
4. The advertiser is a brokerage company.

5. You must be able to express yourself with respect to EDP in nontechnical language for the understanding of general executives, and be able to write and speak clearly in providing instruction manuals and training sessions.
6. You must be continuously aware of the rapid changes in computer technology, hardware and software, and show evidence of your continuing education.
7. The age range sought is 30–35.
8. Previous experience in brokerage accounting systems will be a plus.

When answering any ad, it is worthwhile to list the elements appearing in the ad, to find out, if possible, anything you are unsure of, and to incorporate in your answer everything that is relevant. To answer this particular advertisement you could use a résumé like the following, which emphasizes your familiarity with IBM equipment and the continuing professional updating of your skills. If your age is favorable, mention it; if not omit it. In your covering letter you can refer to the fact that your verbal communications skills are high and that you have been successful in making improvements in systems more expeditiously because you have been able to clarify technical problems to executives who do not possess a computer background. In expressing highly technical qualifications a résumé is a more suitable document than a letter.

43 Ocean Gap
Hermosa Beach, Ca

R E S U M E

JETHRO BALBOA

EDP SYSTEMS DESIGNER

and ANALYST

RESUME TO ANSWER
ADVERTISEMENT FOR
SENIOR SYSTEMS
PROGRAMMER

SUMMARY

Qualified to design online systems, implement
and operate at optimum capacity. Record of
providing cost savings in time, manpower and
equipment and utilizing advanced technology to
accomplish objectives within expedited time
frames.

EXPERIENCE

1985-Present   PACIFIC CONTINENTAL TELEPHONE CO., Los Angeles, CA

ONLINE SYSTEMS DESIGN AND PERFORMANCE ANALYST for one of nation's largest
computer installations.

Responsible for:
A. justifying and devising plan for the following:
    1. conversion of Disbursement Accounting Department's TCAM (Telecommuni-
        cation Access Method) data collection system to CICS (Customer Informa-
        tion Control System) and centralization of online programming
    2. CICS online inquiring to IMS data bases via DL/I interface
    3. eventual migration to mixed CICS-IMS/DC-VTAM environment and
    4. selection of an online text editor to replace TSO for source program
        development and maintenance by application programmers

B. (earlier) headed task force of three analysts to improve Disbursement
    Accounting online CICS Data Entry System.
    - converted from CICS Release 1.2 to Release 1.3 and fine tuned CICS
    - redesigned and reprogrammed the major Data Entry Application Module
    - established Data Entry Problem Determination procedure
    - fine-tuned CICS system to a half-second response time and cut CICS
      CPU resource requirements by 50%
    - installed PAII for workload and performance tracking and capacity planning
    - converted CICS 2260 terminal support to 3270 Native-Mode support

    Accomplished B. above in 6 weeks vs. estimated time frame (by IBM) of 16
    weeks.

C. initial assignment to:
    1. redesign department's Mechanized Work reporting TCAM Data Collection
        System
    2. act as team leader of four Assembly language and COBOL programmers
        during design and implementation of system

Accomplishments overall:
- initiated formation of committee to determine requirements of Disbursement
   Accounting Department for next five years
- designed data collecting system that facilitated maintenance and provided
   additional flexibility
- expanded capacity of system; increased productivity by 100% eliminating the
   need for additional hardware

Over.....Please............

<u>1982-1985</u>   GREAT WESTERN INSURANCE CO., Los Angeles, CA

SENIOR PROGRAMMER for major insurance company.

Responsible for:
- creating a workload Statistics Report program for the Online Data Entry System
- batch program to convert data entry records to card image record for batch processing
- INTERCOMM systems programming
- conversion of Data Entry Application Modules from 2260 to 3270 native mode
- a table-driven, basic editor for online application

<u>1980-1982</u>   EQUIMETRO LIFE INSURANCE CO., Los Angles, CA

PROGRAMMER assigned to COBOL and BAL program maintenance group after employment as trainee.

<u>EDUCATION</u> <u>AND</u> <u>PROFESSIONAL</u> <u>TRAINING</u>:

   <u>B.S.</u>, Mathematics, California Western University, San Diego, CA, 1980

   Stanford University graduate training: 30 hours of Computer applications Information Systems (Computer Management).

   IBM training includes: Performance Evaluation and Capacity Planning;
                           all CICS courses; all IMS/DC courses;
                           TCAM application and systems courses;
                           TSO training; BAL and COBOL programs;
                           3600 Finance System training, INTERCOM
                           (TP Monitor) training;
   over a period of eight years.

   Worked at various jobs throughout college years.

<u>HOBBIES</u>: Basketball, track, football, chess, skiing

<u>PERSONAL</u> <u>DATA</u>: Age 30, separated, excellent health

                    <u>REFERENCES</u> <u>AND</u> <u>FURTHER</u> <u>DATA</u> <u>ON</u> <u>REQUEST</u>

Advertisement for Specialty Apparel Buyer

M. M. Deen, nationally known retail and catalog merchandiser, is expanding its buying group. Live and work in a small town near the Maine coast, mountains and forests. Experience with traditional specialty outdoor apparel for men and women to include textiles in general, casual sportswear and active outdoor apparel and accessories.

An exciting position you can only find in a small and professional organization. Responsibility for product development (test products on trips and expeditions), vendor selection, merchandising, buying, and staff development. Position requires strong analytical skills; minimum of 3-5 years experience with major retail/catalog merchant; knowledge of fabric construction.

Attractive salary and benefits.

Write to (name of company and recruiter).

This advertisement discloses the following information:

1. Name of company, and name of person to whom to write
2. Position: Apparel buyer—men and women
3. Outdoor sporting specialties—apparel
4. Knowledge of textiles required
5. The fact that it is a small but national organization
6. A need for product testing ability
7. The importance of personal outdoor interests
8. 3-5 years buying experience = 29-40 years of age
9. Basic textile buying experience desirable
11. Degree probably expected
12. Must be happy to live in small town
13. Analytical skills required

From other sources you can discover that the company has a sales volume of about $30 million, is located in a town of 1822 people about 15 miles north of Portland on Route #1, has 380 employees, three offices, and, in addition to buying, also manufactures footwear, sporting, and athletic goods. Sales per employee are high, suggesting that the executives probably have a variety of responsibilities.

It deserves an answer something like the following:

Reason for letter	This is in response to your advertisement in *The Wall Street Journal* (date).
Expression of analytical skills	In a ten year career with Abercrombie, Sears, Bauer & Co., famous national retail and catalog merchandiser, where I am presently employed, I tripled women's sportwear sales over a period of 7 years, increased markup 11% and gross margin 7.5% on a total departmental volume of $75 million. During this period, we have achieved a national reputation for sports and casual wear.
Describes exposure to outdoor specialty attire	I have done extensive research on sports apparel, fabrics, linings, weight, closures, durability, warmth, and other aspects of correct clothing for scores of activities ranging from casual use to use under the most rigorous conditions of climbing, hunting, fishing, exploring, and the like. I have also been involved in outfitting complete expeditions to the North Pole, Africa, the Himalayas, and other exotic areas.
Describes technical fabric knowledge	I have taken intensive courses at the New York School of Textile Design and am thoroughly knowledgeable about fabric wear, count, texture, sources, and the methods of achieving desired qualities according to end use.

Tells of apparel testing experience and outdoor lifestyle	In connection with my work and for pleasure I have traveled extensively in wilderness and white water areas and overseas to Kashmir, the lower reaches of Mt. Everest, and in Kilimanjaro.
Emphasizes broad retail administrative experience	My background includes buying for both stores and catalog, merchandise presentation, distribution, automatic shipping systems, profit projections, budget administration, promotion planning, and market testing.
Gives reason for interest	I am interested in moving from a giant corporation to a less structured atmosphere where opportunity for greater career and personal development are both present.

My résumé is enclosed.

JOB COMPETITION

Here is a typical response to an attractive advertisement for a senior marketing executive in a Tuesday edition of *The Wall Street Journal*.

Number of answers	310
In the New York area	186
Outside the New York area	124
Résumés received	294
Letters received	16
Applicants who are employed	257
Applicants who are unemployed	19
Not clear whether employed or unemployed	34
Salary stated	198

Salary not stated	112
Undergraduate degree	180
Master's degree	80
Doctoral degree	7
No degree	43

EIGHTEEN

CREATING A
MAILING LIST

To create a job search campaign by mail you will need to refer to directories to develop your personal mailing list. Your list should be tailored as closely as possible to the kinds of companies, geographic areas, and other special characteristics that reflect your personal needs and preferences. The following are to be found in most public libraries.

Dun and Bradstreet Reference Book of Corporate Management.

Dun and Bradstreet's Million Dollar Directory.

Dun and Bradstreet's Middle Market Directory.

America's Corporate Families. Published by Dun and Bradstreet.

The Career Guide—Dun's Employment Opportunity Directory.

Directory of Directors.

Rand McNally Bankers International Directory.

Fortune's annual supplement listing the 1,000 largest corporations (no individual executive names) and other listings.

Forbes annual list of 2,500 corporations (no individual executive names).

Hardware Age Directory (published by Chilton Co., Radnor, PA).

Pharmaceutical Handbook.

The Standard Advertising Register.

American Management Association publications (such as Executive Search Firms).

The Literary Marketplace.

MacRae's Blue Book.

Standard Rate and Data Service.

United States Government Organizational Manual.

Trade magazines.

Directory of Foundations in Massachusetts.

College Placement Annuals.

Association of Consulting Management Engineers (New York City).

The Wall Street Journal daily list of corporate operating reports.

Standard and Poor's *Register of Corporations, Directors, and Executives* contains an alphabetical listing of the names of about 35,000 corporations, 300,000 officers, directors, and principals, and 70,000 officers, directors, trustees, and partners. *Fortune* magazine annually lists the 1,000 largest industrial corporations as well as the largest financial institutions and the largest overseas corporations. *Stores,* a National Retail Merchants Association publication, annually lists, by volume, the leading department stores. *Forbes Magazine* has an annual listing of 2,500 major companies.

If you prepare your own list of companies to write to, make use of the S.I.C. (Standard Industrial Classification) numbers to identify a company's business. Many companies have multiple S.I.C. numbers. The first two digits of the four-digit S.I.C. number show the major industrial group to which a company belongs:

01 to 09   Agriculture, forestry, fishing

10 to 14   Mining

15 to 17   Construction

20 to 39   Manufacturing

40 to 49   Transportation, communications, utilities

50 to 59   Wholesale and retail

60 to 68   Finance, insurance, real estate

The last two digits classify each company more closely; for example, 3172 and 3199 refer to leather goods and 2844 to cosmetics. A cross-reference to the main body of the register (Standard and Poor's for example) will then give you the address and size of the company and names of executives. Many fine companies are unexpectedly missing, as are some divisions resulting from mergers. Most lists, as distinguished from directories, do not include location, area code, names of executives, and products. Creating your own list is an arduous and time-consuming task, but the result is invaluable. You may also purchase lists containing the information you need from specialist list companies and other sources such as some of the better résumé writing/career guidance companies.

The executives of the 500 or 1,000 largest companies are bombarded with résumés. You might find it worthwhile to address your mailings to smaller, equally fine and growing companies.

The *Yellow Pages* is another good source of local company names, but does not provide names of executives and area codes.

In using lists and "broadcasting" your availability you take the best, quickest, and surest route to employment, other than knowing someone who can place you or having some other "inside track" to a position. Note the following in mailing your material:

- Address your letter or résumé to a specific individual by name, and include the name on the envelope.
- If possible, include the individual's name on the letter as well, though this is not mandatory.
- If you are an upper-middle or top-level executive or adminis-

trator, send a sales or broadcast letter to one of the top executives or to the chief executive officer (by name).

- If you are a lower-middle executive, send a covering letter and your résumé to the personnel director (by name if possible).
- Make your initial mailing to 100 or 200 companies, or more if possible, in order to obtain a satisfactory number of useful responses.
- Select as special targets for individualized letters companies in which you are particularly interested.

In choosing companies to which to apply for employment, you must consider for which type of company you prefer to work and are best qualified to work.

One factor is company size, which can range from small $1 million to $2 million to very large multibillion dollar concerns. Some large conglomerates contain many surprisingly small units. Some small businesses are highly profitable, and many are the giants of tomorrow, taking advantage of the continuously emerging new areas of technology.

Large single-product companies are apt to be highly structured, with formal channeling (job descriptions) for all functions (some small companies seek to copy the structure). The units of large multidivision companies that allow operational autonomy within their divisions, however, can run the full gamut of management philosophies.

Small companies generally tend to be less rigidly structured, allowing greater participation in more areas.

NINETEEN

JOB HUNTING IN THE COMPUTER/TELE-COMMUNICATIONS AGE

Some day you will be able to conduct a practice job interview with your computer, complete with video and audio. The computer will correct your answers to interview questions and critique your comportment. You will have to wait a while for this.

In the meantime your computer can offer considerable assistance in the job search. With the aid of the word processor and an 80,000 word built-in dictionary, your spelling will be error free; your word selection supplemented by *Roget's Thesaurus,* will be impeccable. You may change words, phrases, sentences, paragraphs at will. A résumé usually has to be restructured several times before it is satisfactory. You may change type faces and create headings. You can print the finished copy.

Let us assume that you have MIS qualifications and have so described yourself in your résumé. In addition, however, you are qualified as a corporation counsel. It is easy to reconstruct the original résumé to redirect yourself without rewriting material that can be retained.

There are programs in existence that will enable you to identify S.I.C. (Standard Industrial Classification) numbers and the corporations suitable for your experience or discipline, including the volume of business done in each of the pertinent S.I.C. classifications. Several universities, including the University of Pennsylvania, have such programs.

You may also hook into electronic bulletin boards for job listings and discover specific requirements for a particular job, more detailed than an advertisement, and adapt the résumé accordingly, without changing the entire copy. (In this sense your résumé is copywriting.)

Developing a mailing list by computer is obviously a great time-saver. (Compare Chapter 18: CREATING A MAILING LIST.)

At the present time the first wave of digital information is entering consumers' homes almost exclusively along telephone lines. (Data distribution in the future may be accomplished by cable television.)

Tele-Communications Inc., Denver, through its X-Press Information Services, Ltd. unit, offers a job-search program with a database of listings.

The New York Telephone Company (Nynex Info-Look) has introduced a service that permits those with personal computers to dial a local number and be connected with a range of more than 60 services such as financial news, real estate, electronic mail, education, and travel.

American Telephone and Telegraph Company, together with other regional Bell System companies, plans to offer similar services to any customer with a computer and a modem within their calling areas.

The leading videotex vendors (*The New York Times,* July 12, 1989) are (with number of subscribers in parentheses):

Compuserve Information Service, H&R Block	(574,000)
Dow Jones News Retrieval, Dow Jones	(280,000)
Eastlink, Western Union	(200,000)
Genie, G.I. Information Service Company	(155,000)

Quantumlink PC-Link, Quantum Computer
Services   (94,000)

Prodigy Service Co. IBM/Sears   (75,000)

Delphi, General Videotext Corp.   (50,000)

Fax (facsimile) machine communication offers an exciting method of sending messages (résumés, letters) anywhere in the world in 15 seconds. Of course, there must be compatible equipment at the receiving end.

If you don't have a computer but do have a VCR and a video camera you can still conduct practice interviews on your television screen.

Because of the increasing sophistication of the job search, it is recommended that, if your speaking skills are poorly developed, you should go to a professional for instruction.

TWENTY

CAREER CHANGES

The following are common career changes:

- From the military to private enterprise or Civil Service
- From education to private enterprise and vice-versa
- From the Church to the private sector
- From government to private enterprise
- From household management to career

The military offers many learning opportunities, and annual personnel assessments provide a solid base for transposing military experience into usable private sector skills. A career in education may establish a strong foundation for entry into the business world, just as business experience may supply a need in education.

For the woman who has managed a household, transition into an earning career is aided by education and avocations, many of which demonstrate outstanding talents. People who worked little in their earlier years may still have much to offer if they can express themselves properly. Productive people are always in demand.

The material in Appendix C is included, among other reasons, to assist career changers to identify their experiences with the needs of private or public administration or professional activities.

The following pages are devoted to résumés and letters that have helped individuals jump the fence into a new pasturage.

Dear Mr. Snow:

I have spent my entire career since graduating from college in the U.S. Army. I am now ready to reenter civilian life hoping for a career that will permit me to utilize skills in analysis, management and languages in a domestic or international setting.

As a Major I have been assigned to duties with the Office of Special Investigations (OSI) as Agent in Charge since 1978, acting in connection with frauds, criminal activities, smuggling, homicides, and related matters in the U.S.A., Sicily, and Korea.

Out of my experience I have formed the ability to see what needs to be done in any particular assignment and how it can be done better. I have been cited for numerous contributions to more efficient operations cost savings, the curtailment of frauds and criminal activities, and dedication to duty.

A few examples:

- adapted PERT and CPM techniques to train Special Agents to bridge the gaps between the business world and the military environment.

- arranged for extensive training of Italian National Police to help contain drug traffic utilizing remote areas of the Adriatic coastline for smuggling.

- set up territories for Special Agents in Texas by counties, to reduce unnecessary repeated trips to the same places.

- reorganized method of credit and security checks with substantial savings in time and money.

I possess B.S. and M.S. degrees in Management Science in addition to much other special training. I am multilingual in Korean, Italian, and French (the last needing brush-up).

I am 34 years of age, married with two children, in excellent health; have resided in Korea and Italy and have traveled extensively in Hong Kong, Thailand, Cambodia, Vietnam, and Europe.

If this suggests that I might have some qualifications of interest to your company I would enjoy a personal meeting with an appropriate executive.

Your reply will be appreciated.

Very truly yours,

Samuel L. Clarkson
(000) 333-0000

Mr. Richard S. Kaley, Chairman
Columbia Broadcasting System, Inc.
Rockefeller Center
New York, NY

Dear Mr. Kaley:

While listening to television recently, I was struck by the misuse of the English language by performers, in commercials, and even by the newscasters.

I am probably oversensitive because in the matter of pronunciation I have what is known in musical terms as perfect pitch. The nuances of pronunciation are my vocation and my hobby.

Although I can hardly add 2 + 2 I am fluent in seven languages including French, Spanish, Portuguese, Italian, German, and Russian, speaking each like a native. This naturally gives me a great advantage in pronunciation because I am able to use the subtle tongue and voice box changes that characterize languages other than English.

It has occurred to me that CBS (I am not pointing a finger at you; I prefer to watch CBS-TV) could well use a language arbiter to assure that all who speak under your jurisdiction use proper English. You have at least this kind of an obligation to listeners who perhaps among their families and friends seldom hear English properly spoken. Furthermore, CBS would come to be preferred by a large segment of the more discriminating audience.

Words like premiere, robust, adult, junta, and a hundred others come to mind as consistently mispronounced. You might well ask, by whose standards? I submit there is room for difference of opinion. I am talking only about vulgar or uneducated mispronunciation.

I am an assistant professor of English at Columbia University and have written extensively on English usage and phonetics. I have been published by Times Books, McGraw-Hill, and several educational publishers.

You would be doing a great public service and satisfying a personal ambition by appointing me to a new position in your organization (or if there is now such a position, it is inadequately filled), as Director of Language Usage.

I would appreciate your consideration of this idea and your response.

Very truly yours,

CAREER CHANGE FROM AIR FORCE

1822 Georgetown Street
Point Pleasant, CA 95000

Home (000) 000-0000
Office (916) 000-0000

R E S U M E

of

J. William Grant

===

OBJECTIVE

Cpportunity to utilize skills in analysis, management
and languages, preferably in an internationl environment.

SUMMARY AND QUALIFICATIONS

***   Captain, U.S. Air Force, Office of Criminal intelligence
dealing with criminal and fraud matters, worldwide. Entire
career of 12 years to present in USAF, and in OCI since
1970 as Special Agent in Charge except when attending
language schools. Achieved M.B.A. while in service. (B.A.,
History, 1975.)

***   Record of utilizing management principles and advanced
management techniques to increase efficiency of operations
during every tour of duty assignment.

***   Able to recognize deficiencies in methods and procedures
and find the means to correct them. Cited by supervisors
for numerous contributions to more efficient operations,
cost savings, curtailing frauds, smuggling, criminal
activities, and dedication to duty.

***   Multilingual in Vietnamese, Italian and French.

(FOR FURTHER DETAILS SEE FOLLOWING PAGES)

191

EXPERIENCE

<u>1968-Present</u>   U.S. AIR FORCE.   Rank: CAPTAIN

<u>1979-Present</u>   SPECIAL AGENT IN CHARGE, San Diego, CA
                 Office of Criminal Intelligence (OCI)

OCI investigates criminal and fraud matters on a worldwide basis for the USAF. Supervise eight Special Agents and three administrative assistants. Line of command is Director (worldwide operations), Supervisor, Special Agent in Charge.

Responsible for:

- Investigation of frauds relating to millions of dollars of Defense Department funds for military contracts.

Accomplishments:

- recognized need of specialized training of Special Agents to bridge the gap between the business world and the military environment, including the proper briefing of senior officers; arranged for their training using an adaptation of civilian PERT and CPM techniques developed by the Western Regional Organized Crime Training Institute for the California Department of Justice.

<u>1974-1977</u>   SPECIAL AGENT IN CHARGE, Boot, Italy
              Office of Criminal Intelligence (OCI)

Supervised three language-trained Special Agents.

Responsible for:
- criminal and fraud investigations
- the territory South of Naples, including Sicily
- working jointly with the Italian National Police in matters such as international terrorism and smuggling.

Accomplishments:

- discovered that the port of Boot and the isolated area along the Adriatic Sea were sources of smuggling contraband through Middle East shipping traffic, to Holland and central Europe.
- arranged for extensive training by the U.S. Drug Enforcement Administration and other U.S. agencies in detection and identification techniques, for Italian National Police personnel; drug traffic decreased substantially.

<u>1973-1974</u>   LANGUAGE STUDENT, Italian
              ORD Language Institute, Monterey, CA

<u>1971-1973</u>   SPECIAL AGENT IN CHARGE, El Paso, TX
              Office of Criminal Intelligence (OCI)

Territory: all of northern Texas. Supervised 12 Special Agents, three administrative assistants.

Over..... Please......

1971-1973 continued
Responsible for:
- criminal and fraud investigations and inquiries regarding security
  clearances

Accomplishments:
- noted repeated trips to same areas resulting in unnecessary extra
  travel; set up territories by counties; concentrated assignments so
  that fewer trips had to be made with resulting lower operating costs
  and central billing instead of multilocation billing.

1970-1971 SPECIAL AGENT IN CHARGE, South Vietnam
           Office of Criminal Intelligence (OCI)

- as Vietnamese linguist represented District Supervisor in matters
  involving the OCI and the Vietnamese National Police.

1969-1970 LANGUAGE STUDENT, Vietnamese Language Department
           Ft. Ord Language Institute, Monterey, CA

1968-1969 SPECIAL AGENT IN CHARGE, Kansas City, MO
           Office of Criminal Intelligence (OCI)

Territory: Metropolitan Kansas City.   Supervised 12 Special Agents,
five administrative assistants.

Responsible for:
- criminal, fraud and security clearance investigations; credit investigations of persons entering the military.

1967-1968 AIR FORCE INTELLIGENCE SCHOOL, Pueblo, CO

1966-1967 USAF OFFICER TRAINING SCHOOL, Boulder, CO

EDUCATION:

B.A., History, Council State College, Bluffs, IA, 1968
M.B.A., Management, Garden State University, Trenton, NJ. Special
     training as noted by the USAF

LANGUAGES:

(proficiency: (1) low, (2) average (3) above average, (4) native:
Vietnamese: oral (3)   written (3)
Italian   oral (3)   written (3)
French   oral (3)   written (3)

HOBBIES:

Fishing, hiking, camping, travel

PERSONAL DATA:

Age 34, married, one child. Resided for extended periods in Vietnam and
Italy. Extensively traveled in the Far East and Europe

REFERENCES AND FURTHER DATA ON REQUEST

Naval Base Quarters   Home (123) 456-7890
Newport News, VA (zip)   Office (987) 654-3210

R E S U M E

of

JOHN P. JONES, IV

MANAGER/EXECUTIVE
in
GENERAL ADMINISTRATION or TECHNICAL CAPACITY

* * *   Entire career to retirement, 1 June at age 39, with U.S.
          Navy with present rank of Captain. Electronics and manage-
          ment specialties.

* * *   Accustomed to command positions involving as many as 600
          officers and enlisted personnel.

* * *   Reported on fitness by commanding officers consistently
          either outstanding or excellent.

* * *   Excerpts from fitness reports include the following:

          "a very dynamic officer" developing "a practical, effective
          and realistic organization" with "happy and well-motivated
          subordinates" . . . "cost conscious."

          "excellent command leadership ability, outstanding combat
          officer; ability to train staff in most effective use of
          new and experimental electronic equipment."

          "excellent manager, approaches all problems in rational
          manner; his Section has continued to respond in a timely
          manner to the numerous and varied demands placed upon it
          and successfully pursued existing programs for equipment
          modernization and improved systems performance."

          "demonstrated capability to handle positions of greater
          responsibility."

          and more.

(FOR FURTHER DATA, PLEASE SEE FOLLOWING PAGES)

EXPERIENCE

1964-June 1985   UNITED STATES NAVY

CAPTAIN, Combat Electronics Specialty. Total of 17 assignments in Meditterranean, Alaska, Bahamas, Charleston, SC, Thailand, Washington, DC and Newport News, VA. Most important assignments as follows:

Aug. 1982-June 1985, CHIEF, ELECTRONICS SCHOOL BRANCH, U.S. Navy Training Center, Training Division. Supervised 20 officers, 93 technicians, eight radarmen, 18 clerks. Responsible for:

- training 600 students yearly.
- establishing the curriculum.
- preparation and administration of annual budget of $2 million.

Accomplishments:
- changed curriculum, which was not relevant to needs of U.S. Navy or students, from mathematical theory to practical utilization, assuring capability to repair electronic equipment under battle conditions.
- changed basic theory of training from one based on negative advance evaluation of students to assumption of student intelligence and positive motivation by description of goals.
- grades curved upward and attrition declined from 28% to near zero.

May 1981-July 1983, CHIEF, FACILITIES SECTION, Electronic Engineering Division, U.S. Navy Headquarters, Washington, DC. Responsible for:

- procurement, system design and installation of all electronic equipment on Neptune submarines.
- justification for and preparation and administration of $500 million budget.

Accomplishments:
- issued specific job assignments to engineers by class of ship and equipment.
- discovered that surface search radar installed previously exhibited design deficiencies such as inadequate antenna rotation, catastrophic power supply failures, poor video presentation, grossly inadequate mean time before failure (MTBF).
- increased MTBF from 16.7 hours to 260 hours within year.
- instituted program to monitor and certify all electronic installations.
- tested, developed, and installed new type of transmitting antennas to better meet operational requirements.
- solved problem plaguing high-endurance submarines for many years.

Sept. 1980-May 1981, ELECTRONICS SYSTEM DESIGNER, Cruiser Design Staff, Electronics Engineering Division, U.S. Navy Headquarters. Responsible for:

- design of communications and navigation systems with bidding specifications.

Accomplishments:

- new U.S. Navy Cruiser (classified) has unmatched electronic fire system versatility and complete equal air control and navigation positions.

<u>Sept. 1979-Sept. 1980</u>, HIGH ENDURANCE DESTROYER SECTION, Communications Branch, Electronic Engineering Division, U.S. Navy Hdqtrs. Responsible for system design, procurement, installation of electronic equipment of 37 destroyers.

Accomplishments:

- developed system design for installation of new UHF, VHF/FM and VHF/AM communication equipment.
- improved upon previous designs of CCTV and MF communications systems.
- procured and installed new cameras capable of adjusting to varying light levels.

<u>Sept. 1977-Sept. 1979</u>, SPECIAL STUDIES.

<u>June 1976-June 1977</u>, COMMANDING OFFICER, U.S. Navy Command Station, Thailand. Supervised one officer, 28 enlisted men. Responsible for transmitting (classified) signal 99.97% each month throughout the year.

Accomplishments:
- transmitted usable (classified) signal of proper power and pulse shape 99.99% each month throughout the year.

<u>HONORS</u>:

Bronze Star, Silver Star, Purple Heart (3), D.S.M.

<u>EDUCATION</u>:

ABC Industries, New York, NY, 1977-1979. Advanced Electronics Technology. Graduated 20th in class of 80.
U.S. Navy Officer Candidate School, 1971 (5 months). Graduated first in class of 103.
U.S. Navy Electronics School. Graduated first in class of 67.

<u>HOBBIES</u>:

Wrestling, karate, hockey, water polo, boxing.

<u>COMMUNITY ACTIVITIES</u>:

Coach, Scout football team.

<u>MEMBERSHIPS</u>:

Retired Officers Association.

<u>PERSONAL DATA</u>:

Born 6/15/46, three children, excellent health.

371 Clinton Avenue
Irvington, NJ 07000

Home (201) 378--1657
Office (212) 377-4444

R E S U M E

of

TORAM XESTROS

HUMAN RESOURCES DEVELOPMENT SPECIALIST

OBJECTIVE: Human resource development and planning specialist providing technical assistance in the evaluation and development of corporate personnel and personnel programs.

QUALIFICATIONS: New York State cerfified Clinical School Psychologist, learning disability specialist, experienced coordinator of educational programs. Psychodiagnostician.

Wide experience in administering batteries of tests, evaluating, and producing recommendations.

Currently employed as corporate personnel consultant with additional assignment to develop stronger corporate image.

Graduate and postgraduate studies at New York University with specialty in Clinical Psychology.

EDUCATION: Advanced Certificate in Clinical School Psychology, Postgraduate work, Columbia University, New York, NY 1975
M.S., Clinical School Psychology, New York University, 1973
B.A., Psychology, Fordham University, New York, NY 1970

ACCREDITATIONS: Permanent New York State certification as School Psychologist
Permanent New York State certification in science and special education teacher at junior high and high school levels.

PERSONAL DATA: Age 36, married, four children, own home; willing to relocate.

197

EXPERIENCE

1978-Present   FOREMOST APPAREL INC., New York, NY

PERSONNEL CONSULTANT for major apparel manufacturer with plants in New
York, New Jersey, Pennsylvania, and overseas; several thousand employees.

Responsible for:
-   analysis of employee records for application of psychological test-
    ing as indicated to be necessary.
-   assistance in adjusting a different cultural background to production
    requirements.
-   assistance in development of workshops on human relations
-   bilingual evaluation system to increase employee effectiveness at the
    administrative level
-   studies to improve trade name perception among buyers

1976-Present   (concurrently)   THE BRIGETON (NJ) SCHOOL DISTRICT

LEARNING DISABILITY COORDINATOR for school district with 10,000 students,
600 teachers and 19 elementary, junior high, and high schools, Supervise
4-8 professionals. Utilize tests familiarily known as Academic Achievement, W.A.I.S., W.R.A.T., Bender Gestalt, Projectives, Myers-Briggs Type
Indicator, etc.

Responsible for:
-   organizing, coordinating, and implementing learning disability
    program (L.D.), developing budget, providing leadership and counsel
    to the faculty; hiring, training, and supervising staff.

Accomplishments:
-   taking into consideration manpower, budget, student and faculty popu-
    lation, and existing programs, selected one of four alternatives for
    presentation to Board of Education; it was accepted and has remained
    in successful effect for 2 1/2 years (success measured by improvement
    in remediation)
-   established all the policies and procedures to ensure uniform
    administration and delivery of the needed services
-   held conferences with principals and teachers to create mutual under-
    standing of procedures
-   set objectives for testing, provided prescriptions and dates of
    completion
-   maintained complete data file and progress reports

1975-1976   BONAVENTURE PSYCHIATRIC CLINIC

L.D. SPECIALIST. Supervised staff of six
-   developed individual remedial programs and education therapy for
    inner city children

198

1975-1976 Continued

L.D. SPECIALIST.
- coordinated the reading center
- developed community workshop to enlarge and improve delivery of
  services

1975-1976 (concurrently)   THE NEW SCHOOL

SCHOOL PSYCHOLOGIST

- created programs for the exceptional children
- provided individual educational-career therapy
- acted as consultant to teachers to assist in providing most suitable
  programs to meet the specialized children's needs

1973-1976   PSYCHASSOCIATES, INC. (partially concurrent)

COORDINATOR of EDUCATIONAL THERAPY and ASSESSMENT

-developed programs and network of communications with staff and outside
  contacts

TEACHING EXPERIENCE

1977 Conducted monthly workshops with school staff to implement and
follow program guidelines at the Bridgeton School District.

1974-1975 Seminar workshops for guidance counselors of the New Jersey
Schools.

1970-1974 SCIENCE TEACHER, Newark, NJ public junior high schools

MILITARY SERVICE: Turkish Defense Forces, Naval, 1961-1964

10 Lockmoor Place   (201) 357-5382
Lawrence, NJ 07000

CURRICULUM VITAE

CANDACE HOLTZ

OBJECTIVE:	Administration or Consulting position in health care institution (recruiting, management, research) or administrative or teaching position in university (Associate Dean, Assistant Professor, Department of Nursing).
QUALIFICATIONS:	Doctoral, Master's and Bachelor's degrees; nursing experience in medical departments of large medical centers, intensive care burn unit, chronic rehabilitation hospital, public and private psychiatric hospitals; experience in supervising nonprofessional hospital staffs and professional nursing students in these environments.
	Experience in teaching and curriculum development.
	Competent in research and statistical analyses.
PERSONAL DATA:	Age 36, married, excellent health.
EDUCATION:	Ph.D., Psychology, Teachers College, Columbia University, New York, NY, 1978.
	M.S., Nursing, University of Kansas, Lawrence, KA, 1969.
	B.S.N., Drew University, Madison, NJ, 1966.
	Graduated Cum Laude.
HONORS, AWARDS & SCHOLARSHIPS:	H.E.W. multidisciplinary scholarship, Psychology, 1971-1976
	H.E.W. graduate traineeship, Nursing, University of Kansas, 1967-1969. Elected to Kappa Gamma Phi for achievement in academic work at the college level. Thesis selected for presentation at Eighth Annual Nursing Conference (1970), Honolulu, HI.

Over....Please....

PROFESSIONAL   1975-1978   See EDUCATION
EXPERIENCE:

                  1969-1974   COLUMBIA UNIVERSITY - NEW YORK HOSPITAL,
                              Medical Center School of Nursing

                      1974   ASSISTANT PROFESSOR, part-time, teach-
                             ing Life-Span Developmental Psychology,
                             Adolescence through Senescence; 110 students

                  1972-1974 RESEARCH ASSISTANT and INSTRUCTOR

                  - jointly with Dean, and in collaboration with
                    faculty, established new curriculum for
                    Department of Nursing focusing on the range
                    of phyiological and behavioral states in
                    consideration of prevention care, chronic care,
                    and acute care
                  - and development of course in life-span
                    psychology

                  1969-1971   INSTRUCTOR. Supervised nursing
                  students in spectrum of hospital settings
                  (rehabilitation, public and private psychiatric,
                  medical department)

                    - taught chronic neurological and psychiatric
                      conditions of patients
                    - established group dynamics sessions to promote
                      professional peer evaluation of nursing care
                    - alleviated chronic friction between non-
                      professional nursing employees and profes-
                      sional nursing students

                  1968 (summer) UNIVERSITY HOSPITAL, Lawrence, KS

                  STAFF NURSE, Burn Intensive Care Unit.

                  - Part of interdisciplinary team implementing range
                    of life-sustaining care for severely burned
                    patients

                  1967 PRESBYTERIAN MEDICAL CENTER,
                        Denver, CO

                  STAFF NURSE, medical. Team leader for nonprofessional
                  personnel. Provided nursing care for acutely ill
                  patients.

                  1966 UNIVERSITY HOSPITAL,
                        St. Louis, MO

                  STAFF NURSE, medical. Team leader and nurse as
                  preceding.

                                          Over....Please....

MEMBERSHIPS: American Association for the Advancement of Science
                      American Association of University Professors
                      American Nurses Association
                      American Psychological Association
                      Society for the Research in Child Development

HOBBIES: Tennis, gourmet cooking, professional organizations

REFERENCES: Dr. Robin Delamatre, Department of Human Learning and
                          Thorndike Hall, Box 64, Teachers College,
                          Columbia University, New York City 10027

                      Dr. Helene Rome, Division of Human Development,
                          St. John's College, Annapolis, Maryland 20686

                      Dr. Rita Meadows, Dean and Director of Nursing,
                          Columbia University - New York Hospital Medical
                          Center, 1300 York Ave., New York City 10021

202

TWENTY-ONE

RELOCATION, HOUSING, AND INFLATION

RELOCATION

If offered a position with, for example, an increase in income, assess the cost of living in the new location. It sometimes happens that higher costs in a new location will use up the amount of the salary increase, leaving you no better off than where you presently live. Include also "quality of life" considerations. Quality of life includes the size and comfort of your present home compared with where you might live if you relocated; freedom from crime; commuting convenience; schools, friends, and/or family; opportunity for future career growth; access to cultural advantages; and more.

It is not unusual for employers to add cost of living increments for moving to a high-cost area.

If you are willing to relocate, it may be easier to find the job you want. The perfect match-up between candidate and employer could possibly be right next door. It could also be 3000 miles away. Finding it is a matter of intelligent multiple choices rather than aiming at few targets. Unless you are an expert horse player, an across-the-board bet is safer than a bet on the nose. If you wanted to get into the fast-food business, would you think of Wayzata, MN, or Baton Rouge, LA? Dun and Bradstreet's directory would lead you there. This author being a stick-in-the-mud winces at the thought of relocation, and perhaps you do, too. But take a look at the boom towns or counties in the U.S. as of this writing (perhaps you live near one):

> Gwinnett County, GA
> Orange County, CA
> Fairfax County, VA
> Johnson County, KA
> Fairfield County, CT
> Princeton, NJ
> Morristown, NJ
> Secaucus, NJ

And look at this (*The New York Times,* May 1987):

How the cities ranked as the best place to locate a business	Percent planning to locate new office space in the next twelve months	
1. Atlanta	New York	23
2. San Diego	Los Angeles	14
3. Tampa	Chicago	12
4. Los Angeles	San Francisco	12
5. Boston	Atlanta	10
6. Chicago	Washington	10
7. New York		

For quality of life (good public schools, affordable housing, low crime rate), Atlanta, San Diego, Boston, and Denver were rated superior while New York, Detroit, and Cleveland had lowest ratings.

The survey was conducted during April 1987, with the chief

executives of 403 companies with annual revenues of more than $250 million. They were most hopeful about the Dallas-Fort Worth area, for which 29 percent saw economic improvement, followed by Houston, San Diego, Denver, and Atlanta. In a well publicized move, J. C. Penney moved from New York City to Plano, TX, and Mobil Corporation from New York City to Fairfax County, VA.

Discontent often hovers around thoughts of:

Retirement.

Inflation (making ends meet).

Possible illness.

Lack of adequate resources.

Looking for employment.

Cloudless skies shine on:

High income.

A life-style one enjoys (this could be exclusive).

The exuberance of health. (Life is an endless succession.)

A job one likes.

What has this to do with résumés? I will make the connection. Inflation is a topic of considerable speculation. Here is a retrospective. My first job paid me $50 a month, or 17¢ an hour, based on an eight-hour day, a 5½-day week, and 4⅓ weeks in a month. The minimum wage is now $3.35 an hour and soon to go up (in 1990 to $4.25). This is about twenty times greater, but because of a more common 35-hour week, the monthly wage is only 10 times greater, slightly above $6,000.00 a year. (I have read that airline porters earn up to $45,000 per year.)

In the 1940s, in the suburban town of which I shall speak, starter homes sold for $10,000 to $15,000 (3–4 bedrooms, 1–2 bathrooms). The same houses sell today for $275,000–$325,000. This averages 24 times greater.

Today's cost of carrying a 30-year, $300,000 mortgage at 11 percent is $34,284 annual amortization, plus upkeep of 2½ percent, and taxes of $4,850.00. If one wants to spend no more than 35 percent of income on housing and has no house to trade in, so to speak, that has not benefited from inflation, one needs an income after taxes of $138,850 to live in a starter home. The reason for the recent phenomenon of two-income families becomes apparent. The community to which I refer is among the more expensive places to live, chosen for commuting convenience, quality of life, excellent public and private schools.

The demographic profile supplied by the Chamber of Commerce provides the following information:

1980 population	19,523
Land area	10 square miles
Age groups	
0–14	4,664
15–24	2,575
25–34	2,000
35–54	5,456
55 and up	5,846
Median age	40.9
Total households	6,969
Median household size	2.44
College: 4 or more years	6,642
Household income distribution (1979 figures)	
under $14,999	1,174
$15,000–29,999	1,563
$30,000–74,999	3,258
$75,000 and over	1,400
Average household income	$53,155

(The 1990 census will show substantial changes in all these figures.)

The average selling price of 102 homes in this community in 1988 was $514,000. The price range was from $220,000 to $1,325,000.

To place these data in perspective, around 1968 people earning $50,000 or more were in the top 1–2 percent of earners. Executive-level homes cost $70,000–$80,000. In 1989 these same homes sold for $550,000 to $750,000. The top earners of 1968 could no longer afford them at their prevailing salaries. Fortunately, in the 1970s and 1980s incomes rose about three times.

The median household size (2.44) is a function of the age distribution of the population; 44.5 percent of the residents are 45 years of age or older, and in many cases their children have moved away. Many retired people have retained their homes (3,208 people are 65 years of age and older).

According to Wharton Econometrics the highest-priced single-home markets are:

Area	Current price (in thousands of dollars)	1997 projection (in thousands of dollars)
1. Bridgeport–Stamford Norwalk–Danbury	$342	$485
2. Anaheim–Santa Ana– Garden Grove	268	425
3. Newark, NJ	266	430
4. Honolulu	264	439
5. New York (including N.J. suburbs)	247	442
6. San Francisco–Oakland	241	371
7. Hartford–New Britain	232	385
8. Los Angeles–Long Beach	227	342
9. Boston	224	316
10. San José	216	389

Projections are at best dangerous to make. If a depression occurs, present prices might be 50 percent lower instead of the 42 percent to 80 percent higher shown preceding. However, Wharton Econometrics suggests that single-home values will

exceed inflation by 1 percent a year. The best markets for existing single-family homes (projected) will be:

State	Gain, 1989 (%)
New Hampshire	85
Vermont	85
Oregon	83
New York	78
California	71
New Jersey	69

According to a Chicago Title and Trust Co. report, home
prices continued to rise *nationally* in 1988. The average price of
a house, nationally, rose 9 percent in 1988, from $133,410 to
$145,500.

Housing affordability by income for December 1988:

Annual income	Mortgage amount	Home price
$20,000	$ 49,000	$ 61,250
30,000	73,500	91,875
40,000	98,000	122,500
50,000	122,500	153,125
60,000	147,000	183,750
70,000	171,150	214,375
80,000	196,000	245,000

The mortgage amount was determined by qualifications for a
conventional loan covering 80% of the home cost.

In thinking about your career consider where the greatest
business opportunities prevail, at the same time keeping in mind
the qualify of life you want. Your approach to new employment
by way of writing offers *unlimited geographic choice*. We have
given you an analysis of one community. Chambers of Com-

merce can be found for any locality. Send for profiles of the places that interest you. Then visit. If you have school-age children and find that the schools are poor, this might mean the added expense of private schools. It is true that using a résumé as an employment tool can take you anywhere, but equally true that "anywhere" may not be desirable.

In examining a demographic profile (having your own needs in mind), look particularly at age groups, school quality, median household size, income distribution. Inflation, currently around 5 percent, is theoretically under control, certainly when compared with the double-digit inflation of a decade ago. Nevertheless, 5 percent inflation over five years is 28 percent, over ten years 63 percent, over 15 years 108 percent. Keep this in mind in your planning. Buying a single-family home will probably keep you ahead of inflation. For some people, in the past, it has been the best investment they ever made.

Some day you will retire. Your retirement benefits are a very important part of your employment benefits. If you are employed for 30, 40, or 50 years, even relatively low inflation will have multiplied your financial needs for the time when you will have no employment income. Social Security is not enough. And remember, in your retirement planning, if you die, your wife must be suitably provided for. (Or should I say your spouse?)

So remember your résumé may banish *discontent* by providing cures for inadequate income, retirement worries, inflation concerns, substandard life-style, an unsuccessful job search. Really a magic carpet.

TWENTY-TWO

JOB INTERVIEWS

Preparation for interviews means:

- Knowing your qualifications so you can talk about them unhesitatingly.
- Rehearsing your lines ahead of time.
- Remaining optimistic even if you have a series of unsuccessful interviews.

Research indicates that five candidates are interviewed before one hire takes place. The ratio of hires to interviews for top-level executives may be greater. *The New York Times* reported in February 1989 that in seeking a successor for Dr. Vartan Gregorian, President of the New York Public Library, 100 candidates were screened and 18 interviewed. These were narrowed to four until one was selected. The man was 65 years of age. As St. George slew the dragon, so qualification conquered age.

The interview is weighted in favor of the employer. The interviewee is the salesman. The relationship is originally adversarial. Do not let it upset you. To an interviewer an interview is like unwrapping a mummy. What's under all those bandages? Unwrap the bandages yourself. Pity the poor interviewer. If there is a mistake in hiring it can cost the employer from $400 minimum to millions of dollars at top levels.

Ask yourself what you would look for if you were doing the hiring.

210

Interviewers pounce on:

Evasions.
Hesitations.
Illogic.
Unsupported claims.
Poor employment background.

Questions to be expected when being interviewed:

Tell me about yourself.
What did you think of the company (or people) you worked for?
Where do you want to be in five years?
What's your problem with your present employment?
What do your associates think of you?
What references can you give me?
What books have you read recently?
Why did you get fired?
How do (did) you get along with your boss?

Chemistry between people has a big role in hiring. You can't control it. Your chemistry will be favorable with some, adverse with others.

Knowing what kind of manager you are will help you to explain yourself to an interviewer. Here is an almost universal definition of a good manager:

Has integrity.
Knows job thoroughly and those of immediate superiors (has prepared himself for promotion).
Constantly updates with respect to determining how the job can be done better.
Teaches subordinates and trains a successor.
Is never mean or vindictive.
Has an objective.

Knows how to lead others.

Is motivated.

Continues to educate self.

Can work under pressure without losing temper.

Can act decisively.

Is more often right than wrong in business judgments.

Can act with subtlety and finesse when required to do so.

INTERVIEW EXAMPLE

Tell me about yourself.

"I increased the sales of our company by eight times in a period of nine years." This may have appeared in your résumé in this manner, and for its purpose is a good statement.

But it is an unsatisfactory answer at an interview. The interviewer wants to know how you did it, hear how you express yourself, find out what kind of manager you are, and also wants to get some ammunition, if possible, for questions that may trip you up.

Here is the way you should answer this question at an interview:

"During my tenure at Swan and Cook Manufacturing Company as vice-president and general marketing manager, I was able to double our sales in about five years. It still seemed to me, however, that there was a further potential of some magnitude. I spent a considerable amount of time studying our statistics— measuring distribution against population and demographics, analyzing variations on product sales by customer, and a lot of other comparisons. When I started, I really didn't know exactly what I was looking for.

"A pattern finally began to emerge. We had about 30 categories of products. Of these, five were in strong demand, and each had characteristics and uses that were different from the others.

"It seemed to me that we could build a consumer campaign around these five products. I assigned jobs to our inside sales department: devise a display, create an advertisement, dummy up some catalog pages, develop a formal sales presentation. When this was put together we spent a couple of days practicing among ourselves in making a sound sales presentation suitable for various kinds of buyers—wholesale and retail.

"When the plan was ready, I asked for a special meeting of the executive committee and presented the whole program, from concept to plan of execution.

"The committee was enthusiastic. We brought our salesmen in and presented the idea, and set up a plan to have home-office sales executives travel for three or four days with each salesman.

"The idea worked so well that after a few days our salesmen were able to sell the plan to nine out of ten of their customers.

"It became necessary, because of the overwhelming response, to withdraw customer presentations from most territories and confine ourselves to a few regions, until we could meet production projections.

"The end result was a tripling of our business over a period of three years."

TWENTY-THREE

THE EMPLOYMENT APPLICATION FORM

Some personnel executives place great stock in the hand-written application form. They believe they can detect candidate characteristics from the way it is completed. For reasons mentioned hereafter have your résumé with you when doing this exercise.

- A sloppily filled out application form is a poor advertisement for you. It may express carelessness, muddled thinking, attempts at evasion.
- If a question requires a narrative answer, the reader will look for coherence, unity, and brevity. If you refer to your résumé, it might help you to express yourself more clearly.
- The reader looks for contradictions, gaps in employment, misspellings, errors in chronology, too frequent changes of residence, grammatical errors, and the like. Refer to your résumé to eliminate such flaws.
- Be ready to indicate why you left your last job. You should be ready to answer this from prior self-examination. Putting the blame on others, even if true, makes a bad impression.
- Be ready to disclose your salary history.
- Be prepared to explain why you would like to work for the company.

TWENTY-FOUR

ESTABLISHED SERVICES AVAILABLE TO THE JOB SEEKER

Help-wanted advertising appears regularly in the classified section of newspapers in two forms:

Classified advertising.

Display advertising.

Employment agency advertising usually appears with the classified section. Almost every newspaper carries help-wanted classified advertising. *The New York Times* and *The Wall Street Journal* have national distribution and are of importance to anyone seeking employment. A typical edition of *The Sunday New York Times* contains approximately 3,000 or more classified help-wanted ads and an equal number of openings advertised by employment agencies. Many large employers work closely with employment agencies for original screening of job candidates. Employment agencies charge a fee for their services. The fee is often paid by the employer, but sometimes by the job candidate who is placed. If you utilize an employment agency, make sure you know who has the payment obligation. The words "fee paid" in an ad mean the employer pays.

The following is taken from *EMA Reference Guide*, Annual Edition, 1979, published by the Employment Management Association. It is entitled "How to Select and Effectively Use an Employment Agency" and is written from the employer's point of view.

> "Choosing the right employment agency involves a number of things not the least of which is how to use your other applicant sources such as advertising, write-ins, employee referrals, etc."

When an employer uses an employment agency in this manner, it pays the fees. Many employment agencies specialize in certain kinds of employees, accountants, secretaries, fashion, Wall Street, legal, and so on. Read their ads to determine if their job offerings are compatible with your objectives.

Despite the multiplicity of job offerings in classified advertising, many job seekers cannot find a match between positions available and their own skills. Problems of location, people, compensation, type of company, and opportunity, may not meet the requirements of the candidate. Also, jobs available may be misrepresented. Keep in mind also that 60 percent or more of job openings are never advertised. Scanning help-wanted advertising is nevertheless mandatory. In the help-wanted *display* advertising section, the jobs available are upper-level without exception. *Open house* advertising appears in the display section.

Available openings for careers in education, librarian openings, hospital, health care, medical employment, and university programs are advertised in "The Week In Review" section of *The New York Times*, Sunday edition, and elsewhere in other newspapers.

Trade Journals. Journals are an important source of employment opportunities for their industries.

Corporate Personnel Departments. If you are at an entry, clerical, or lower middle-management level, these departments in large employment centers such as department stores, insurance companies, utilities, factories, and the like, may be visited without invitation. A stroll through a large retail mall discloses many job openings.

Executive Search Firms. These are hired by corporations to find top-level managers. "Search" is the key word. They conduct an active search, usually among employed executives who have already established successful records. Therefore, it is far more likely for an executive to be discovered through "search" than for a candidate to find a position through solicitation of such firms. The field is dominated by six to eight large companies out of more than 2,000 operating nationally. Some job seekers, nonetheless, have found employment by soliciting these firms.

Temporary Help Agencies. These are among the fastest-growing segments of the employment field. Employers avoid their normal obligations to employees: pensions, medical coverage, insurance—in fact, all fringe benefits. At the same time they gain qualified personnel. Look in the Yellow Pages under EMPLOYMENT CONTRACTORS—TEMPORARY HELP.

Outsearch Specialists. These are employed by companies to ease the search for new jobs by dispossessed employees, that is, fired, restructured out, or disemployed for whatever reasons. In today's world, large, publicly recognized, enlightened corporations do not dismiss established and effective employees without lending a helping hand, particularly if unemployment is no fault of the employee. Some outplacement firms will work with individuals who are willing to pay their fees. In general, they are not important factors in individual job search.

Career Guidance. These companies offer their services to help individuals look for employment. Such companies will write a résumé for you, offer help in improving your interview techniques, seek out potential employers, and mail out résumés. The fee is 10 percent of expected first year's compensation. A gimmick offered by some is that you will be reimbursed for your expenses if the company is successful in getting paid by the hiring company. The manager of one such office admitted to me that in his five-year association with the office not one client had been so reimbursed and few had actually gotten jobs. One who chooses this route should investigate carefully before signing up.

College Placement Offices. If well staffed, they are useful, especially to recent graduates.

Public Libraries. Librarians sometimes offer assistance to job seekers.

Over Forty Clubs. These are organized to help mature people find employment. They are usually operated on a nonprofit basis. The members help each other do the chores necessary for the job search. Desk space and telephone service are supplied at cost. You will find them listed in telephone directories if they are active in your area.

Management Consultants. They are aware of openings among their own clients. The larger accounting firms also offer consulting services.

Conventions and Trade Association Meetings. Jobs are often originated and nailed down at these convocations.

Government Hiring. Federal, state, and some local governments provide employment services. You will find comprehensive listings in telephone books.

EXAMPLES:

New York—City of

New York—State of

- Jobs, household.
- Industrial, construction, and transportation.
- Office personnel.
- Professional placement.
- Labor Department. (There are extensive listings under this heading.)

Careers in Education, Librarian Openings, Health Care, Medical Employment opportunities and University programs are advertised in "The Week in Review" section of the New York Times, and elsewhere in other newspapers.

CLASSIFIED ADVERTISING
Ten most wanted categories

Administrative ass't.	510
Accountant/bookkeeper	480
Sales	416
Household help	375
College graduates	309
Receptionists	292
Programmers	274
Word processing	245
Bank positions	236

(From a recent survey)

TWENTY-FIVE

JOB-SEARCH SUGGESTIONS

For letters, Monarch size stationery (7″ x 10″) is preferable to 8½″ x 11″ size.

When involved in a job search, install a telephone answering system to avoid missing important calls from possible employers.

After an interview, be sure to write a "thank you" letter to the interviewer.

Copy-test your writing. If you are not getting replies to your mailings, change your copy. Well-written and well-directed letters and résumés should elicit a 5 to 10 percent response.

If you have an important customer following, be sure to mention it in your writing.

Make a list of your acquaintances. It will probably be a greater number than you think. Distribute résumés among them.

Discover poorly managed businesses in your area of expertise and write to them.

If your work produces samples of what you have done, take them with you to an interview.

If you are at an established management level, seek out growth companies and smaller rather than giant companies for employment.* Large organizations often promote from within.

*Of interest, *Forbes'* annual survey, The 200 Best Small Companies in America, usually published in a November issue.

Some companies are "dressy," but some think blue jeans are acceptable. Dress your best until you know which are which.

Do not fail to keep in mind that fully 60 percent of all available jobs are never advertised. Seek them by the use of directories and by talking with people.

Statistics show that two-thirds of all jobs are created in businesses with fewer than 20 employees. Some are mom and pop enterprises, but others have large revenues.

IDENTIFY YOUR ACCOMPLISHMENTS

Many job applicants find it difficult to identify accomplishments that they consider worthy of writing about. Doing their jobs day by day, they fail to recognize that the completion of daily tasks results in the achievement of certain goals, such as expedited work flow, more timely reports, improved customer service, reduction in complaints, greater productivity, and better morale.

Almost everyone has accomplishments if he or she will search for them.

- Increased profits.
- Increased sales.
- Identified new markets.
- Improved work efficiency.
- Saved money.
- Reorganized.
- Integrated office systems.
- Reduced staff.
- Earned additional income (for employer).
- Improved competitive position of company.
- Devised new products, improved existing products.
- Expanded markets.

- Arranged financing (for company).
- Improved asset security.
- Increased value of corporate securities.
- Trained.
- Solved problems.
- Contributed new ideas.
- Reduced overdue accounts.
- Reduced inventory.
- Increased turnover.
- Improved financial reporting.
- Found acquisitions.
- Reduced taxes.
- Improved management reporting.
- Reduced employee turnover.
- Upgraded personnel.
- Used cost-saving purchasing techniques.
- Discovered better copy theme.
- Introduced better filing system.
- Increased typing speed and accuracy.
- Relieved boss of administrative details.
- Planned better meetings.
- Improved employee morale.

Have you thought of your accomplishments in these ways?

TWENTY-SIX

JOB-SEARCH MAXIMS

- Department managers frequently know what they want better than the personnel department, but the latter will be responsible for finding and screening the several suitable candidates who may then be referred to the department manager for the actual hiring decision.
- In a labor-intensive company the personnel department can be so busy with labor grades, or so oriented to that kind of employment, that it has no responsibility for other than blue-collar and clerical hiring.
- In giant companies the top officers will seldom participate in employment decisions except at the highest levels, and then only after all the necessary screening has been completed by others.
- In big companies personnel executives have been upgraded to top organizational status and are of increasing influence in hiring decisions.
- Many large, mature companies have fewer openings at mid-level and in upper management than might be expected because of a policy to promote from within.
- Jobs at mid-level and in upper management are frequently easier to get with smaller companies under $100 million, at salaries comparable to those paid by big companies.

- The increase in the number of M.B.A. graduates and their employment, the increase in women managers, the trend towards promoting from within, and the growing number of acquisitions have had an unfavorable impact on the hiring of mature executives.

- *After age 45 one should never leave existing employment before getting another job* (unless financially secure or widely known). Age 45 is rather arbitrary; it could just as well be 48 or 55 or 43.

- If you are conducting a mail campaign for a job, do not address the heads of giant companies; they are not interested in you at the approach stage.

- If you are conducting a mail campaign, make it comprehensive—100 to 200 companies; don't use half measures. Careful selection can improve the response and reduce the size of the mailing. To put it more strongly, selection is subordinate only to superior writing.

- Any job search is affected by the time you can devote to it, your age, your accomplishments, your particular field, the time of year, the state of the economy, and many other factors; it must be adjusted accordingly.

- The liberal arts degree, downgraded in past years, is now recognized as excellent employment preparation.

- Many obscure companies employ 10 to 1,000 people and are good targets for employment applications because they are not bombarded by candidates.

- Rapidly growing companies should be primary targets of job seekers; they have had no time to establish management depth.

- Large diversified companies remain a good target for employment because they are frequently composed of small divisions; if what you offer seems interesting, your résumé or correspondence may be circulated among many other divisions. The personnel department is invaluable in this respect.

- Do not be upset if you are interrogated by a person at a lower level than your own; this is an essential time-saver in a large corporation.

- For corporations that list (in directories) an assistant to a president (or chairman or other top executive), address yourself to him/her rather than to the top executive; screening you is part of his/her job.

- Going over the head of an existing manager by writing to or talking with the chairman or president can be irksome, irritating, or insulting to a departmental manager and can be the "kiss of death" to your job hopes; on the other hand, if you have something truly unusual to offer, go to the top.

- Financial people such as accountants, treasurers, controllers, and corporation counsels can apply to almost any company for employment, regardless of what it makes or does. Marketing and production people more often need to choose companies related to their experience.

- Very small industries should be avoided even if a job often sounds good; there is no place to go if the industry doesn't grow or if technological change overcomes it.

- For maximum career progress and job-getting ability avoid career gaps: a year off to travel or write a book, activity as a self-employed consultant over a period of a couple of years, or any self-employment that you do not expect to continue.

- Make a habit of thinking about yourself on a regular basis. Review your accomplishments, keep a continuing record of them in writing.

- Plan steps to remove yourself from any company in which you are stymied through no fault of your own; on the other hand, offers implicit in "afraid to quit?" advertising by career advisers are dubious invitations.

- The lower the level at which you apply for a job, the easier it is to get one, and vice-versa.

- Many people find jobs by a lucky chance or by being in the right place at the right time; you can give luck a chance to be on your side by circulating the fact of your availability.
- Never become so involved in your job that you don't have time to think about yourself.
- Never hesitate to seek advice, if needed; even if it is expensive it may be very cheap in terms of your career development.
- Even if you are secure in your job, plan for what you would do if you lost if; there is more uncertainty in any job now than at any time in the past.
- The expansion of government carries with it the enlargement of job opportunities in government.
- It frequently requires as much as a year of hard work to find a new job.
- Employment letters to top executives of large companies marked "confidential" or "personal" are sometimes irritants to the addressee, particularly to the heads of major corporations.
- If unemployment is 6%, there remains a 94% chance of finding the job you want (if you are qualified).
- Companies in need of management talent are just as interested in hiring as you are in getting a job.
- Executives or those hoping to be executives should not permit their activities in a present job to become so narrow in scope that they become specialists in an area of little use to other companies. Examples: attorneys dealing with nuclear regulatory agencies; systems analysts for very small companies; utility rate experts; supervisors of small departments (order handling, customer service); certain specialized banking jobs.
- From time to time return to academia to brush up on new management techniques; knowledge accumulates in geometrical progression every five or ten years.
- Analyze your talents and your work preferences in anticipation of the possibility of a second career.

- Learn how to handle the next job above you and the one above that as well. To have done so will be helpful in looking for another position.
- As you grow older, make an increasing effort to review regularly what you are doing and what you have done in order to discover how it can be done better; executives are replaced or downgraded because they have become complacent.
- Employers tend to overestimate the average qualifications necessary for adequate job performance; and candidates usually offer less than average qualifications.
- Job candidates miss out on job opportunities more often for lack of interview preparation than for lack of qualifications.
- Interviewer misjudgment is the cause of both excessive job turnover and weak employee selection.
- More people fail in their jobs as a result of their own or their boss's personality defects than for lack of competence.
- If the awarding of jobs were based on an accurate assessment of qualifications existing at the time of appointment, there would never be, for example, a President of the United States; people create their qualifications on the job if they are any good—or crack up in the process.

A TYPICAL EXECUTIVE*

He was born in 1941 and spent most of his childhood in the urban Midwest. Eldest of three children, he attended public schools, helped put himself through college (a large public institution) by working part time, and then earned his M.B.A. at a top private university. He started with his employer 19 years ago as a functional specialist. He is married, has three children, and his

*Survey of Fortune 500 companies.

wife has no outside career; his family has had to relocate during his career, but not often.

He believes concern for results, integrity, and desire for responsibility increase one's chances for success—more so than creativity, ambition, and aggressiveness. And he should know. Though he may never assume the company presidency—and he doesn't seek it—his success is indisputable, because these preponderant characteristics describe senior executives of America's largest corporations.

How These Executives Started Their Careers

Marketing/sales	27%
Finance/accounting	60
Professional/technical	30

Percentage of these executives in general management now:

Of those starting in marketing/sales	52%
Of those starting in finance/accounting	31
Of those starting in professional/technical	51

APPENDIX A

SUPPLEMENTARY RÉSUMÉ EXAMPLES

In this appendix we reproduce 29 résumés, in addition to the 23 résumés scattered throughout the book. To find résumés by vocation, see Résumés Index. To locate types of résumés (chronological, functional, etc.) consult the General Index.

120 East 83rd Street
New York, NY 10033

Home (212) 700-6666
Office (212) 800-1111

R E S U M E

GRETA SORENSON

OBJECTIVE

Project direction, product management,
sales promotion, general administration
for consumer goods company

SUMMARY and QUALIFICATIONS

*** Skilled organizer, trainer, administrator, marketing
manager research analyst. Able to conceive and
implement marketing strategies; hire and supervise
staffs; set up office policies and procedures.
*** Experience includes advertising agencies, network
television, film production, with record of significant contributions in all assignments.

EXPERIENCE

MARKETING
PROJECT
DIRECTOR

TRANSATLANTIC, LTD., New York, NY
(Client is a wholly owned subsidiary of Philips
International, Amsterdam, Holland). The company
is a marketing firm and advertising agency with
15 employees; supervise four.
Report to President

Responsible for (1980-Present):
- analysing market and providing sales direction for marketing distilled spirits product
new to the U.S. but consumed overseas

Accomplishments:
- identified key markets by location and demographic data, directing distributor salesmen
to best prospects
- tracked sales and established sales goals for
salesmen and territories; administered sales
report system and inventory depletion report

Over....Please....

- organized sales data as basis for marketing strategies
- organized and supervised field research; pro moted successful product testing
- instituted sales incentive programs
- instituted direct mail campaign to salesmen
- developed office information system for client: systems handling, sales data areas of responsibility, organization chart
- currently achieving sales enthusiasm, and product growth, with account expansion and repeat business on schedule

ADMINISTRATIVE MANAGER

For same company
(1979-1980)
Responsible for:
- setting up offices for new company

Accomplishments:
- staffed office with receptionist, secre- tary, bookkeeper, traffic manager, clerical; made arrangements for free-lance assistance (artists); established systems and procedures, insurance and benefits
- purchased equipment and supplies
- established good relationships with supplier
- coordinated and participated in West Coast field research, analyzed results and made recommendations that were adopted

LEGAL CLEARANCE MANAGER

DELLAFEMINA - HICKS, New York, NY
Major international advertising agency, 1971- 1972
Reported to Executive Vice President.

Responsible for:
- clearing advertising for compliance with F.T.C. and other broadcast regulations

Accomplishments:
- advised creative and account management through development and production stages
- reviewed research supporting advertising claims
- avoided legal problems

BROADCAST CLEARANCE EDITOR

NATIONAL BROADCASTING CO., New York, NY
1970-1971. Reported to Vice President of Broadcast Standards.

Responsible for:
- reviewing commercials for acceptability on network television

Over....Please....

- judging claims and product performance
  reports
- evaluating and editing children's programs
  and feature films

Accomplishments:
- conducted effective administration

FILM PRODUCTION ASSISTANT	HAL PRINCE PRODUCTIONS, INC., New York, NY 1966-1969. The company produces animated children's shows, commercials, and training films. Reported to President/Executive Producer.

ASSISTANT   Responsible for:
TO PRESIDENT   - purchasing and editing scripts, screening
                   talent, supervising recordings and mixes
                   for final film
                 - hiring office personnel
                 - coordinating all areas of production of
                   animated films for network television,
                   including timing on animation, voice-over
                   recordings for film and final production,
                   clearances, deliveries and copyright reg-
                   istration.

PART-TIME   1976-1978 HARRIET ADAMS COMMUNITY CENTER,
ADMINISTRATOR   New York, NY
                 - counseled; coordinated meetings and
                   seminars for senior administrators while
                   handling family obligations and rearing
                   young daughter

EDUCATION   B.S., Rhode Island School of Design,
                 Providence, RI
                 Certificate, New School of Design, New York,
                 NY

PERSONAL DATA   Divorced, 9-year-old daughter, excellent health

REFERENCES   On request

232

27 86th Street   (212) 777-7777
Staten Island, NY 10000

R E S U M E

of

JOHN GRANT HEFNER, C.P.A.

OBJECTIVE

Tax Manager, Supervisor or Director for financial,
service or industrial corporation.

SUMMARY

***   Extensive successful experience as Tax Manager and
Supervisor for "Big 8" certified public accounting
firm for 13 years; credited with significant contributions to tax law interpretations in aid of
clients, including large and small corporations,
and individuals.

***   Earlier, for five years, agent with the Internal
Revenue Service responsible for initiating and
winning a precedent-setting action in a famous
case.

***   Although a tax specialist, possess credentials and
competence in all areas of accounting services.

(FOR FURTHER DETAILS SEE FOLLOWING PAGES)

EXPERIENCE

TAX MANAGER   1970-Present: CROON, BABSON & CO., New York, NY
                              Certified Public Accountants with 60
               partners, staff of 375 and diversified corporate clients
               from large to small in a great variety of industries.

               Responsibilities:
               - as manager, below partner level, supervise entire staff
                 on tax matters

               Contributions to firm:
               - added about $3 million in new clients to firm's volume
               - conducted seminars on regular schedule for entire staff
                 on tax matters; prepared advisories used by entire firm
                 on tax procedures
               - acted as personal tax consultant to high elected
                 political figures, senior partners of international law
                 firms, famous designers, realtors, stockbrokers, tele-
                 vision personalities, and sports figures in addition to
                 corporate work
               - provided solutions for complex tax issues
               - was recognized authority in certain tax areas
               - expedited intraoffice paperwork; improved quality of
                 correspondence

               Areas of activity include tax shelters (oil and gas, com-
               modities, real estate, equipment, cattle), joint committee,
               farm losses, accumulated earnings tax, travel and enter-
               tainment, officers' salaries and loans, leasebacks, bad
               debts, etc.

               Contributions to clients (examples):
               - increased pension benefits by restructuring a corpora-
                 tion into six corporations
               - saved $1/2 million in connection with a proposed dividend
               - saved $20,000 in the use of a yacht for business enter-
                 tainment
               - liquidated a real estate corporation that did not have
                 an attorney
               - saved $1 million for famous designer with a plan in-
                 volving a personal holding company
               - arranged substantial tax and personal benefits to two
                 feuding family officers; represented both of the two
                 surviving corporations
               - and much more

I.R.S. AGENT   1965-1970 U.S. INTERNAL REVENUE SERVICE
                              Office of International Operations,
               Washington, DC, and at Camden and Trenton, NJ

               - examined returns of U.S. citizens residing abroad, non-
                 resident aliens, and foreign corporations

I.R.S. AGENT (continued)

- as agent in New Jersey, audited returns of corporations, partnerships, and individuals
- assigned also to tax problems involving celebrities such as John Wayne, Clark Gable, Clara Bow, Mark Twain, Norman Rockwell and others
- initiated a precedent-setting case involving income exclusion for a U.S. citizen residing abroad; position was sustained

EDUCATION: B.S., Drew University, Madison, NJ.
                Elected to Honor Society

                Graduate work in Accounting at University of Pennsylvania

                Continuing education with NY State Certified Public Accountant Society

ACCREDITATION: Certified Public Accountant

PROFESSIONAL   American Institute of Certified Public Accountants, Board
AFFILIATIONS: of Examiners

                New York State Certified Public Accounting Society, Committee on Federal Taxation

                Columbia University Tax Study Group

PERSONAL DATA: Age 42, married, excellent health

REFERENCES: On request

DISCUSSION

Accounting Résumé. The résumés of public accountants (if they are not partners) are often difficult to write using the formula of "What were your responsibilities?" and "What did you accomplish in the exercise of those responsibilities?" In practice, accountants do segments of a client's work—payroll, audits, reconciliations, taxes, investments, consolidations—and are unaware of the total influence of the package on the client's affairs.

The preceding accounting résumé has interest because the subject analyzed his involvement carefully.

Hefner, in his tax work, had many interesting experiences, including his tenure as an IRS agent, and named some of the people (fictional here) whose returns he had worked on. He also became such an expert in the tax area that he was called upon to give seminars for the entire staff of his large firm.

In accounting résumés, experience in a variety of industries or institutions lends breadth; advisory work with clients provides authority; and work on tax shelters, EDP techniques, estate advisories, corporate reorganizations, and reversing IRS decisions shows a sophisticated competence.

EXECUTIVE SECRETARY

510 Governor Clinton Apartments   (212) 867-3410
New York, NY 10009

R E S U M E

of

TUESDAY WELT

OBJECTIVE: Position in private industry as EXECUTIVE SECRETARY
                  to busy manager.

QUALIFICATIONS: Skills included ability to plan and organize work for
                  expeditious completion; to work under pressure; to
                  accept responsibility; to supervise effectively and
                  coordinate the work of others. Harmonious with people
                  at all employment levels. Possess typing speed with
                  accuracy of 75-80 wpm; shorthand speed of 100-120 wpm.
                  Experience in research. Able to handle correspon-
                  dence with minimum supervision when desirable. Accus-
                  tomed to summarizing important happenings during ab-
                  sence of executives; to setting up agendas, acting
                  as liaison among executives, making itineraries,
                  scheduling travel. Administratively competent in
                  record-keeping, forecasting work loads, arranging
                  and reporting meetings. Multilingual. Have highest
                  nonprofessional Civil Service rating.

EXPERIENCE: 1962-Present Rockefeller Foundation, New York, NY
                  EXECUTIVE SECRETARY, Office of the Chairman, Council
                  on National Alternatives (1974-present). Responsible
                  for preparing summaries of committee meetings; for coor-
                  dinating work of secretarial staff, often under pressure
                  sometimes throughout the night to draft reports, reso-
                  lutions and amendments for distribution prior to next
                  day's meeting; for organizing and processing document
                  publication. Responsible for attending conferences in
                  Mexico City, Rio de Janiero, Buenos Aires; monitoring
                  results.

                  PERSONAL ASSISTANT to Executive Director of Grants
                  (former U.S. Ambassador to Albania) (1971-1974),
                  requiring attendance each year at Economic and Social
                  Council meetings in Berne; handled protocol at offi-
                  cial dinners.

                  PERSONAL ASSISTANT, formerly Secretary, to Director of
                  South American Trade and Development (1967-1971). Re-
                  sponsible for coordinating and supervising work of
                  secretaries. Aided in setting up conference committees.
                  Attended conferences in New Delhi and Geneva.

EXPERIENCE: SECRETARY to Director of Public Information Division
(continued)   (1962-1967). Responsible for keeping Director briefed
                during extended absences; for supervising office staff.
                Attended meetings in Paris and Mexico City.

LANGUAGES: Fluent French and Spanish.

EDUCATION: King's University, London, England, 1957-1958.
                Pace Institute, New York, NY, 1958-1959.
                Hold certificate in report and letter writing.

PERSONAL DATA: Divorced, age 40, excellent health. Want to relocate.

REFERENCES AND FURTHER DATA ON REQUEST

```
27 Alexander Hamilton Hill                          (201) 618-7423
Hoboken, NJ 07000
```

CURRICULUM VITAE

CAROLYN COMFORT

OBJECTIVE: Administrative or Consulting position in health care in-
                  stitution (recruiting, management, research) or admin-
                  istrative or teaching position in university (Associate
                  Dean, Assistant Professor, Department of Nursing).

QUALIFICA-   Doctoral, Master's and Bachelor's degrees; nursing ex-
TIONS: perience in medical departments of large medical centers,
                  intensive care burn unit, chronic rehabilitation hos-
                  pital, public and private psychiatric hospitals; ex-
                  perience in supervising nonprofessional hospital staffs
                  and professional nursing students in the environments
                  mentioned above. Experience in teaching and curriculum
                  development. Competent in research and statistical
                  analysis.

PERSONAL DATA: Born 2/24/46. single, excellent health.

EDUCATION: Ph.D., Psychology, Teachers College, Cornell University,
                  New York, NY, 1979.

                  M.S., Nursing, University of Chicago, Chicago, IL, 1970.

                  B.S.N., Saint Aloysius College, Cincinnati, OH, 1967.
                  Graduated Cum Laude.

HONORS,   Rhodes multidisciplinary scholarship, Psychology, 1972-
AWARDS &   1977. Rhodes graduate traineeship, Nursing, University of
SCHOLARSHIPS: Michigan, 1968-1970. Elected to Kappa Gamma Phi for
                  achievement in academic work at the college level. Thesis
                  selected for presentation at Eighth Annual Nursing Con-
                  ference (1970), Albuquerque, NM.

PROFESSIONAL   1976-1979   See EDUCATION
EXPERIENCE:
                  1979-1975   COLUMBIA UNIVERSITY - PRESBYTERIAN HOSPITAL
                              Medical Center School of Nursing

                  1974   ASSISTANT PROFESSOR, part-time, teaching Life-Span
                  Psychology, Adolescence through Senescence; 110 students

                  1973-1975   RESEARCH ASSISTANT and INSTRUCTOR

                  - jointly with Dean, and in collaboration with faculty,
                    established new curriculum for Department of Nursing
                    focusing on the range of physiological and behavioral
                    states in consideration of preventive care, chronic
                    care, and acute care
                  - and development of course in life-span psychology
```
```

1970-1972   INSTRUCTOR. Supervised nursing students in spectrum of hospital settings (rehabilitation, public and private psychiatric, medical department)

- taught chronic neurological and psychiatric conditions of patients
- established group dynamics sessions to promote professional peer evaluation of nursing care
- alleviated chronic friction between nonprofessional nursing employees and professional nursing students

1969 (summer) UNIVERSITY HOSPITAL, Kansas City, MO
STAFF NURSE, Burn Intensive Care Unit

- part of interdisciplinary team implementing range of life-sustaining care for severely burned patients

1968   PRESBYTERIAN MEDICAL CENTER, Denver, CO
STAFF NURSE, medical. Team leader for nonprofessional personnel. Provided nursing care for acutely ill patients

1967   UNIVERSITY HOSPITAL, Kansas City, MO
STAFF NURSE, medical. Team leader and nurse, as above

MEMBERSHIPS: Federal Association for the Advancement of Science
American Association of University Professors
New York Nurses Association
American Psychological Association
Society for the Research in Premature Births

HOBBIES: Tennis, gourmet cooking, skiing

240

44 Tracay Avenue   Home (321) 098-7654
Kansas City, MO 12345   Office (123) 345-6789

R E S U M E

of

ROBERT SOLON

PUBLIC ADMINISTRATOR/FOUNDATION EXECUTIVE

Skilled in creating programs, setting and accomplishing goals for the alleviation or elimination of minority group grievances by persuasion, conciliation, arbitration dealing with administrators at the highest levels of City, State and Federal Government and with minority groups; with effective results in averting crises, resolving disputes, developing mutual respect in confrontive situations.

As Regional Director U.S. Department of Justice	Over a period of four years, hired, trained and led a professional, racially mixed staff of 30 and 12 clerical employees in the handling of conflicts, disputes, demonstrations in the North Central United States.
	Motivated staff to encourage and accomplish problem solutions by the citizens themselves in a matter of their own best self-interest.
	Established Agency liaison with Governors of various States and their staffs to use Agency programs to handle potential crises.
	Accomplished liaisons with major businesses, major Federal funding agencies and with Departments of Labor and Transportation to ensure that solutions were fully understood at all levels.
	Averted riot in Detroit, Michigan, by use of Department "Task Force" approach.
	Resolved school conflict in Cleveland, Ohio, by coordinating administrators, teachers, community groups and students under a program that identified areas of mutual interest before attacking areas of disagreement.
As Community Relations Specialist, U.S. Dept. of Justice	Aided in averting violent confrontations in Watts area, Los Angeles, California.

241

Settled conflict regarding Indian hunting and fishing rights in New Mexico. Chaired group to set up critical analysis of methods of solving urban problems in Newark, Paterson, and Plainfield, NJ; developed modus operandi; established training seminars for administrative officials under Federal auspices; techniques now being extensively utilized by local' and state governments.

As Trial Attorney U.S. Dept. of Justice

Prepared, filed and conducted civil rights cases, involving police restrictions of freedom in connection with demonstrations by large groups.

Analyzed litigation procedures and developed new procedures for expediting litigation. Worked with U.S. Supreme Court Administrative Assistant to create plans for a sublevel of jurisdiction to eliminate case overloads. Plan is under consideration.

Chronology of Employment

1972-Present: U.S. Department of Justice, Community Relations Service.

1969-1972: U.S. Department of Justice, Inter-Government Liaison Service.

1968-1969: U.S. Department of Justice, Civil Rights Division.

1962-1968: U.S. Department of Justice, Administrative Division.

Military Service

U.S. Army, 1954-1964, Aide-de-Camp to General Symington, Tenth Combat Division, Vietnam.

Education

L.L.B., Harvard University School of Law, Cambridge, MA.

B.A., Political Science, University of Denver, Denver, CO.

Accreditations

Member of the Bar, District of Columbia, Maryland and Virginia.

Personal Data

Age 39, married, three children, excellent health.

REFERENCES AND FURTHER DATA ON REQUEST

242

ADVERTISING

```
Olympic Tower                          Home (000) 000 0000
391 Fifth Ave.,                        Office (000) 000 0000
New York, NY 00000
```

R E S U M E

of

RALPH W. EMERSON

ADVERTISING EXECUTIVE

OBJECTIVE   Percentage ownership and profit sharing in
             large, successful advertising agency.

EXPERIENCE

CREATIVE   1974-Present RUBICAM, THOMPSON, AYER, WELLS &
DIRECTOR   DOYLE, New York, NY

             Credits:
             - created Alka-Seltzer campaign
             - developed Miller Light campaign
             - received Anny award for Coca Cola campaign
             - established Joe DiMaggio and other celebri-
               ties in bank, coffee, Fortunoff and other
               campaigns
             - continued A.T.&T account direction
             - conceived Marlboro campaign
             - 27 awards in five years for copy, art,
               concepts, leadership, best advertising
               campaigns, and best individual advertise-
               ments

COPY   1970-1974   RUMRILL, FOOTE, McCANN, D'ARCY
CHIEF   ADVERTISING, New York, NY
             - copy and lyrics, Chrysler Corp
             - copy for Rolls Royce and Volkswagen
             - copy for XEROX Corp.
             - campaign for British Airways
             - developed theme for A.T.&T., still used
             - received 18 awards for excellence.

ACCOUNT   1966-1970   OGILVY, MARSTELLER, GUENTHER
EXECUTIVE   INTERNATIONAL, New York, NY
             Responsible for the following accounts:
               Chemical Bank, XEROX Office Systems,
               United Technologies, TV Guide

                                                      243
```
```

ACCOUNT   <u>1960-1966</u>   HICKS & DeGARMO, New York, NY
SUPERVISOR
                 Aided in market analysis campaign develop-
                 ment and new business presentations. As-
                 sisted in handling such accounts as Welch
                 Grape Juice, J. Wiss & Sons Co., Time Maga-
                 zine and State of West Virginia. Wrote
                 copy, recommended media, participated in
                 concept planning, met with clients.

PUBLICATIONS: The Thorn Birds (national best seller)
                 The Advertising Murders (selected by The
                    Crime Club)
                 Advertising Made Easy (Macmillan Book Club)
                 Sex and People (co-author with Chapman and
                    Jong)
                 Back Packing Around the World (selected by
                    the Wilderness Club)
                 Official handbook, U.S. Department of the
                    Interior and the U.S. Army
                 Extensive published writing for trade
                    publications

EDUCATION: <u>M.B.A.</u>, Harvard Graduate School of Business
                    Administration, Cambridge, MA
                 <u>B.A.</u>, English, Bucknell University, Lewis-
                    burg, PA, Phi Beta Kappa, Summa Cum Laude

HOBBIES: Platform tennis (runner-up, national cham-
                 pionship, men's doubles); tennis, court
                 tennis, squash (A player)

PERSONAL DATA: Age 37, married, three children, excellent
                 health

REFERENCES: Anyone in the advertising business

244

12 Duse Street   (516) 000-0000
Liberty Square, NY 11000

R E S U M E

of

WILLIAM R. STOCKHOLM

BANK OFFICER

* * *   Entire career in banking as Assistant Vice President and
          Branch Manager (earlier Teller and Chief Clerk), with
          responsibility for new business and operations. Record
          of developing significant volume of new business in
          every branch assignment and of effective management and
          good judgment.

* * *   Experience and competence also include accounting,
          financial analysis, branch location planning, commercial
          and consumer lending, foreign transactions, money market
          operations, mortgage loans, personnel administration,
          municipal finance.

* * *   Qualities include leadership, innovativeness, selling
          skills, ability to train and motivate, analytical ability,
          broad financial acumen, comprehensive branch bank operations
          management knowledge.

          (FOR FURTHER DETAILS, SEE FOLLOWING PAGE)

EXPERIENCE

1955-Present   BENJAMIN FRANKLIN TRUST COMPANY
New York, NY with 2,000 employees.

1977-Present   ASSISTANT VICE PRESIDENT, MANAGER of Radio City Branch,
Superville, NY. Supervised assistant and ten clerical employees.
Reported to Senior Vice President.
Responsible for:
- profitability, policies and procedures, carrying out the precepts
  established by general management to recapture losses resulting
  from the problems of an acquired bank

Accomplishments:
- with aid of staff recovered more than 40% of the lost deposits.

1955-1977   ASSISTANT V.P. and MANAGER, successively appointed to
larger branches rising from start as Teller, Chief Clerk, Manager,
Assistant V.P.
Responsible for:
- new business, operations, profitability, policies and procedures

Accomplishments:
- directed three branch openings; managed branches and brought them
  to profitable operating levels
- developed new business programs; met potential customers; multiplied
  membership in local organizations to widen business potentials
- opened Selden office (1959); started at zero, built deposits to $6
  million by 1964, increasing to $15 million by 1969
- opened Lefrak City branch October 1970; from zero, gained deposits
  of $2.5 million in five months

1951-1955   BANK OF SMITHTOWN, Smithtown, NY. TELLER.

MILITARY SERVICE:
U.S. ARMY, 1943-1948. Graduated from O.C.S. as 2nd Lt. Graduated from
Pilot School. Assigned to European theatre; promoted to Captain division
artillery, Air Section; supervised 30 officers, 50 enlisted men. Awards:
Air Medal with four Clusters

EDUCATION:

Rutgers University, New Brunswick, NJ, two years
Major: Accounting, Business Management
Graduate: American Institute of Banking

LANGUAGES:

Fair Spanish

HOBBIES:

Local community activities and clubs; golf

PERSONAL DATA:

Married, one child, own home, excellent health

REFERENCES AND FURTHER DATA ON REQUEST

572 Park Avenue   (212) 800-8000
New York, NY 10032

R E S U M E

of

HELEN McREADY TARBEL

SUMMARY

***   Extensive experience for six years in advertising
         copy and promotion, public relations, sales,
         planning sales strategies, new product development,
         conducting research, training, for major companies.

***   M.B.A. candidate, marketing; multilingual.

EXPERIENCE

1980-Present   LAWRENCE PRINCETON ADVERTISING, New York, NY

ACCOUNT EXECUTIVE for award winning agency billing about $8
million annually.

Responsible for:
- market planning and strategy for the following clients:
  Styleset International, DeBeers Jewelry Corporation,
  Mabelline Corporation
- media planning and selection
- direct mail and sales promotion campaigns
- public relations
- recommendations for market research and evaluation of
  results
- coordinating projects within agency and with outside
  suppliers

Accomplishments:
- working with art director, developed widely acclaimed
  and innovative campaign for STYLESET Jeans; company has
  since attained leadership position in industry
- effectively repositioned DeBeers Jewelry in the
  marketplace

Over....Please....

President of DeBeers was interviewed on the new approach by
THE NEW YORK TIMES: reported in the Times business section,
April 8, 1982

1979-1980   MORROW & COMPANY New York, NY

EASTERN SALES MANAGER, for trade magazine for major book
and trade magazine publisher (50 trade magazines). Reported
to publisher. The magazine is circulated nationally to
manufacturers of women's wear, mills and fiber companies

Responsible for:
- advertising sales along the eastern seaboard and west to
  Denver
- advertising copy and strategies for customers
- recommendations for corporate advertising, promotional
  copywriting, circulars and brochures, market research

Accomplishments:
- doubled number of advertising accounts
- responsible for selling more than half of total
  advertising over period of employment

1977-1979   WESTERN PUBLICATIONS, New York, NY

SPECIAL PROJECTS MANAGER (newly created position); worked
with President in planning new marketing programs for
publisher of 17 trade magazines.

Examples:
- planned and conducted advertising seminars for prospective clients
- conducted acquisition studies; issued reports on competitive publications
- carried out field research on reader attitudes and made
  qualitative analyses of data
- organized trade shows for MODERN JEWELER and CONVENTION
  NEWS magazines
- created promotion material and direct mail campaigns

Accomplishments included:
- gaining new accounts through the advertising seminars
  and trade shows
- aiding in the selection of successful acquisitions
- improving existing magazines as result of research and
  promotions

Recruited by executive search firm for position with
Morrow.

                                    Over.... Please....

248

1975-1977   GARDEN CITY PUBLISHING CO., Garden City, NY

ASSISTANT PRODUCT MANAGER for Educational Development
Laboratories, a division of one of the world's largest
publishers.

Responsible for:
- assisting in the marketing of audio/visual aids to public
  and private schools
- implementing research proposals and writing reports
- developing sales training seminars
- aiding in budgeting, sales and analysis, creating
  marketing strategies

Accomplishments:
- recommended expansion of sales effort to include Spanish
  language alternatives

Originally employed as PROJECT EDITOR producing sales
training materials; promoted.

1973-1975   COMMUNITY DAY CARE CENTER, New York, NY

ADMINISTRATIVE DIRECTOR of day care program for approximately
100 children. Supervised eight teachers, assistants, and
accountant.

Accomplishments:
- led center to 33% growth
- raised funds through public relations campaigns and
  presentations to hospital directors

1971-1973   ASSEMBLY OF THE CARIB HOMETOWNS:
                 HEAD START PROGRAM

DIRECTOR and CONSULTANT of federally funded pre-school
bilingual program for inner city area. Supervised five
teachers, custodian, cook, social worker, bookkeeper, and
secretary.

1968-1970   BRONXVILLE BOARD OF EDUCATION

TEACHER. Initiated successful new techniques.

EDUCATION:

   B.A.   Psychology, University of Pennsylvania, Philadelphia
          PA, Regents Scholarship. Dean's List. Matriculated
          at age 16

                                    Over....Please....

249

EDUCATION: (Continued)

M.A.T.   (Master of Arts in Teaching) University of
         Pennsylvania, 1968. Selected by Philadelphia Board
         of Education to participate in new program for
         talented liberal arts graduates. Course included
         internship.

M.B.A. in Progress at New York University. Marketing major.
Sponsored originally for this Texaco Foundation Graduate
Management Program for Women, by Garden City Publishing
Company

Attended public school in New York City; selected as
participant in special accelerated science program.

LANGUAGES: French and Spanish

PERSONAL DATA: Divorced, excellent health

REFERENCES AND FURTHER DATA ON REQUEST

250

1837 Caldwell   (123) 456-7890
Los Angeles, CA (zip)

RESUME

of

WILLIAM CLEVELAND

***   Record of achievement in advancing to Vice Presidency
        of major construction firm, after starting as super-
        visor of foremen.

***   Strong profit orientation with exposure in public
        relations, marketing and sales; grasp of advertising
        strategy, direct mail campaigns, brochures; budget
        planning and forecasts; successful track record in
        competitive bidding situations.

***   Strength in planning new objectives, finding methods
        of implementation, creating millions of dollars of
        extra sales and profits.

***   Practical experience in project management, complete
        administration of work from start to finish; payment
        breakdown, monthly billing, percentage of completion
        CPM or progress completion scheduling.

***   Proven skills in field supervision, evaluation of
        field personnel, labor relations, negotiations,
        material scheduling and expediting; purchasing-
        materials and vendor subcontracts.

***   Experience in quality assurance - quality control
        analysis and administration; job cost analysis, spec
        interpretation and negotiating.

        (FOR FURTHER DATA, PLEASE SEE FOLLOWING PAGE)

251

<u>1965-Present</u>   (NAME OF COMPANY ON REQUEST)

With current annual sales of $50 million, this Mechanical
Contractor employs 50 office personnel and from 200 to 400
people in the field engaged in a variety of construction
projects, including a recently acquired complete plant
with heavy R&D investment in a patented module unit.

Scope of activities includes; piping-heating, ventilating,
air conditioning; industrial piping for manufacturing,
chemical, petroleum, natural gas processing; gas for turbines, instrumentation, pollution control, power generation, cryogenic facilities, cold boxes, vaporizers, barge
unloading systems, liquid natural gas storage plants,
vehicle loading stations for LNG service, liquid propane
handling and storage systems, and alterations to existing
systems

Employed as Supervisor (1966-1969); moved up to Senior
Supervisor (1969-1970) and on to Assistant Manager (1970-
1971). Since then have successfully met challenges in the
following succession:

*   Chief Project Manager
*   Assistant to V.P., Marketing
*   Assistant to Executive Vice President
*   Vice-President, Marketing Services

* Specific Achievements

As Assistant Manager:
-   developed new and better methods for estimating both
    HVAC and power piping
-   Increased sales by ten million dollars by end of year
-   was given added responsibility as Project Manager

Analyzed market conditions, made recommendations and won
approval for a plan to specialize efforts in power piping.

As Assistant to Vice President of Marketing:
-   given full responsibility to head all industrial project
    including such areas as estimating, project manager,
    customer relations, subcontracts, engineering expediting
    purchasing and cost control
-   increased sales every year since 1970

*Personal Data:

35 years old, married, enjoy golf and sailing; active in
community affairs; excellent health.

<u>REFERENCES AND FURTHER DATA ON REQUEST</u>

230 Albemarle West
Constantine, NY

Home (000) 123-4567
Office (000) 890-1234

R E S U M E

of

WILLIAM R. HAYES

OBJECTIVE

Position in corporate development department of corporate finance division
of bank.

EXPERIENCE

1978-Present BAXTER CYANAMID CORP, Camptown, NY

MANAGER, BUSINESS DEVELOPMENT, for $1 billion international
manufacturer of ethical pharmaceuticals, proprietary
medicines, toiletries and household products. Report to
Senior Vice-President, International Products

Responsible for:

- defining targets and criteria for acquisition program
  at an expenditure level of $30-50 million annually,
  and for proposing and implementing strategy for acquiring
  approved companies or products

- accumulating, maintaining and analyzing a broad base of
  information suitable for making evaluations

- presenting reports and recommendations; conducting
  acquisition negotiations

- coordinating all activities in support of the responsibilities assigned

Accomplishments:

- investigated dozens of acquisition candidates, of which
  five acquisitions were made

1974-1978 INTERPOLE S.A., Aix-la-Chapelle, Belgium

DIRECTOR of MERGERS and ACQUISITIONS (starting in 1976) for
investment company engaged in consulting and arranging
mergers and acquisitions among manufacturing corporations
for clients in the U.S. and overseas. Staff of eight,
including accountants.

Accomplishments:

- reorganized existing research and acquisitions department which had been ineffective
- researched hundreds of major companies in Europe and the
  U.S., identifying size, financial strength, product line
  and areas of potential mutual interest among these compani
- expanded firm's contacts with banks and corporations,
  and outside of firm's European sphere; opened up American
  market
- introduced strict cost-controls within the merger/acquis-
  ition activity
- designed more effective method of recognizing acquisition
  candidates
- concluded nine successful acquisitions since 1975;
  acquisitions of U.S. and European corporations; participated in all negotiations

Earlier, trained in arranging financing for major manufacturers in heavy industry for worldwide contracts.

EDUCATION:

B.S., Business Administration, Oxford University, Cambridg
1977. Attended evening classes, 1975-1978.

University Captain (top student leadership position).
Captain of crew. Debating Society (honor student).

LANGUAGES:

French, German, Spanish, Hungarian

PERSONAL DATA:

Age 27, (born in Vienna, Austria); married.
Extensively traveled. Wide professional and personal
contacts throughout Europe.

REFERENCES AND FURTHER DATA ON REQUEST

254

27 Ogilvy Drive   Home (201) 999-8888
Monkton, NJ 07823   Office (212) 888-9999

R E S U M E

of

ORIN THOMPSON

EDP EXECUTIVE

***   Extensive experience for more than 15 years in development of
       management information systems, EDP audits, EDP reorganizations,
       project management to accomplish improved reporting systems and
       lower costs for such major companies as Prudential Insurance Co.,
       Citibank, Interpublic and Airco.

***   Competent in the utilization of medium, large-scale and mini-
       computer installations for comprehensive range of reporting,
       accounting, production, marketing.

***   Excerpts from letters of commendation include: Studebaker
       (Interpublic) client: "I would especially like to single out
       Orin Thompson for the important contributions he made to the
       overall success of the project" (LCS Industries).

       Interpublic: "We also want to recognize, in a very special
       way, the involvement of Orin Thompson. He provided Inter-
       public with the most professional guidance available any-
       where" (Army Recruiting Command).

***   Age 42, married, M.B.A. and B.A. degrees

(FOR SUBSTANTIATING DATA PLEASE SEE FOLLOWING PAGES)

255

EXPERIENCE:

1981-Present   DATA CONSULTANTS, INC., New York, NY

SENIOR CONSULTANT, New York Office, for senior systems and project management consulting firm, for users of broad spectrum of large and minicomputers, with home office at Boston, MA and another branch in Richmond,
VA.

Current Assignment:
-   development of seven multidivision users manuals for use with about-
    to-be-implemented wholesale Demand Deposit Accounting System (in-
    volving 20,000 customers and 90% of bank revenues) for Citibank,
    requiring the translation of a functional specification and a tech-
    nical systems specification manual into user language for all levels
    of management and clerical operations: Reference Manual, Operation
    Manual, Data Dictionary, Bank Control File, Account Officer Manual,
    Cash Management Manual.

Earlier:
-   Project Manager and Senior Analyst responsible for designing and
    implementing online computerized system covering 15,000 parolees
    for Albany County Parole Department
-   responsible for development and implementation of comprehensive
    business support systems for new line of insurance by METROPOLITAN
    LIFE with annual premiums of $80 million and agent field force of
    8000

    Excerpt from letter from Metropolitan executive: "His (Thompson's)
    efforts in developing procedures, organization planning, personnel
    training, procedures documentation, and site planning were vital to
    the success of our project. The tasks set . . . were significant
    and the deadlines critical."

-   for INTERPUBLIC RESPONSE DIVISION, evaluated responses to an RFP
    for a computer-based fulfillment system for the U.S. Army Recruiting
    Command; evaluated and selected new systems vendor and aggressively
    supervised the design and installation of the new system, resulting
    in savings of $1 million per year and capability of answering
    inquiries overnight, installed error-free; influential in retention
    of $45 million in annual billing by Interpublic, and in substantial
    follow-up contracts for Interpublic client.

Recruited for position by former boss at Airco.

1977-1981   AMERICAN BIBLE SOCIETY, New York, NY

MANAGER, INFORMATION SERVICES, for international organization with
revenues of $80 million, 500 employees.

Accomplishments:
-   reorganized data processing, systems, and programming functions into
    a single Information Services Department with resulting increase in
    efficiency; accomplished timely distribution for first time in
    three years.

256

AMERICAN BIBLE SOCIETY (continued)
- Represented Society at international data processing conferences in Europe. Addressed conferences on data processing systems and utilization
- planned and coordinated move of entire EDP staff and equipment to new installation; introduced major innovations: new documentation standards, tape library functions, data input/output control, a files program, and production scheduling; reduced operations from three shifts to two and increased production
- directed major systems implementation of forecasting program permitting accurate assessments of sale and distribution of modern bibles in scores of variations

1971-1977   AIRCO, INC., Parsippany, NJ

MANAGER OF STANDARDS, AUDITS AND CONTROLS (1973-1977) after progression as follows: Senior Systems Analyst, Project Manager, Systems Training Administrator for billion-dollar international company.

Accomplishments:
- wrote and implemented corporation-wide procedures manual for standardization of documentation of systems and programming; wrote and implemented handbook of tested and proven techniques to guide systems analysts and programmers; volumes were distributed to the Airco family of companies worldwide
- handled transfer of all systems and operations of newly acquired $10.2 million company from Michigan to New Jersey
- established corporation-wide training program for systems, programming and supervisory personnel
- performed systems audit of British subsidiary and reorganized entire EDP system to give improved performance
- designed personnel information system now used throughout Airco companies
- directed major systems conversion to IBM 1410 and later 360 under DOS

1962-1971   METROPOLITAN LIFE INSURANCE COMPANY, New York, NY

SYSTEMS ANALYST (1966-1971) after earlier clerical supervisor and administrative trainee

Accomplishments:
- participated in study of General Division resulting in reorganization and reduction of turnaround time in answering inquiries from 5-7 days to 2 days with fewer people
- participated in study of Group Insurance Department lasting over a period of two years; achieved substantial cost savings
- conducted study of New Business Office resulting in speedup of processing applications from five days to two
Received management training in all major departments earlier over a period of two and a half years (1962-1964).

MILITARY SERVICE:

U.S. Army, active duty VietNam, one year.

257

EDUCATION:

  M.B.A., Administrative Management, Rutgers University, 1965.
  Attended evening classes

  B.A., New York University, New York, NY, 1962

ADDITIONAL STUDIES:

  Project Management, IBM, 1981
  Data Processing Operations Management, IBM, 1981
  Systems Seminar, 1970

                REFERENCES AND FURTHER DATA ON REQUEST

258

Holly Lane   Home (203) 100-1000
Greenwich, CT 06903   Office (203) 900-6000

R E S U M E

of

ELSIE JOYCE

OBJECTIVE

> Participation in a program for the elderly
> at a local or national level, involving all
> or some of the following: health care and
> quality of life; housing; communications;
> education; administration.

EXPERIENCE

1970-Present   STEPHENS GARDENS, GREENWICH, CT

Director (1976-Present) of 100-unit retirement residence for 116
senior citizens, including nursing facilities. This is a retirement
home offering the opportunity for independent living in gracious
surroundings providing complete food, service, recreation, educational
activities, and living accommodations.

EARLIER, DIRECTOR OF PUBLIC RELATIONS (1970-1976)

Concurrently (since 1969) Radio Show Host, weekly, Station WAAV
"Making the Most of Modern Maturity"; and frequent lecturer to
senior citizen groups and paraprofessionals in the health care field
on concerns of the aging. Member since 1973 of Greenwich's Commission
on Aging, with recent citation for "dedication, generosity and
service to senior citizens of the community."

Responsible for:
- administration of "4-star hotel for older adults" recognized for
  sound and innovative leadership in the field of geriatrics

Over....Please....

259

Accomplishments and activities include:

- seminars and symposia by leading experts for residents (examples): Dealing with Modern Maturity; Speak Out (on legislation); Heart Attacks and Strokes; Your Health; Salute to Volunteers, and scores more
- lectures coordinated with the University of Connecticut, I.B.M. Corp., Health Consultation Center, Adam Careers Educational Service, Greenwich Hospital, School of Dental Hygiene, and others
- contest in letter writing
- "Afternoon with the Stars" (Connecticut Broadcasters Association)
- "Fashions for the Young in Spirit" (Marlo Beck)
- Series with the University of Bridgeport
- B. Altman fashion show
- organization of golf, tennis, horseback riding, swimming at nearby country club
- organization of in-house activities: bridge and other recreation, chapel services, parties, visitor planning and the like
- creation of food and living facilities at the highest levels of quality
- budgeting and financial management
- levels of care required by patients
- dealing with psychiatric, alcoholic and other problems of the true elderly
- counseling residents' families
- maintaining good relationships with the professional and political communities
- gaining state and national recognition for high performance of Stephens operation

EDUCATION:

Cornell University

Credits toward Masters degree in Communications

PERSONAL DATA:

Married, excellent health

REFERENCES AND FURTHER DATA ON REQUEST

260

1843 Niles Street
Antrim, NY 23456

(516) 300-3000

R E S U M E

of

WILLIAM McKINLEY

Qualified as

PROJECT ENGINEER-STRUCTURAL

Experienced, capable, innovative Structural Engineer with
record of effective participation and leadership in
vitally important and complex projects such as MOREX
Building of the (ABM) System, Kansas City Mall Power Plant
Units.

Demonstrated management competence and broad engineering
comprehension by coordinating diverse engineering disciplines to effect optimum results in adhering to completion schedules and maintaining high quality, safe design
and construction.

Excellent educational background with supporting graduate
courses in important engineering areas.

Record of remaining on job from inception to completion.
Recalled by former employers as new projects develop.

Registration; LICENSED PROFESSIONAL ENGINEER, State of
New York, No 123456, December 1960.

B.S. Degree, age 43, married.

(FOR FURTHER DATA, PLEASE SEE FOLLOWING PAGES)

EDUCATION AND ACCREDITATIONS:

B.S., Civil Engineering, Structural Option, College of
Engineering, University of Denver, Denver, Colorado, 1961.

Graduate courses in Structural and Industrial Engineering,
New York University, New York, NY, 1966, 1967, 1968.

Read, write, speak German, Arabic, Polish.

EXPERIENCE:

1979-1983   ELY & SIMPSON, INC., Wichita, Kansas

1983-Present   ELY & SIMPSON, INC., Wichita, Kansas

SENIOR STRUCTURAL ENGINEER for consulting engineering firm.
Responsible for major part of review and revision of design
engineering of the Library and Museum Building in the "New
Kansas City" Project. Checked design of posttensioning systems
coordinating with contractor on manner and sequence of systems.

1979-1983   ELY & SIMPSON, INC., New York, NY

As SENIOR STRUCTURAL ENGINEER for Criteria and Design worked on:

Criteria:

- Complex Attack Umbrella Module System (AUMC) component in
  conjunction with mechanical, electrical, architectural and
  other engineering disciplines developing design criteria and
  specifications for structures designed to sustain nuclear
  blasts. Prepared cost estimates of project components. On
  project from inception to completion. (Studies available for
  inspection.)

- Specifications and design criteria for structures capable of
  withstanding nuclear blasts.

Design:

- Updating drawings to conform to latest Atlas Arms Convac
  interface requirements.
- Made field site visits, resolved deficiencies indicated in
  engineering memos.
- Supervised preparation of criteria for interdisciplinary
  groups.
- Maintained contact with all engineering groups, including
  mechanical and pipe support groups.
- Chosen to confer with A.U.M.C. Contractors and outside
  manufacturers' representatives.
- Remained on projects to completion.

Jan. 1979-July 1979   BALL & CHAIN ENGINEERING CORP., Kew
                       Gardens, NY

As SENIOR STRUCTURAL DESIGNER:

- Supervised preparation of design drawings and reviewed industrial structures in steel mill plant (Italy) and gas
  processing furnace (Kuwait).

1975-1978 SENIOR STRUCTURAL DESIGNER employed through job
shops for design, coordination of other engineering disciplines, and supervision of drawings for the following firms:

- U.S. Electric Power, West Point, NY, floor systems and air
  intake enclosure ducts of Cape Horn thermal power plant.

- Maywood Corporation, Hopewell, NC, design of compresser
  building, foundations, superstructures, coordinating with
  other engineering disciplines to completion of project.

- Pasco Corporation, New York, NY, copper processing plants
  (Peru). Designed complete building in processing system
  from foundation to superstructure; remained on job to
  completion of project.

1974-1975   BALL & CHAIN ENGINEERING CORP., Smithtown, NY

As SENIOR STRUCTURAL DESIGNER in charge of:

- design and layout of reinforced concrete underground coal-
  handling structures and equipment for two 1000 MKW units,
  Wheelock Power, PA, project for Florida Electric and Power
  Company

- design, layout, checking and supervising drawings of 500 KV
  substation switchyard, structural steel framing, on project
  for Charlestown Electric Power Company.

- complete superstructure and foundation - transmission
  towers for 500 KV switchyard on Denver Power Project.

Remained on all projects to successful completion.

1972-1974 MAKAIGH & FINCH, New York, NY

As STRUCTURAL DESIGNER participated in design of high-rise
commercial and institutional buildings such as: Columbia
Medical School, Church of the Holy Virgin, Settlement, NY;
Pownall College buildings; B'Nai Brith Congregation, Pittsburgh, PA; Foley Square Arena, New York, NY; participated
in stress and stability investigation and preparation of a
report on Kansas City Civic Center

1970-1972 ELY & SIMPSON, INC., New York, NY

As STRUCTURAL ENGINEER, participated in design of Terminal
Building, Kennedy International Airport, New York, NY, and
approach viaducts. Designed floors and columns. Prepared
complete pilot analysis and design of prototype concrete bent
of viaduct fronting terminal; design used as guide for design
of other vents.

<u>1969-1970</u>   ARCO CONSTRUCTION COMPANY, Somaliland

ASSISTANT FIELD (CIVIL) ENGINEER for construction of underground reinforced concrete hangars for Somali Air Force.
Supervised preparation of concrete mixes, earth removal, road-
beds, paving.

<u>1968</u>   DIANA STEEL COMPANY, Jupiter, FL

STRUCTURAL DESIGNER working in structural steel detailing.
Member of team of seven structural engineers training in
preparation for management of consulting engineering business
in Israel.

<u>1967</u>   SUSS, INC., New York, NY

STRUCTURAL DESIGNER. Designed various steel and reinforced
concrete structures on a Chemical Processing Plant project
for zinc plant.

<u>1966</u>   CHRYSLER ASSOCIATES, Chicago, IL

Worked as CIVIL ENGINEER in design, layout, drafting of
municipal projects involving highway drainage, sewer and
water services.

<u>PERSONAL DATA</u>:

Age 43, married, six children, own home and car. U.S. Citizen.

Defense Department Security Clearance: SECRET

Traveled extensively in Europe and Africa

Member of American Steel and Aggregate Association

<u>REFERENCES AND FURTHER DATA ON REQUEST</u>

3040 River View   (914) 123-4567
Hastings-on-Hudson, NY 10021

R E S U M E

of

ANNE MARIE TODD

qualified as

FASHION/FABRIC EDITOR

or for

FASHION-RELATED POSITION IN ADVERTISING, PUBLIC RELATIONS

---

* * *   Recognized authority and analyst in fashion and fabrics for
        men and women, with ability to write, lecture, train; imag-
        inative in coordinating fashion elements; technical fabric
        knowledge; excellent trade relationships.

* * *   Experienced in large segment of fashion industry, in mer-
        chandising and promotion, store operations, fashion shows,
        public relations, organizing, editing. Familiar with home
        sewing and craft industries. Accept responsibility and
        execute. Trained in budget preparation and presentation.

* * *   Eighteen years as successful associate editor, fabric
        editor, promoter, trend forecaster, for three of the most
        important magazines in the field of fashion.

* * *   Made patterns and crafts segments of one magazine so
        attractive to readers that pattern pages were doubled and
        crafts pages increased fourfold.

* * *   Consistent record of career development in fashion industry.

FOR FURTHER DATA PLEASE SEE FOLLOWING PAGES

265

BUSINESS EXPERIENCE

<u>1980-Present</u> SYNTHETIC YARN ASSOCIATION, New York, NY.

DIRECTOR of promotional unit of synthetics industry representing
about 90% of all U.S. producers, including all major mills. Report
to Board of Directors of Council. Responsible for:

- publicity, merchandising, promotion, using all communications
  media in all markets for Men's, Women's and Children's Fashions

Accomplishments:

- Put together and staged fashion shows for TV across the
  country and arranged publicity, tying in with leading department stores; acclaimed by manufacturers, designers, retailers
  and public for excellence; strong press coverage, radio
  interviews.
- conducted important fashion show annually, including Men's
  Wear; attended by more than 1,000.
- prepared and presented budgets for board approval on monthly
  basis; made quarterly presentations to industry.

<u>1978-1980</u>   VOGUE-BAZAAR MAGAZINE, New York, NY

Employed in Fashion Department as Fabric Editor, working for Executive
Editor of this internationally famous magazine directed to the 13-19
age market.

Responsible for:

- coverage of fabric and fashion markets to be continuously
  current and ahead of trends in order to plan, coordinate and
  execute monthly fashion pages; study and report on color
  evolutions.

- conducting public relations programs, representing magazine
  as lecturing fashion authority; attend fashion shows and
  business conferences around U.S. and overseas; consulting
  with clients with respect to outlooks, fashion guidance.
- autonomy to approve fashion pages in absence of editor.

Accomplishments:

- pages devoted to fabrics doubled and tripled respectively
  due both to increased reader interest and better, more
  interesting pages.
- first Fabric Editor at magazine to be sent to Europe to
  cover Frankfurt Fair to report on European influences.
- made successful presentations to advertisers of such companies
  as Monsanto, J.P. Stevens, DuPont, Celanese.

266

- new promotions, such as Dior Daytime Patterns, tied in with major department and specialty stores nationally.
- responsible for new section and magazine cover tying in with Nieman Marcus and Post-Teen Department.

1976-1978   CITY, TOWN & COUNTRY, New York, NY

ASSISTANT TO DIRECTOR OF MERCHANDISING AND PROMOTION with responsibility for fabric and fashion promotion.

- edited and supervised production of promotional brochure, including fabric reports.
- made presentations to retail buyers on importance and effectiveness of editorial pages; worked cooperative advertising programs with multimillion-dollar corporations.

1965-1976   BUTTERY PATTERN COMPANY, New York, NY

Successively ASSISTANT SERVICE EDITOR, ASSOCIATE EDITOR.

- as Fabric Editor, covered fabric market intensively, presented ideas and prognostications to staff, clients, buyers; acted in PR capacity.
- predicted color and design trends; maintained library; epitomized market.

Work was widely recognized, resulting in unsolicited job offers from three of the major fashion magazines.

EDUCATION:

    Jesuit College, Kansas City, MO, 1963-1967
    B.S., Merchandising.

HOBBIES:

    SCUBA diving, gourmet cooking, travel.

PERSONAL DATA:

    Age 39, married.

REFERENCES AND FURTHER DATA ON REQUEST

387 Western Drive
St. Louis, MO (zip)

(123) 456-7890

CONFIDENTIAL RESUME

of

THOMAS MELLON

FINANCIAL EXECUTIVE

***   Consistent record, with various companies, of utilization of financial expertise to improve earnings, increase asset values, establish important lines of credit. Experienced in all facets of financial management; in handling financial public relations and corporate legal matters. Extensive experience in public accounting, taxes, E.D.P., corporate financing.

***   Using sophisticated financial techniques, sound accounting practice, advanced management methods, turned ailing company into highly profitable corporation, doubling its listed stock value in a period of three years.

***   Restructured multimillion-dollar corporation by changing established policies and eliminating losses after years of marginal operation. Accomplished outstanding turnaround for a third company.

***   Now employed, but seeking larger opportunity to exercise competence.

(FOR FURTHER DATA, PLEASE SEE FOLLOWING PAGES)

1973–Present   (NAME OF COMPANY ON REQUEST)

TREASURER, CHIEF FINANCIAL OFFICER, Member, Board of Directors for AMEX-listed industrial products manufacturer, with approximate annual sales of $35 million, four manufacturing plants, three warehouses. Supervise staff of 25, including Controller, Chief Accountant, Cost Accounting Manager, Manager, Inventory Control Manager.

* Responsible for all financial affairs and financial reporting of the Company, Legal Liaison, Financial Public Relations.

* Responsibilities:
  — set up corporate budgets, departmental operating budgets, factory overheads, R.&D., sales and G.&A. expenses; capital appropriations budget.
  — set up standard cost system and departmentalized overheads.
  — recommended profit goals as related to sales; as return on investment; measured progress by 15 relevant financial ratios.
  — calculated cash requirements, evaluated proposed capital expenditures.
  — invested cash in short-term commercial paper or otherwise as indicated currently.
  — handled Company insurance. Set up Company pension plan, secured Government approval; administered stock option and profit-sharing programs. Consulted with other officers on all compensation plans.
  — responsible for S.E.C. filings and all corporate taxes.

* Accomplishments:
  — recommended sale of and sold losing Division.
  — reduced factory costs by approximately $1 million lowering cost of goods sold from 67% of sales to 61%.
  — saved G.&A. expenses by over $1 million annually or a reduction of 37%.
  — reduced audit expenses by $80,000 annually.
  — speeded up billing and reduced receivables turnover time from 90 days to 48 days, with resulting increase of $1.5 million in cash flow.
  — earned $60,000 to $80,000 annually through short-term investments.
  — eliminated all short-term borrowing, reduced long-term debt, improved debt-equity ratio; created high credit rating.
  — increased utilization of EDP by 100% to include all corporate reporting at a cost increase of only 20%.
  — achieved Company turnaround from loss and poor credit position to annual profit after taxes of 9% and R.O.I. of over 22.7%, doubling value of stock in 3 years.

* Additional Accomplishments:
  — set up sales forecasting system for Sales Department using regression analysis techniques.
  — created successful PR effort for financial community
  — reduced legal fees by $100,000 annually by handling matters within own competence.

1971–1973 SHERIDAN CANDY CORP., Hicksville, OH

GENERAL MANAGER, FINANCE and ACCOUNTING, Assistant to President of $10 million company with staff of five including Vice President-Finance, Treasurer and Controller.

* Administered all financial affairs of Company by analysis of operations and effective application of financial techniques, succeeded in overcoming losses and achieving breakeven point in first year.
  – established breakeven point for products; closed out production of poor sellers.
  – established departmental budgeting that signaled loss areas, permitting correction and reducing expenses by $25,000.
  – successfully led Company defense against attempt to unionize.

1968–1971 LEED CORP., Hudson, CT

CONTROLLER for this manufacturer of electrical components.

* Operations much as described previously.

1954–1968

Provided financial management for N. HOPPER CO. INC. (paper manufacturer), OVERHEAD DOORS CORP. (garage doors); worked for Certified Public Accounting firms.

* *Education:*
  B.S., Accounting, 1955, University of Michigan
  M.B.A., Finance, 1979, University of Chicago (attending evenings)

* *Accreditations:*
  C.P.A.

* *Membersips:*
  The National Association of Financial Executives

* *Personal Data:*
  Age 49, married, one child, excellent health

<u>REFERENCES AND FURTHER DATA ON REQUEST</u>

270

Seranade Drive
Las Vegas, NV 00000

(107) 000-7711

R E S U M E

of

HENRY SCARNE

HOTEL EXECUTIVE

for

HOTEL CHAIN or FIRST CLASS HOTEL

***   Comprehensive early training and education in all phases of hotel management and for the last ten years significant successes in profitable operations and in turning losses to profits in large enterprises; in directing construction and accomplishing successful opening of major resort hotel complex.

***   Accustomed to complete management responsibilities for accounting and controls, front office, food and beverage, golf course, club house, entertainment and all other facilities: and to financial reporting, profit and cash flow projections; planning and development.

***   Accomplished also in developing convention business, arranging entertainment, providing gourmet food service and high level of other services. Experienced in close analysis of operating figures and correction of trouble areas; in the use of E.D.P. to assist the managerial function.

***   Capable in selecting, training and developing management talent; possess leadership and empathy.

(FOR FURTHER DATA, PLEASE SEE FOLLOWING PAGES)

271

BUSINESS EXPERIENCE

<u>June 1974-Present</u>   CAESARS HOTEL, Las Vegas

GENERAL MANAGER of 800-room hotel, with additional 400 rooms scheduled for opening in January 1976; six specialty restaurants, 600-seat main dining room, three golf courses, club house, beach operation, two pools, convention hall and meeting rooms, night club, discotheque and restaurant, water distillation and recycling plants, housing for staff of 1,000 with staff cafeteria and transportation service.

Responsible for:
- supervision of construction and opening of new $74-million hotel complex.
- staffing and training, marketing, pricing, menu planning.
- September 1975 opening with reception and five-course banquet for 1,100 with floor show.
- reaching occupancy rate in October 1975 at 87% with gross October sales of $1.3 million and average room rate of $80.00 MAP.
- attaining immediate results of 37% food cost, 24% beverage cost; with monthly payroll of $400,000.
- complete plans which will permit additional 400 rooms to be available for occupancy with full service immediately upon completion.
- booking $8.0 million conventions back to back September through June 1976 and similarly for 1977.

Other responsibilities included union negotiations, advance planning, budgeting, guest relations, advertising and all other management activities for entire operation.

<u>1963-1974</u>   KNOTT INTERNATIONAL HOTEL CORP., Bermuda

VICE-PRESIDENT and GENERAL MANAGER: Hotel opened in 1969 with poor start. Persuaded by President of Knott International to operate this new hotel.
Accomplishments included:
- made complete necessary reorganization to save money, including Sales Department.
- by 1971 an increase in gross sales of $1.2 million.
- improvement in operating profit by $800,000.
- sell-off of unprofitable operations reducing corporation to half its original size.

<u>1965-1973</u>   BERMUDA BEACH HOTEL, Bermuda

VICE-PRESIDENT and GENERAL MANAGER. Unit suffered loss of $453,000 in 1962. Following four-month loss of $301,000 in four months 1961.

- instituted immediate cost reduction programs.
- reoriented marketing and advertising to highlight travel agency sales.
- established personalized services.
- created management development program.
- took other necessary steps.

The following figures show results accomplished (000 omitted):

1967	$277
1968	$325
1969	$375
1970	$427
1971	$482
1972	$523
1973	$670
1974	$940

The audited results for this 200-room hotel in 1969 showed $4.2 million gross revenue with a gross operating profit of $1.7 million. Corporation recovered all losses during this period.

1964-1965 CORAL BEACH CLUB, Bermuda

RESIDENT MANAGER

1963-1964 KNOTT INTERNATIONAL HOTEL CORP., New York, NY

NEW YORK SALES MANAGER for Coral Beach Club

1962-1963 WATERLOO HOUSE, Bermuda

U.S. SALES MANAGER. Directed sales activities of hotel until sale of property was announced.

1961-1962 HENRY ADDISON, 800 Fifth Avenue, New York, NY

NEW YORK DISTRICT SALES MANAGER for Hotel Representative firm. Handled sales in the New York District.

- responsible for 59% of convention sales ($2.3 million).

MILITARY SERVICE:

1959-1960 U.S. ARMY, Lieutenant

EDUCATION:

B.S., Hotel Administration, Cornell University
Seminars in Advanced Management, Decision Processes
Grid School. T. Groupings
Worked in hotels during summer vacations.

PROFESSIONAL MEMBERSHIPS:

Board of Directors, A.H.M.A.; Executive Committee, A.H.M.A.; Member, Board of Directors, Florida Knott International Corp.; SKAL; ASTA

PERSONAL DATA: Born 5/14/40; married. two children, excellent health.

REFERENCES AND FURTHER DATA ON REQUEST

1831 Log Cabin Drive   Home (201) 327-5251
Cuyahoga, OH 23320   Office (212) 001-1111

R E S U M E

of

WILLIAM ABRAM GARFIELD

OBJECTIVE

Vice President or Director of Marketing, domestic and/or international, or General Manager in the U.S. of division of multinational company.

SUMMARY and QUALIFICATIONS

*** Nearly 18 years of success in the chemical and textile industries
     for major companies, plus extensive educational background in
     both areas.

*** Experience includes full marketing direction with staff of 70
     after stages in R.&D., manufacturing, production planning, sales
     management, product management, technical promotion, advertising,
     key account liaison, pricing strategy, profit margin improvement.

*** Experience also encompasses these activities both in the U.S. and
     overseas. Possess intimate understanding of European business
     attitudes and needs with the ability to merge differing philosophies
     into successful common objectives. Multilingual.

*** Record of success in introducing new products and increasing market
     share with continuously increasing responsibilities to present posi-
     tion. Participated in spectacular turnaround for present employer.

*** Able to train, lead, motivate; to recognize and exploit business
     opportunities.

*** Chemical Engineering degree and continuing educational involvement.

(FOR FURTHER DATA PLEASE SEE FOLLOWING PAGE)

EXPERIENCE

<u>1971-Present</u>   STEVENS & BURLINGTON CORP., Cleveland, OH
                 (Dyes & Chemicals Div.)

VICE PRESIDENT, Marketing and member of Management Committee for $100 million division of $720 million manufacturer of dyes and chemicals for the textile and paper markets, fragrances, and other chemical products.

Earlier (1976-1980), Director of Marketing with staff of 40-50 and direct reporting group of eight.

1973-1975, successively Sales Manager, Middle States; Product Manager, Senior Product Manager.

Achievements:
- accomplished spectacular turnaround for Division, which since 1976 has become a leader in the industry noted for its marketing and earnings.
- earlier as Product Manager produced significant sales gains.

<u>1960-1970</u>   AAKEN A.G., Geneva, Switzerland, and Dayton, OH

<u>1970</u>   Permanently relocated to the U.S. to aid company in divestiture of Division, caused by merger. Aided in formation of Estoril Corp. for acquisition by Stevens & Burlington.

<u>1969-1972</u>   Temporarily relocated to U.S. to introduce chemical agents for textile industry. In 1971, additional responsibilities were assigned for the promotional coordination of dyes and chemicals in the U.S.
- accomplished high share of market for synthetic fabrics.
- increased company market share in all dyes and chemicals.

<u>1962-1968</u>   APPLICATION and DEVELOPMENT GROUP LEADER, Geneva
- aided in development of FWA application technology; awarded patents
- created technical literature, including comprehensive volume on new technology.
- wrote for many publications; held many speaking engagements; made promotional visits to the U.S. and many other markets; became leading expert in the field.
- Aaken became leader in chemical agents worldwide.

<u>EDUCATION</u>	C.E., Chemical Engineer, Stevens Institute, Hoboken, NJ, 1962. Subsequent training included spinning, weaving, dyeing finishing, printing, accounting, supervisory experience in departments of two of the largest companies in New Jersey.
<u>LANGUAGES</u>:	German, French, Spanish, Portuguese, Italian
<u>HOBBIES</u>:	Tennis, skiing, soccer, opera
<u>PERSONAL DATA</u>:	Age 40, married, three children, excellent health. Father was a chemical executive who traveled extensively in Europe with his family, giving me an opportunity to exercise my ability to learn languages with relative ease.

<u>REFERENCES AND FURTHER DATA ON REQUEST</u>

28 Bainbridge Place   Home (212) 123-4567
New York, NY (zip)   Office (212) 765-4321

R E S U M E

of

RICHARD STERN

Qualified as

SALES/MARKETING EXECUTIVE

***   Learned the techniques of sales management in the field
as a salesman. Developed new accounts, opened up new
territories. Handled key accounts.

***   Devised programs, displays, assortments to meet the
needs of new classes of trade. Expanded distribution.
Created new selling units producing better profits.
Recruited, trained, managed salesmen.

***   Excellent contacts nationally among mass merchandisers,
chains, department stores, stamp and mail order companies, drug chains and hardware wholesalers, supermarkets.

***   Experienced in budgeting, forecasting, advertising,
sales presentations, sales meetings, remuneration, new
product development.

(FOR FURTHER DATA, PLEASE SEE FOLLOWING PAGES)

EXPERIENCE

Sept. 1983-Present   (NAME OF COMPANY ON REQUEST)

NATIONAL SALES MANAGER for manufacturer of household products, casters, waxes, stains, cleaners, venetian blinds, plastic covers; 200 employees and a sales force of 40 covering the entire United States. Report to President. Responsible for:

- recruiting, training and directing salesmen.

- planning participation in appropriate trade shows.

- key account development, sales and supervision.

- sales forecasts, budgets, pricing and profitability.

- new product development, displays and packaging.

- preparation of essential sales tools such as sales training material, catalog pages, advertising planning.

Successful in:

- replacing unprofitable line with highly profitable new lines, increasing volume.

- effective repackaging of entire line.

- increasing sales by means of unique and exclusive exchange plan.

- opening new accounts, which added 20% to Company volume.

- developing strong accounts throughout the U.S. in areas where Company had been traditionally weak.

- meeting and outselling competitors in such accounts as Mass Merchandiser Catalog and Mail Order Companies, Variety Chains, Drug Chains, Supermarkets.

- making Company number one in field among all above classes of trade.

Travel extensively throughout the U.S.; maintain excellent contacts with major buyers nationally.

1980-1983 HAMILTON CREATIONS, INC., New York, NY

1979-1980, FIELD SALES MANAGER (Assistant to National Sales Manager) super vising sales force of 40 manufacturers' representatives with department st line and separate brand for mass merchandisers.

Responsible for:
- discovering ways to increase sales.

Accomplishments:
- worked with salesmen on short trips; achieved immediate results in opening new accounts for new department store line; appointed Field Sales Manager.
- found Company department store oriented; developed concepts for mass merchandisers to fit individual customer needs such as prearranged assortments using existing displays, for drug and hardware chains.
- sold hundreds of small new accounts and rack assortments without which new line would have been dropped.

1978-1979, SALESMAN, New York Metropolitan Area, for parent company and subsidiary selling consumer equipment: hampers, space savers, baskets, brushholders, tank cabinets, ice buckets, picnic kits, etc.

Responsible for:

- selling to major department stores and independent retailers.

Accomplishments:

- created effective promotions with major accounts.
- sold to new accounts including major home furnishing chain.
- increased volume over 20% in one year.

MILITARY SERVICE:

U.S. Navy, 1971-1973, Boatswain's Mate First Class.

EDUCATION:

B.S., Rutgers University, New Brunswick, NJ, 1977.

HOBBIES:

Tennis, bridge, chess.

PERSONAL DATA:

Age 31, married, two children, own home, excellent health. Willing to relocate.

REFERENCES AND FURTHER DATA ON REQUEST

278

100 Pound Ridge Road   Home (123) 456-7890
Clayton, MO (zip)   Office (246) 321-4567

R E S U M E

of

JOHN T. MORRIS

Qualified in

FINANCIAL MARKETING

***   Strong personal motivation with successful background in manage-
      ment, sales, corporate and individual financial planning, systems
      and organization and excellent record of volume and profit con-
      tributions in every position held from beginning of career. Able
      to conceive and implement broad, complex programs to reach new
      goals.

***   History of numerous top awards and commendations for setting
      and achieving high sales objectives as well as for developing
      marketing plans, motivating staff and raising branch offices
      to national leadership.

***   Experienced recruiter and trainer of top producers in the
      industry, consistently sought by competitive firms because of
      known qualities of outstanding leadership and empathy and ability
      to communicate.

***   Accustomed to negotiations at highest levels, assigned responsi-
      bilities for large accounts with resulting growth and develop-
      ment to major status under most competitive conditions.

***   Experienced in profit sharing, pension and insurance planning
      for major corporations, and in maximum EDP utilization.

(FOR FURTHER DATA, PLEASE SEE FOLLOWING PAGES)

EXPERIENCE

<u>1980-Present</u>   NEW HORIZONS RESEARCH CORP., St. Louis, MO

DIRECTOR of CLIENT RELATIONS for investment research company providing
investment management for portfolios of individuals, pension and
profit sharing funds, corporate accounts, trusts and institutions.
Investment recommendation featured in Forbe's (1/15/78). Responsible for:
- marketing management, marketing research, gaining new clients, liaison
  with existing clients.

Accomplishments:

- created complete marketing program where no program existed.
- trained network of Registered Representatives working for N.Y.S.E.
  member brokerage firms to sell our services.
- gained listing on Hemphill, Merrill, Hayden, Bache & Smith, Inc.
  approved list of investment advisors.
- initiated tax advisory program for professional individuals through a
  prominent Missouri law firm to assist with:

  * incorporating individuals
  * pensions and profit-sharing plans
  * deferred compensation
  * Keogh plans

- achieving letter of intent to manage $50 million in-house investment
  management program for large brokerage firm to begin in January upon
  expiration of contract with another firm.

<u>1975-1980</u>   CORVATH, HAYES CO., St. Louis, MO

MANAGER, St. Louis Office (earlier Assistant Manager), for national
brokerage with 80 offices from coast to coast and total assets
approaching $1 billion. The company handles retail, commercial and cor-
porate accounts and deals in preferred and common stock, corporate and
municipal bonds, mutual funds and insurance for corporations. Supervised
29 salesmen through three Assistant Managers and back-office staff of
nine. Responsible for:

- setting up new salesmen, training program, establishing guidelines for
  sales approaches, encouraging customer contacts.
- handling new stock and bond offering calendar.
- personal selling, providing investment ideas, generating sales.
- liaison with leading corporations whose stock is recommended.
- corporate profit-sharing, pension and insurance planning for major
  companies.

(continued)

Accomplishments:
- brought office to second most profitable nationally from a position
  seldom among top 20.
- recruited and trained the two top producers in the office who now
  rank among the top ten nationwide.
- personally generated substantial sales while concurrently effective
  in administrative duties.

1969-1975   CONROY ELLIMAN SECURITIES, Mission Hills, KS

SALESMAN FOR BROKERAGE FIRM.

- increased personal sales production over 200% in six years.
- awarded gold prize for generating $10,000 in commissions in one month.
- awarded diamond prize for generating $20,000 in commissions in one
  month.
- chosen to speak to 200 salesmen on Salesmanship at headquarters meeting
- won five-day trip to Hawaii in Mutual Funds Sales Contest.

1967-1969   MERRILL, SMITH & MORGAN, New York, NY

SECURITY ANALYST, RESEARCH TRAINEE for large brokerage firm. Received
excellent training for future personal development in financial selling,
service, and analysis.

EDUCATION:

B.S., Economics, University of Kansas, Kansas City, KS 1967

OUTSIDE ACTIVITIES:

Instructor, Adult Education Classes, N.Y. Stock Exchange program.
Coach, Youth Athletic Association baseball team.

MEMBERSHIPS:

Bond Club of Missouri, Member, Chamber of Commerce

PERSONAL DATA

Age 37, married, three children, own home, excellent health.

REFERENCES AND FURTHER DATA ON REQUEST

281

102 New Amsterdam Street   (213) 000-4441
Montebello, CA 00100

R E S U M E

of

MARION HOKENSON

OBJECTIVE

OFFICE, SALES and/or
GENERAL MANAGEMENT RESPONSIBILITIES

SUMMARY

***   Broad-based manager accustomed to supervision and
      leadership, with strong background in accounting,
      financial analysis, organization and sales direction.
      Record of contributions to improved policies,
      expanded sales and the implementation of efficient
      management procedures.

***   Extensively traveled throughout the U.S., attending
      and managing sales producing shows at major national,
      regional, and local conventions.

***   Earlier conducted own tax practice for individuals.

***   In short, thrive on responsibility, and able to
      supply wide range of skills.

EXPERIENCE

1979-Present   NEEDLE NOODLES, INC., Los Angeles, CA

MANAGER of multimillion dollar needlework company. Supervise
staff of five, plus art department with full-time and free-
lance personnel.

Responsible for office supervision, finance and sales:
- maintain all books of corporation, compile and analyze
   financial statements
- purchase all raw materials for production and all
   supplies for other operations
- supervise production in absence of owner
- set up, attend and manage trade shows throughout the
   U.S.; hire and supervise sales representatives; guide
   salesmen in their territory coverage and new account

Over....Please....

Responsible for: (Continued)

   generation and development; sell to thousands of
   specialty accounts

Accomplishments:
- upgraded reputation of company which had retrogressed
  under previous sales manager
- organized office which had been without direction
- participated effectively in all operations of this new
  successful business, with continuing significant contributions to growth, cost savings, policy and strategy

1975-1979   HENRY AUSTEN, ESQ , Garden City, CA

OFFICE MANAGER for attorney/C.P A. with tax practice

Responsible for:
- work distribution of accountancy clients
- writeups for accounts through 1040, 1120 and partnership
  tax return
- handling smaller clients from inception; setting up bookkeeping procedures for clients and indoctrinating them in
  maintaining the system
- supervision of internal per diem accountants
- checking all returns produced by firm

1974-1975   FRONTIER FABRICS, San Antonio, TX

ASSISTANT TREASURER for $5 million multicorporate company
with factored receivables handled by three different factors
Supervised from 5 to 25 employees in factor and sales, depend
ing on volume and production requirements.
- completely responsible for all factors' statements

Held same position with this company 1961-1964. In interim
period conducted tax practice for individuals while raising
family of three children.

PERSONAL DATA:

   Educated at San Francisco State College

   Excellent health

                REFERENCES AND FURTHER DATA ON REQUEST

37 East Corsica Street   Home (212) 765-4321
Blooming Grave, NY (zip)   Office (212) 123-4567

R E S U M E

of

FLORENCE DeW. HARDING

PERSONNEL EXECUTIVE

***   After receiving Master's Degree in Sociology at the
         University of Chicago, employed as Stewardess by
         United Airlines; promoted after six months to PR and
         training assignments.

***   Since that time and for 12 years to present, engaged
         in Personnel Administration and continuing study
         with increasingly important responsibilities for 3
         employers. Currently Personnel Director of $50
         million manufacturing company.

***   Experienced in labor relations, new employee indoc-
         trination programs, benefits, remuneration, job
         descriptions, employee review programs, security,
         recruiting to $50,000 annual salary level, Federal an
         State employment laws. Saved present employer hun-
         dreds of thousands of dollars in potential liability
         by instituting wage and salary increases under sal-
         ary equalization program between men and women more
         than 3 years ago.

***   Invited to conduct seminar in labor relations by
         leading international management association.
         Complimented on organization and content.

***   Age 35, married, B.B.A. and M.S. degrees, excellent
         health.

(FOR FURTHER DATA PLEASE SEE FOLLOWING PAGES)

EXPERIENCE

<u>1980-Present</u>   (NAME OF COMPANY ON REQUEST), New York Area

DIRECTOR OF PERSONNEL (started as Assistant Director) for
well-known manufacturer of communication equipment for industry, municipal, State and Federal law enforcement agencies, transit authorities and the Military. Supervise staff
of 10. Report to President. Responsible for:

- recruiting, wage and salary administration, records and
  procedures, employee benefits, employee relations and
  social activities and plant security.
- labor relations, settlement of union grievances, participation in union contract negotiations; appearances before
  the National Labor Relations Board.
- preparation of job descriptions for all clerical, administrative and executive personnel.
- manpower development planning.
- budget administration.
- employee food services.
- development and improvement of work flow forms; continuing study to improve existing programs.

Accomplishments:

- recognized potential impact of Fair Employment Practices
  Act; studied job responsibilities and titles; upgraded
  female employees; avoided litigation for unfair practices;
  estimated saving to company in potential liability of
  $780,000.
- credited with superior judgment in hiring middle and upper
  management executives to $50,000 annual remuneration.
- studied national labor scales by job classifications; recommended upgrading salary and piecework rates; avoided
  strike in 1978 which had previously occurred during every
  three-year negotiation period since 1969.
- improved employee cafeteria with better food quality,
  attractive lounges, recreation area.
- conducted regular program of employee indoctrination;
  reduced turnover rate by 43%.

<u>1975-1980</u>   CONTINENTAL AIRWAYS, INC., Kansas City, MO

MANAGER, Employee Motivation Services. Responsible for:

- in-flight and ground crew uniforms, training, motivation,
  grooming (3,000 women, 2,000 men) involving Flight Attendants, Pursers, Ticket Desk, Passenger Assistance, Mechanics, Porters, Marketing Personnel.
- grievance hearings and settlements as possible.
- budget of $3 million.

285

1975-1980   (continued)

Accomplishments:

- selected uniforms for 14 different employee categories,
  gained management approval, organized simultaneous
  changes for all employees and met established deadline.
  Changes previously had been accomplished in classification segments and were invariably late.
- set up training programs for Flight Attendants in smaller
  groups with superior results as shown by tests.
- improved employee service to public by initiating employee
  relations programs: meetings with top executives, better
  interemployee communications, prizes recognizing exceptional service, better employee ground facilities.

TRAINING SUPERVISOR,   Flight Attendants.

- set up new training program.
- conducted PR seminars throughout Greater Chicago area.

Earlier STEWARDESS (Flight Attendant) for six months.

EDUCATION:

   M.S., Sociology, University of Chicago, 1971.

   B.A., University of Chicago, Chicago, IL, 1970. Dean's
   List Junior and Senior years.   Elected to honorary
   society; Homecoming Queen.

   Special courses over a period of five years (evenings)
   at New York University in Personnel, Labor Relations for
   Non-Lawyers, Manpower Development Planning, Laws Relating to Employment.

HOBBIES:

   Golf, tennis, swimming, travel.

PERSONAL DATA:

   Married, one child, excellent health.

               REFERENCES AND FURTHER DATA ON REQUEST

286

213 Seesaw Avenue   (201) 00u-1234
Belmar, NJ 07000

R E S U M E

of

OTTO HELMSTETTER

PLANT/PRODUCTION MANAGER
METALWORKING AND PLASTIC

***   Qualified manager, experienced in metalworking production,
      equipment maintenance and supervision. Learned as apprentice
      in Germany; added to skills in assignments in the U.S. over
      a period of 19 years.

***   Competent in tool and die making, fixturing, welding, pro-
      duction planning and scheduling, purchasing equipment and
      materials, adapting equipment to accomplish better produc-
      tion, fabricating machines or parts from blueprints or
      sketches, engineering development work; and repair and re-
      building of industrial equipment.

***   Experience includes forging, heat treating, machining, EDM
      machines, design of fixtures and custom-made tools, plastic
      extrusion, compounding machinery, packaging machinery, in-
      dustrial and marine pumps.

***   Record of improving production efficiency, reducing costs,
      minimizing downtime, contributing to profitability.

***   Accustomed to supervision, setting standards, leading. A
      shirt-sleeve manager who can accomplish any mechanical job
      personally and show others how it should be accomplished.

(FOR FURTHER DETAILS SEE FOLLOWING PAGES)

287

EXPERIENCE

<u>1977-Present</u>   S.M.C. COMPANY, Carlstadt, NJ

PRODUCTION MANAGER of the largest shop for freight car and industrial repair on the East Coast. Report to the Vice President.

Responsible for:

- entire plant production

Accomplishments:

- improved planning and flow of work through shop by establishing new
  procedures and methods
- increased production and profits by proper delegation of responsibili
- competed successfully against other O.E.M.'s by providing quality
  workmanship with shorter delivery times

<u>1975-1977</u>   WESTINGHOUSE ELECTRIC CO., Service Shop, Saddle River, NJ

MECHANICAL SPECIALIST in the mechanical department of one of the largest
Westinghouse service shops in the U.S.A.

Responsible for:

- quoting, selling, planning and follow-through of all mechanical work
- repair and rebuilding of industrial equipment

Accomplishments:

- promoted from mechanical supervisor to mechanical specialist within
  four months
- designed custom-made tools to perform equipment repairs in the shop,
  as well as for on-site work
- made suggestions and submitted cost improvements resulting in savings
  in excess of $125,000.

<u>1969-1975</u>   WILLIAMS STEEL CO., INC., Purchase, NY

PLANT SUPERINTENDENT of $1.5 million manufacturer of tools and dies, en-
graving tools, molds, hobs and coining dies. Supervised 20 to 30 machinis
tool and diemakers, engravers; with complete general machine shop.

Responsible for:

- all manufacturing operations

Accomplishments:

- reorganized inefficient shop
- changed production flow; purchased new equipment; built new fixtures;
  separated inefficient personnel; reduced work crew from 36 to 16 top
  craftsmen and increased production

1968-1969   WESTOVER EXTRUDER CORP., Irvington, NJ

Manufacturer of plastic extruders, compounding machines and blow molding equipment. GENERAL FOREMAN of fabricating, welding, grinding, assembly, machine shop, auxiliary department and plant in Ohio. Supervised labor force of 100 to 125.

Responsible for:

  - administrative supervision

  - production from engineering to finished products

Accomplishments:

  - made needed corrections in disorganized and unsafe shop

  - set up new procedures, reduced downtime

Company moved to South Carolina.

1966-1968   STUMPF & KOERNER CORP., Chadwick, NJ

This U.S. branch of Germany-headquartered company manufactures plastic extruders and compounding machines. TECHNICAL SERVICE ENGINEER.

Responsible for:

  - installation of equipment, startups and troubleshooting

  - customer service

1960-1966   PROCTER & GAMBLE, Elizabeth, NJ

TOP ENGINEERING/DEVELOPMENT MACHINIST in packaging machinery plant of this giant international company. ACTING SUPERVISOR in absence of Supervisor.

Responsible for:

  - parts fabrication and assembly of prototype packaging machinery

Accomplishments:

  - fabricated automatic and semiautomatic machines from engineering instructions and drawings

  - started as machinist first class; promoted after six months

1956-1959   M. M. HOECHST GmbH, Waldenheim, Germany

WORKING FOREMAN, MAINTENANCE for manufacturer of paper-making machinery, power turbines, hydraulic transmissions and clutches.

1951-1956   FIELD SERVICE TECHNICIAN for above. Traveled throughout Europe.

1950-1951   IN TRAINING with above company.

1945-1949   Served MECHANIC APPRENTICESHIP with Zuyderzeeschleiferel Oelze, Waldenheim.

EDUCATION:

    Junior College, Germany, 1944-1945; Trade School, Germany, 1945-1948
    B.S., Rutgers University, 1964-1965.

LANGUAGES: Fluent German

PERSONAL DATA:

    Born March 31, 1930, married, two children, excellent health
    U.S.A. citizen

REFERENCES AND FURTHER DATA ON REQUEST

30 Hermitage
Chappaqua, NY 00000

Home (212) 070-3131
Office (212) 111-2222

R E S U M E

of

JOSEPH R. MAZDA

MANUFACTURING/OPERATIONS/GENERAL MANAGER

SUMMARY

***   From beginning of career, 1964, to present with leading manu-
facturer of metal components, starting as Engineer in Training
through seven promotions to present position as Director
of Manufacturing.

***   Record of creating cost savings, increasing R.O.I., consistently
gaining greater productivity, innovating in technology. Hold
three patents. Author of papers on worker motivations and precision instrument ball bearings.

***   Accomplished turnaround for deficient division, including new
products, new image, new customers and tripling of sales.

***   As head of new products committee, worked with major consultants,
found new product now ready for marketing, participated in two
acquisition negotiations.

***   Experienced in all forms of metalworking from forging and stamp-
ing to plating and assembly. Able to lead, communicate, motivate, decide.

(FOR FURTHER DETAILS, SEE FOLLOWING PAGES)

EXPERIENCE

<u>1964-Present</u>   PNEUMATIC BUSHING CO., DIV. DATRON INC.
                 Belgrade, NY

<u>1977-Present</u>, DIRECTOR OF MANUFACTURING for $160 million manufacturer
of precision parts. Operations include forging, stamping, heat treating, machining, precision grinding, polishing, plating, coating,
assembly. Supervise five U.S. plants with 5,000 employees.

Responsible for:
- complete operations of all plants, which includes 12 profit centers;
  participation in labor negotiations.

Accomplishments:
- monitor and document continuous cost performance analysis; reorganized staff to achieve 13% productivity improvement in 1979;
  reached 6% productivity improvement in 1978 with saving of $5 mil-
  lion.

- sponsored foreman efficiency reward programs involving series of
  personal meetings with 140 foremen providing leadership and communications, and establishing goals and incentives.
- improved on-time performance with customers; reduced overdue commit-
  ments.

- set, and with few exceptions met, R.O.I. objectives by profit centers.

- participated in factory computer control project expected to contribute further improvement in productivity.

- appointed to represent Company at elite Industrial Machinery Institute, member of Manufacturing Council; delivered paper before Institute "Improved Operations Through Tier Training."

- company received two awards for plant safety record - from Datron -
  and more are forthcoming in 1980.

- appointed to labor negotiating committee.

- improved scrap by 12%.

<u>1974-1977</u>   GENERAL MANUFACTURING MANAGER

Responsibilities much as described before, for four plants in New
Jersey.

<u>1973-1974</u>   DIRECTOR OF PRODUCT DIVERSIFICATION

Headed new products committee; employed and worked with management
consulting firms such as Booz, Allen, Hamilton; personally recommended
new product (transmission units) now ready for marketing. Also involved
in two acquisition negotiations.

1970-1973   PROJECT MANAGER

Assigned to correct operating deficiencies in division:

- conducted marketing research; called on prospective customers;
  created new product line and identity; added major new high
  precision product line for computers, missiles, space vehicles;
  tripled sales.

1964-1970 Successively, Engineer in Training, Application Engineer,
Senior Engineer in Charge, Engineering Manager.

EDUCATION:

Degree, Management Engineering, M.I.T., Cambridge, MA. Minor:
Mechanical Engineering with Electrical Engineering, 1964.

Harvard University School of Business Administration, intensive Executive Development Program sponsored by Datron.

EXTRACURRICULAR ACTIVITIES:

Secretary and Honor Board (elected) Interfraternity Council.
Summer jobs each year 1958-1961; Engineering Assistant; Crib Attendant
(Pratt & Whitney); Maintenance, Connecticut General.

PROFESSIONAL MEMBERSHIPS:

Science Foundation, Air Force Association, Component Manufacturers
Association (Tech subcommittee), MPI (Machinery Products Institute).

COMMUNITY ACTIVITIES:

Vice Chairman, Zoning Board of Appeals, Chappaqua
Chairman, Corporate Gifts (raised $250,000, 1977-1978)
Vice Chairman, Board of Special Assessor
President, High Gee Association
Justice of the Peace

COMPANY ACTIVITIES:

Chairman, U.S. Savings Bond Drive
Company won three awards for percent of participation, increases in
 new enrollments, increases in amounts deducted, 1977.
New York Committee on Business Planning.

HOBBIES:

Tennis, platform tennis, sailing, cross country skiing, hunting,
fishing, travel, electronic assemblies.

PERSONAL DATA:

Age 38, married, three children, own home, excellent health.

REFERENCES AND FURTHER DATA ON REQUEST

196 Garth Road   Home (914) 725-5687
Scarsdale, New York 10583   Office (212) 687-2323

R E S U M E

of

ALLEN ROOSEVELT

OBJECTIVE

Involvement in real estate analysis and acquisition
for company with large funds available for investment
in real estate at optimum yields.

SUMMARY   AND   QUALIFICATIONS

* * *   Competent in real estate portfolio evaluation, and real
          estate appraisal and analysis, including all elements
          involved in the decision-making process for investment,
          divestment or use.

* * *   Special expertise in analysis and valuation of regional
          shopping centers; in the restructuring of all components
          of an income statement to estimate market value of income-
          producing properties of all kinds; for "Blue Ribbion"
          clients.

* * *   Experienced in interfacing with and advising clients--
          developers, bankers, corporations, major law firms.

* * *   Record of reliable analysis and creativity in the
          identification of real estate investment opportunities.

* * *   J.D. AND B.A. degrees. Age 32.

(FOR FURTHER DATA, PLEASE SEE FOLLOWING PAGES)

294

EXPERIENCE

1982-Present   ANALYTICAL ASSOCIATES, INC., Houston TX

ASSOCIATE (investment analyst/appraiser) for widely respected real estate consulting firm with "Fortune 500" clients.

Responsibilities and Accomplishments:
- land use, valuation, investment analysis, market and feasibility studies from inception to consummation; including net operating income and expense projections, tax and operating expense escalations, lease expirations, overage and/or percentage rent projections, discounted cash flow analyses; after considering physical condition, demographics (trends), location, debt structure and costs; to arrive at market value for the purposes of investment, portfolio review, disposition, mortgage financing, internal financial planning
- work of this nature nationally involving such diverse projects as regional shopping centers, office buildings, land development, apartments, industrial complexes, ranging in value from a few million dollars to $350 million or more

- specifically, such assignments include valuation of fees underlying major office buildings on Michigan Avenue (Chicago); land use and market studies for proposed large scale multifamily residential developments; appraisal of regional shopping centers in Ohio, Indiana and New Mexico; portfolio reviews of major REITS; valuation of properties net leased to A & P, Burger King, Singer Co. and other major retailers; appraisal of 25 industrial warehouses in eight different cities; investment analysis of real estate arm of major investment banking institution; valuation of office buildings and air rights over buildings in Houston involving such clients as B.I.G. Property Investors, Standard and Poor, Metropolitan, Houston Public Library, Illinois Consolidated Gas, Citibank, Baltusrol Development Corp., Western Pacific

- the preparation of opinions used as the basis for multimillion-dollar investment or divestment decisions

- most of the above activities require the computation of pretax and aftertax yields

- interfacing with clients as to advisability of purchasing fees, air rights, major tenant equity interests in proposed office buildings, and lease negotiations (for major office space)

1980-1982   EQUITABLE LIFE ASSURANCE COMPANY, Dallas, TX

REAL ESTATE INVESTMENT ANALYST for insurance company with assets of $1.4 billion.

Responsible for:
- analysis of purchase and development of raw land into apartments, condominiums and office buildings

295

- recommendations with respect to problem loans
- legal review of purchases, sales, underwritings; selection of and
  coordination with local counsel for bankruptcies and foreclosures
- appraisals for insurance and valuations for sales
- work on major bankruptcy involving company loans of $8 million

Accomplishments:
- recommended better utilization of accelerated depreciation, prepaid
  interest and other tax advantages to shelter income
- recommended studies of residual value of property, maximization of
  useful life, projection of income and expenses, capital gains, and
  the recapture of excess depreciation on individual properties to
  increase return on invested assets
- instrumental in arranging $6 million in tax-free income by putting
  together a package of five wholly owned apartment complexes and
  avoiding a capital gain from their sale by retaining ownership and
  mortgaging through a California S&L company

1979   CLAYTON ADVERTISING INC, Dallas, TX

ASSISTANT ACCOUNT MANAGER. Decided to return to real estate field.

1978-1979   SMITH & CO., Salt Lake City, UT

REAL ESTATE BROKER for largest full-service real estate company in the
Rocky Mountain region, managing more than $250 million in property and
sales exceeding $100 million.

1976-1978   DOBERMAN & PINCHER, Salt Lake City, UT

LAW CLERK, INSTRUCTOR in real estate school owned and operated by this
law firm. Students achieved the highest examination-passing percentage
in the state.

EDUCATION:

J.D., Moravian University, Logan UT; Legal Aid and Defender Program;
    National Moot Court Competition, Interschool
B.A., History, Miami University of Ohio, 1973. Active in intramural
    sports. Editor of Compos Mentis paper.
Rice University Real Estate Institute, 1974-Present (six courses)
Courses 1A and 1B sponsored by the American Institute of Real Estate
Appraisers

ACCREDITATIONS:

Licensed Real Estate Salesman in third year at law school
Licensed Real Estate Broker immediately upon graduation
Member, Real Estate Board of Texas, Inc.

296

HOBBIES:

Handball, platform tennis, tennis, bridge, riding

PERSONAL DATA:

Single, engaged to be married, excellent health

REFERENCES AND FURTHER DATA ON REQUEST

1905 Plymouth Street
New York, NY 10023

Home (212) 362-9232
Office (212) 736-8900
X39

R E S U M E

of

GRACE COOLIDGE

OBJECTIVE

Sportswear buyer; buying office market
representative

QUALIFICATIONS and SUMMARY

Experienced sportswear buyer (5 years) for chain of
23 quality department stores with record of planning
and producing volume multiplication, and introducing
new departmental subdivisions, new concepts and new
lines.

EXPERIENCE

1979-Present   FEDERATED RETAILERS, INC., New York, NY

1983-Present   BUYER, SPORTSWEAR, for chain of 23 department stores
in 12 states throughout the Midwest. Total volume approximately
$41 million; sportswear $12 million. Quality moderate to better;
emphasis on brand names using such resources as Trissi, Devon,
Fire Islander, Ship 'n Shore, Koret, Levi, Dunloggin and some
lower-priced lines. Report to Divisional Merchandise Manager.

Responsible for:
- buying for all stores, with an open-to-buy of $5.0 million
- all missy sportswear - coordinates, separates, blouses, skirts
  sweaters; also large sizes
- all swimwear, with $500,000 O-T-B
- junior and missy designer jeans
- exercise wear
- planning; accompanying individual store executives on market
  trips

Accomplishments:
- instituted Danskin program using warehouse as a distribution
  center; developed volume as follows: 1983, 4,000 units; 1984,
  10,000 units (est.)
- introduced Calvin Klein jeans in 2 stores, now featured in all
  stores; volume rose from zero to 7,000 units (denim and corduroy),
  1984
- developed "large size" sportswear department started in 4 stores,
  now expanded to 13, all successful
- started rapidly growing basic denim and stretch gabardine
  programs throughout chain

1979-1983 FEDERATED RETAILERS CORP., Dayton, OH

DEPARTMENT MANAGER, Sportswear Department, for $1.5 million junior
department store. Reported to Store Manager.

Responsible for:
- all aspects of day-to-day departmental management including stock,
  inventory, scheduling, markdowns
- regular New York buying trips

Accomplishments:
- increased departmental volume from $230,000 in 1974 to $480,000 in 1978;
  doubled space of department
- found and built important new resources
- contributed highest percent increase in sportswear of any store in
  chain in 1977-1978
- promoted and assigned to buying for all stores at New York City
  headquarters

EDUCATION:

B.A. degree, Bowdoin College, Brunswick, ME, 1979
Major: Fashion Merchandising and Retailing; Dean's List.
As extracurricular activity, coordinated four fashion shows, two each for
Butterick and Vogue. Designed the sets, arranged lighting, selected models,
prepared and did the commentary.

SUMMER JOBS (high school and college):
1977-1979 THOM McAN SHOES, Hanover, NH, SALESPERSON, CASHIER
1975-1977 BELLIN'S DEPARTMENT STORE, Portland, ME, STOCKROOM CLERK; CASHIER

HOBBIES:

Reading, skiing, tennis, cooking

PERSONAL DATA:

Age 24, single, good health

REFERENCES AND FURTHER DATA ON REQUEST

37 Robe Boulevard   Home (123) 456-7890
Pasadena, CA (zip)   Office (123) 654-3210

R E S U M E

of

TAYLOR GIMBEL

RETAIL EXECUTIVE/DIVISIONAL MERCHANDISE MANAGER/STORE MANAGER

***   Progressive and successful career in retailing
            from Trainee to Merchandise Manager with major
            Los Angeles department store.

***   Record of efficient departmental reorganizations,
            consistent volume increases; innovative promo-
            tional ideas, new display and packaging concepts.

***   Develop buyer confidence and find strategies to
            maximize profits and volume.

            (FOR FURTHER DATA, PLEASE SEE FOLLOWING PAGES)

300

BUSINESS EXPERIENCE

<u>1977-Present</u> WILSHIRE DEPARTMENT STORES, Los Angeles, CA, internationally known $1 billion plus department store retailer with branches in major metropolitan areas.

<u>1984-Present</u>, MERCHANDISE MANAGER, Pasadena, CA, with additional assignment as Supervisor of $24 million branch store. Responsible for:

- merchandising Major Appliances, Television, Radios and Stereo Sound Studio, Air Conditioners, Housewares, Budget Store, Auto Shop; with departmental sales of $10 million.

Examples of Accomplishments:

- overcame poor sales of T.V.'s, stereo systems and service contracts.
- changed location, improved display with new display concept, improved product emphasis and sales presentation; increased sales 27% in first year (20% over plan and best increase among all branches).
- surmounted loss of housewares space reduction of 40% by better identification of potential bestsellers, placing orders accordingly, conceiving new display presentation; increased sales 12% above plan, and only 15% below previous year in larger space.

<u>1984</u>, MERCHANDISE MANAGER, San Diego, CA, for Leisure Living, Housewares, Budget Store, Toys, Auto Shop.

Examples of Accomplishments:

- developed new floor plan for poorly organized Housewares Department; created new displays, impulse shopping atmosphere, improved traffic flow. Major elements of play were adopted as prototypes for all Wilshire stores; increased Fall sales 13% in first year (10% above plan), the highest percentage increase among all departments and stores in Division. Increased spring sales 9%, second largest Housewares increase among all stores.
- for entire departmental responsibilities achieved first, second or third best percentage increases among all stores.

<u>Jan. 1983-Jan. 1984</u>, MERCHANDISE MANAGER, Long Beach, CA, for Men's Store, Silver, Luggage, Cameras, Fine Jewelry.

- increased volume 7%.

<u>July 1981-Feb. 1983</u>, BUYER, Men's Underwear, Hosiery, Handkerchiefs, and Scarves, Los Angeles, CA.

- started new trend in men's accessories; imported new and different products from Europe; created $100,000 new volume in six months.
- conceived handkerchiefs promotion based on new approach; used with great success by manufacturer nationally after Wilshire introduction.
- designed new men's underwear display fixture now used in all stores.

301

<u>1978-1981</u> BUYER, Men's Underwear and Hosiery, Main Store

- originated theme "Look as Well Inside as Outside"; sold $27,000
  in three days.
- rated most profitable Buyer for Company 1968.
- gave vendors responsibility for departmental mark-on percentages.
- appointed Chairman, Corporate Buying Committee.

<u>1970-1978</u> MEYER AND DANIELS, Portland, OR

<u>July 1978-Dec. 1978</u> BUYER, Men's Shirts, Hosiery, Pajamas, Robes

<u>1976-1978</u> BUYER, Men's Dress Shirts, Hosiery

- created unique promotion still used by Company; at first promotion sold
  entire stock in one day.
- achieved departmental net profit of 20.5%.
- increased volume from $4 million to $6 million in one year.

<u>June 1975-Feb. 1976</u> BUYER, Appliances

<u>1970-1975</u> Successively Trainee, Head of Stock, Assistant Buyer,
           Associate Buyer.

<u>MILITARY SERVICE</u>: U.S. Navy, Shore Patrol, 1968-1970

<u>EDUCATION</u>:   <u>B.A.</u>, History and Business Administration, University
                  of California at Los Angeles.

                  <u>Ph.D.</u>, Political Science and Philosophy, 1967.
                  Certificate, Stanford University of Retailing, 1972.

<u>PUBLICATIONS</u>:   "What's Wrong with Housewares," Housewares Magazine.
                  "Merchandise Review," Men's Furnishings.
                  "Merchandise Review," Men's Underwear.

<u>HOBBIES</u>:   All sports, hiking, travel.

<u>PERSONAL DATA</u>:   Born 2/15/39, married, two children, excellent health.
                  Willing to relocate.

<u>REFERENCES AND FURTHER DATA ON REQUEST</u>

302

845 Fifth Avenue
New York, NY 10003

Home (212) 000-0000
Office (212) 000-0000

R E S U M E

SUSAN ANTHONY

OBJECTIVE: Position in sales

QUALIFICATIONS: Experience in dealing with people and problems in present position and in earlier part-time jobs during high
school and college years. Extensive theater experience
and education. Some earlier teaching experience in
drama and dance.

PERSONAL DATA: Age 22, single, excellent health.

EDUCATION: B.S., Theater/Literature, Vassar College, Poughkeepsie,
NY, 1980. Dean's List. Departmental Honors. Served
Theater Internship at Kansas City Theater Center,
December 1979-February 1980, and at Connecticut Theater
Festival, June-August 1979. Managed Vassar Theater box
office; brought Broadway actors to Vassar.

EXPERIENCE: 1983-Present   TICKETRON, INC., New York, NY

TICKET AGENT. Responsible for:

- booking groups from around the world into a variety
  of cultural events in the U.S., including Broadway
  productions.

- suggesting suitable visits for various kinds of
  groups: club, religious, singing, etc.

On own initiative, provided itineraries, hotel and
restaurant reservations, activity schedules, tours,
and meetings with performers. (This is not a regular
service of the company.)

SUMMER JOBS: 1981   LORD & TAYLOR, New York, NY

ASSISTANT TO GENERAL MANAGER, Better Dresses

- analyzed sales reports from 11 stores

- analyzed inventories

- aided in selection of Fall merchandise

303

<u>1980-1981</u> (two years) DANA WOMEN'S FASHIONS,
                          New York, NY

ASSISTANT SALES MANAGER

<u>1979</u>, Taught drama at the New School; drama and dance
       in Afghanistan
<u>1978</u>, Taught drama at children's camp

THEATER: Participated in leading or chorus parts in 9 shows,
                  Vassar

EXTRACURRICULAR: Student of ballet and modern dance

HOBBIES: Skiing, tennis, dance, gourmet cooking

REFERENCES: On request

304

1874 Blacksmith Drive   Home (201) 123-4567
West Branch, NJ (zip)   Office (212) 654-3210

R E S U M E

of

WILLIAM HOOVER

DISTRIBUTION/TRANSPORTATION EXECUTIVE

***   Record of profit contributions in millions of dollars to two
employers in 15 years through transportation cost savings
and efficiencies arising from wide experience and continuing
studies of transportation administration.

***   Qualified for executive management of corporate operations
involving personnel, facilities, equipment, procedures,
inventory control and policies. Strong experience in using
computer technology to establish programs and arrive at answers
to complex problems including inventory control and better turnover to generate improved cash flow.

***   Experienced in organization structure, manpower development,
space analysis and layout including sophisticated warehouse
planning. Demonstrated leadership qualities.

***   Experienced conference, association, seminar speaker, negotiator with government commissions and all major rate bureaus.

(FOR FURTHER DATA, PLEASE SEE FOLLOWING PAGES)

RECORD OF EMPLOYMENT

January 1970-Present   ESBEE QUALITY PRODUCTS CO., INC., Boonton, NJ

MANAGER, TRANSPORTATION of $250 million Company with 1,000 direct-to-
dealer salesmen calling nationally on retail stores. Staff of 15 including Analysts, Routing, Passenger, Travel, Private Transportation
Supervisors, Automobile Fleet Coordinator, Transportation Clerks.

Responsible for:

- direction and coordination of all transportation functions including
  recommendations of policies and procedures.
- coordination of established programs and procedures.
- providing direction to Branches and Manufacturing Units in establishing and maintaining adequate and efficient transportation services.
- all transportation costs and expenditures.
- administration of leasing of 1,250 automobiles for salesmen and
  executive staff and 250 delivery trucks.
- personnel travel and hotel accommodations.

In execution of responsibilities:

- issued Transportation Department Manual, Delivery Service Manual,
  Guidelines for Transportation Profit.
- assisted all units by counseling during periodic visits.
- participated in selection of Transportation personnel.
- maintained and communicated data in connection with newest development in transportation.

Accomplishments include:

- development of expanded own carriage program with a 1979 saving of
  $318,000.
- trucking cost savings: 1977, $100,000; 1978, $200,000; 1979, $400,000.
- utilization of Air Freight Forwarding for a $300,000 saving in first
  year.
- substitution of an automobile lease program for automobile allowance
  program reducing salesmen's out-of-pocket expenses and saving Corporation $100,000 annually.
- establishment of LCL and Truckload Commodity Rates to eliminate
  premium rates on mixed shipments resulting in annual corporate savings
  of $400,000 (prior to expansion of own carriage program).
- setting up additional consolidation terminal in Omaha supplementing
  New Jersey terminal. Created transportation savings of $250,000
  annually.
- by computer program eliminated scales, UPS and postage meters and
  operators in 12 branches. Saved $175,000 annually.
- developed Unitized Shipping Plan in-bound from Vendors. Expanded
  plan to include out-bound shipments to branches. Annual saving of
  $600,000.

306

1963-1970   ALLIED STORES, INC., New York, NY

GENERAL TRAFFIC MANAGER for $1 billion plus chain of 100 leading
department stores, supervising department of 85 people.

Accomplishments included:
- reduction of staff from 85 to 70 with annual saving of $150,000.
- development of Company Vendor Routing Guide.
- reduction in number of Shipper Association Memberships.
- improvement of shipping time to West Coast.
- increase in claims recoveries of $250,000.
- establishment of New York warehouse to handle imports.
- computer program to control imports. Reduced pier handling time by
  seven days per shipment.

1958-1963   PROPANE GAS COMPANY, Indianapolis, IN

Tank Car Supervisor, Rate Clerk, Transportation Clerk.

EDUCATION:

B.A., University of Indiana, Indianapolis, IN. Major, Business;
Minor, Transportation. Attended evening classes.

SPECIAL SEMINARS:

Attended advanced seminars in Transportation 1965-1975, evening classes.
The Management Grid, Scientific Methods, Inc., Washington, DC

COMMUNITY PARTICIPATION:

Chairman, Community Chest, three years. Citizen-of-the-Year Award.

MEMBERSHIPS:

President, The National Shippers Association
Board of Directors, Carrier Conference of BNT
American Traffic Club.

HOBBIES:

Chess, bridge, golf.

PERSONAL DATA:

Born 8/30/41, married, 2 children, excellent health. Willing to relocate.

REFERENCES AND FURTHER DATA ON REQUEST

307

APPENDIX B

USEFUL WORDS AND PHRASES

There are certain words that may help you to express yourself better and phrases and sentences typical of the succinct and vivid language of a résumé. The examples given below are intended only to guide you and to suggest style. Appraise them carefully before choosing a word or phrase that fits you best. Your résumé should be as distinctive as your fingerprints.

ABOUT YOUR EXPERIENCE

consistent record (of progress, growth, achievements, promotion)
demonstrably (successful, capable, effective)
effective
experienced
extensive
intensive
successful

in-depth, comprehensive, of wide scope, wide, broad, diversified, varied
intimate (familiarity with rules, regulations, procedures)
progressive
solid
complete
thoroughgoing

ABOUT YOU

---

accustomed, used to
administrator
analytical
broad gauge
(possess) communication skills
competent, capable, able
contest or award winner
contributor
contributory
controlled
coordinator
dedicated
developer
distinguished
dynamic
educated, schooled, trained
efficient, effective
exceptional (avoid
   "unexceptionable")
executive
generalist
harmonious
imaginative, conceptual
indoctrinated (with)

ingenious, inventive
talented
innovative, creative
leader
manager
motivated
motivator
multilingual, bilingual
negotiator
organizer
outstanding
planner
producer
reliable
responsible
skilled
specialist
strategist
stress resistant
student of
supervisor
trainee
trainer
traveled

ABOUT YOUR SKILLS AND ABILITIES

---

analyze
assist
communicate

lead
organize, systematize, install
plan

conceive (an idea)
contribute
create
create profit, profitability
delegate
develop
economize, save money
implement
innovate
learn

qualify for
recruit
solve problems
supervise, manage, administer
train, indoctrinate, teach
understand
work well with others, work in
   harmony
write, compose, create copy

ABOUT YOUR ACCOMPLISHMENTS

accomplished
achieved (example: company
   or division turnaround)
activated
administered
analyzed
composed
conceived
coordinated
contributed
created
designed
developed
directed
expanded
generated
guided
invented

launched
led
managed
marketed
motivated
originated
planned
produced
progressed
reduced (expenses)
reorganized
restored (profit)
saved
streamlined
succeeded
supervised
trained

ADVERTISING

Credited with novel concepts and creative approaches to the production of scores of recognized 30- and 60-second prime-time TV spot commercials for leading national advertisers.

Complete knowledge of the application of graphics to good design with ability to curtail cost.

Developer of creative response-generating themes for major national advertisers. Worked on Chrysler, ALL (cereal), Mr. Coffee, Alka Seltzer, Clairol, other accounts. Exciting copywriter. Award winner.

ADMINISTRATION

After 15 years in public service, interested in making a career change to the private sector and qualified in personnel, college administration, recruiting, manpower development, general administration.

ADMINISTRATIVE ASSISTANT

Six years of secretarial and other office experience as receptionist, bookkeeper, filing clerk, and PBX operator with a variety of service companies: law firm, management consultant, insurance company, advertising agency. Type accurately 60 to 65 words a minute, with skills increasing continuously.

CONSTRUCTION

Comprehensive experience in the financial and administrative management of large engineering and construction projects overseas and in the United States involving diverse heavy industrial and military installations; assured their profitable completion.

Demonstrated management competence and broad engineering comprehension in coordinating diverse engineering disciplines to effect optimum results in adhering to completion schedules and maintaining high quality, safe design, and construction.

ENTRY

Single, young, motivated, willing to travel, willing to relocate.

Good education, consistently high academic grades, willingness to work hard to establish capability; concerned with and interested in major U.S. and world problems; experienced in working with general public during summer jobs and in retail selling since graduation from college last year. Harmonious, articulate, diligent. Knowledge of French and German.

EDUCATION

School psychologist and counselor, self-starting and innovative.

Eleven years of experience in the development of sound educational systems, administration and teaching. Cited in *The Last Twenty Years of Education in the United States,* 1st edition (1960–1980), Langston and Rhodes, 1981.

Listed in *Who's Who in Colleges and Universities,* 1967, 1968, 1969. Captain U.S. Army (Vietnam), Bronze and Silver Stars.

Publications (if any, list)

ENERGY

Record of major contributions in increased revenues, cost savings; in leadership and revitalization of underproductive departments; in research, analysis, and recommendations with respect to feed-stocks, tankage, storage, production and marketing optimization, cost control, economics, forecasting, budgeting.

EXECUTIVE (GENERAL)

Exceptionally consistent record of turning loss-operated companies into profitmakers; recently increased sales and production four-fold in less than three years.

Record of continuous promotion to positions of greater responsibility; currently holding P & L responsibility for multi-million dollar division where sales have tripled and a profit objective has been met. Fully equipped in all aspects of management; in developing management information systems; in full utilization of data processing; in long-range planning and implementation.

FINANCE

Author of program to expedite critical data to management leading to expansion (other).

Proven skill in defining requirements, procedures, methods, display, and report formats to keep management informed of progress.

Comprehensively trained and experienced in brokerage and investment banking, in both front office and back office procedures: portfolio management, Exchange, and S.E.C. compliance.

Record of strong profit contributions to employers.

Successful career as financial analyst, securities salesman, knowledgeable in all areas of brokerage, including municipal bonds, commodities, underwritings, placements, individual and corporate portfolio management. Competent trainer, leader, developer of manpower. Excellent public speaker, widely experienced in conducting seminars and adult education courses in securities and investment.

GENERAL

Comprehensively trained in every aspect of procedures.

Able to bring effective solutions to complex (mechanical, engineering, financial, marketing, pricing) problems.

Willing to undertake training. Capable of learning. Possess imagination to conceive goals and find ways to accomplish them, quality of leadership, and ability to communicate.

Labor intensive, capital intensive (industry).

Talent for recognizing better ways to accomplish business objectives through coordination, consolidation, systematization, retraining.

Able to see interdisciplinary relationships and express them effectively.

Ability to see what needs to be done, to do it or get it done in a general management capacity.

Ability to conceptualize and implement broad, complex programs to reach new goals.

HOTEL/RESTAURANT

Accustomed to complete management responsibilities for accounting and controls, front office, food and beverage, golf course, club house, entertainment, and other facilities; financial reporting, profit and cash flow projections; planning and development. Accomplished also in developing convention business, arranging and providing gourmet food service and high level of other services. Experienced in close analysis of operating figures and correction of other areas; in the use of EDP to assist the managerial function.

INSURANCE

Experienced in most aspects of insurance, with emphasis in the investigative and adjusting field, which includes extensive legal negotiations and autonomous discretion from major insurance companies to settle cases at the highest levels. Also general brokerage experience, including solicitation and development of accounts, counseling relative to insurance needs, complex underwriting evaluations, and placement of coverages by various carriers.

LAW

Awareness of legal needs of business and ability to provide clear answers and effective remedies for corporate legal problems.

MARKETING/SALES

Product student, market researcher, competition evaluator, sales planner, salesman.

Competent in developing existing customers; in finding new customers; in implementing sales plans; in maintaining customer loyalty.

Experienced in managing salesmen, training, recruiting, sales planning, utilizing all techniques (audiovisual, flip charts, advertising, contests, tie-ins, advance merchandising) to stimulate sales.

Intimately familiar with U.S. markets, business methods, requirements, and strategies. Record of creating sales and profits of significant proportions, measured in millions of dollars in diverse industries involving marketing to supermarkets, chains, department stores, government agencies, institutions, wholesalers, using brokers, agents, direct salesmen.

Expert in marketing wide range of ethical and proprietary pharmaceuticals and complex electronic health instrumentation products, with in-depth knowledge of markets, sales techniques, training methods. Skilled in communications. Numerous company awards for sales and other achievements. Accustomed to leading, training, and motivating large staffs and hundreds of employees.

Leader and developer of sales personnel for effective administration of greater responsibilities.

Expert in developing innovative packaging to enhance consumer response.

Effective market researcher, sales leader, and trainer with expertise in all kinds of packaging and creative sales ideas.

Demonstrated management ability in national marketing with strong following among chains, discounters, distributors; excellent personal salesman.

MANAGEMENT INFORMATION

Experienced in establishing effective management information systems; in the expanded use of EDP to provide critical data expeditiously; in cost accounting, inventory control, production control; in reducing lead time; in measuring productivity; in creating controls at all levels of production to identify profit leaks; in applying innovative methods of accomplishing corporate objectives and increased profitability.

OPERATIONS

Ability to analyze and reorganize corporate administrative procedures and use advanced techniques (word processing, communications center, electronic data processing) to achieve greater efficiency at lower cost.

PERSONNEL

Experienced recruiter and trainer of top producers in the industry; known for leadership and ability to communicate and identify with others.

Extensive educational background and practical experience in human relations, the latter as program developer for nonprofit organization working in Africa to improve the effectiveness of the organization's structures, human relations, and economic and health conditions of the nationals of Tanzania and Kenya, and of the organization's personnel. Conceived program and assigned to implement it.

PRODUCTION

Accomplished in organizing efficient production, in production control planning, and in the effective utilization of the complete range of metal fabricating equipment.

Successful record as president of own business, formerly director of industrial engineering for multimillion-dollar corporation. Experienced in the selection and evaluation of capital equipment needs, production control, rate setting, productivity standards and measurement, systems and procedures, plant layout, incentive plans, in power plant operation.

APPENDIX C

JOB RESPONSIBILITIES IN MAJOR JOB CLASSIFICATIONS

You may find it helpful to review the activities in certain job classifications. The list below does not include *all* job responsibilities.

Not all companies specify the same responsibilities. R&D as well as warehousing and shipping may sometimes be assigned to marketing and sometimes elsewhere. As a vice president of marketing you would be expected to be familiar with all the elements listed under that heading, depending on a company's organizational structure. As a sales manager you would be responsible only for the areas shown under that heading. You will get ideas about other responsibilities, such as product manager, from one or more of the résumés reproduced.

The classifications include most of the duties within the major functions of a company: marketing, finance, and production. Select your area of activity within these categories.

The list also includes personnel, purchasing, retail, data processing, and others selected somewhat arbitrarily; it could have been expanded *ad infinitum*. We wish to show that whatever the job classification, your résumé should discuss the responsibilities and accomplishments normally associated with that job. A sales manager, for example, must know the markets of the industry in question.

Use this section as a reminder of your responsibilities, so that you do not omit relevant and important activities with which you should be familiar.

ACCOUNTING

Act as cashier
Adjust entries
Age accounts receivable and accounts payable
Analyze intercompany expenses
Approve petty cash and checks
Bank reconciliations
Budgets, forecasts, and financial planning
Closing entries
Collect from debtors; pay creditors
Consolidate reports for parent company with recommendations
    as to standing and results of operations of local branches
Correspondence
Dispose promotional items
Examine salesmen's collections and promotional remittances
Examine weekly reports of branch managers and regional offices
Footings
Maintain books of original entry, general ledger, and subsidiary
    ledgers
Maintain records and control costs of inventory
Posting to the general ledger
Prepare regular payroll
Prepare reversing entries
Prepare taxes
Prepare various supporting schedules
Take off and post closing trial balance
Trial balance

AUDITING

Age receivables and payables

Analysis and evaluation of cash flow, fiscal and interim statements, and projected statements

Analytical audit of books of original entry and records

Analyze turnovers of receivables and payables

Cash counts

Close books

Comparative analysis of sales and financial statements between two or more fiscal periods

Compute breakeven inventory, estimate inventory, and estimate profit or loss

Conduct physical inventory

Confer with company's officers and accountants

Continuous reconciliations

Detailed analysis of balance sheet and P&L

Evaluate D&B ratings

Examine and check other audit reports

Examine bonds, stocks, important documents, contracts

Examine canceled checks and checks being held

Examine notes

Examine pension fund, welfare fund, vacation fund, unemployment fund, education fund, accrual fund

Examine shipping documents

Examine taxes

Financial and accounting analysis of diversified multidivisional corporations

Observe factory inventory flow and operations

Post to general ledger

Prepare entries: journal, adjusting, correcting, reversing

Prepare financial statements with opinions

Prepare, present, discuss, explain reports

Prepare taxes

Prepare various schedules

Send out trade checks and verifications
Systems suggestions
Take off trial balance and post closing trial balance
Work on books of original entry

DATA PROCESSING

Applications to inventory, production, accounts receivable, accounts payable, payroll, sales, shipping order processing

Budgets
Data centers
Diagnostic systems
Econometric models
Economic models
Educational systems
Forecasting
Hardware, selection of
Leased time
Management information
 systems

Minicomputer use
Models—financial, marketing,
 production
Procedural manuals
Programming
Real time
Scientific systems
Softwear, selection of
Training
Utilization, maximum

FINANCE

Acceleration of financial reporting
Accounting
Acquisitions and mergers
Audits and controls
Balance sheets
Bank reconciliations
Bank relationships
Budgets
Capital resource planning
Cash flow

Cash handling
C.P.A. accreditation
Chart of accounts
Compensation
Consolidations
Cost analysis
Credits and collections—bad debt ratios, accounts receivable, aging
Economic correlations
EDP systems
Financial models
Financial public relations
Financial reporting
Financing
Forecasting
Foreign currency fluctuation
Insurance
Inventory control, turnover
Investment
Invoicing systems
Long-range planning
Management information systems
Negotiations
New York Stock Exchange, AMEX listings
New York Stock Exchange, AMEX reports
Pensions, fringe benefits, profit-sharing plans
Pricing formulas
Profit and loss reporting
Profitability
SEC reports, registrations, prospectuses
Staff training
Taxes
Terms of sale
Training
Underwritings

MARKETING

Sales management
  Budget
  Compensation
  District sales
  Expenses
  Field sales
  Incentives
  Markets
  National sales
  Organization
  Quotas
  Regional sales
  Sales meetings
  Sales planning
  Sales training
  Territory routing
Sales promotion
  Brochures
  Budget
  Circulars
  Direct mail
  Display
  Merchandising
  Packaging
  Presentations
  Promotions
Public Relations
  Budget
  Employee public
    relations
  Media liaison
  Planning

Press releases
Speech writing
Legal liaison
  Advertising agreements
  Co-op advertising
  Discounts, pricing
  Sherman antitrust
Computer utilization
Planning
Product management
  (marketing in microcosm)
Research and development
  Budget
  Market products
  New products
  Obsolescence
  Old products
  Product evaluation
  Quality comparisons
Advertising
  Agency relations
  Budgets
  Contests
  Copy, copy testing
  Legal liaison
  Media: print, TV, radio
  Production
  Themes
Market research
  Cost projections
  Demography
  Market testing

New market planning
Pricing
Forecasting

Pricing (pricing for profit)
Warehousing and shipping
(distribution)

PERSONNEL, INDUSTRIAL RELATIONS, AND MANPOWER DEVELOPMENT

Administration, wage and
salary
Arbitrations
Bonding
Budget
Community relations
Computer utilization
Credit unions
Disability
Discipline
Employee orientation
Employee productivity
reviews
Employee public relations
Fair Employment Practices
Act
Food service
Grievances
Group insurance
Hiring
Interviewing
Job description

Labor negotiations
Legal liaison
Loans
Major medical insurance
Manpower planning
Medical department
Morale
National Labor Relations
Board
OSHA (Occupational Safety
and Health Administration)
compliance
Policy and procedure
Records
Security
Social functions
Training programs
Unemployment compensation
Unemployment insurance
Welfare and pension plans
Worker's compensation

PRODUCTION

Automatic equipment
Automation
Budgets
Chemical engineering
Civil engineering
Computer utilization
Construction
Conveyorization
Cost control
Electrical engineering
Electronics engineering
Environment
Industrial engineering
Inventory control
Manpower planning
Mechanical engineering
Metallurgy
New construction, startup
Patents
Personnel

Plant layout
Power
Production control, scheduling, planning, flow
Purchasing, materials management
Quality control
Quality engineering
Recruiting
Research and development
Safety engineering
Space planning
Stampings, forgings, castings, extrusions
Systems
Tools and dies
Training
Warehousing and shipping
Waste disposal, recycling

PURCHASING AND MATERIALS MANAGEMENT

Alternate option purchasing
Blanket and annual contracts
Budget
Computer utilization
Economic Order Quantity (EOQ) purchasing
Economics
Environment
Inventory control

Legal liaison
Make or buy
Market studies
Packaging
Price trend analysis
Shortages
Strikes
Turnover
Value analysis

RETAIL

Acquisition
Administration
Advertising
Branch store administration, expansion
Budgeting
Buying
Cash flow
Computer utilization
Credit
Department layout
Display
Expansion
Financial planning
Financial reporting
Housekeeping
Inventory control
Leadership
Management information systems

Market analysis
Market changes
Markup, mark-on
Merchandise selection
Merchandising
Open-to-buy
Operations
Promotion
Quality control
Receiving
Retailing mathematics
Security
Shipping
Staffing
Store layout
Systems
Training

APPENDIX D

A DEFINITION OF EMPLOYMENT LEVELS USED IN THIS VOLUME

DEFINITIONS OF THE THREE MANAGEMENT LEVELS

In these pages I have referred to entry level, middle management, and upper management. The following broad definitions are a general guideline.

CLERICAL OR ENTRY LEVEL (NONDECISION MAKERS)

Any job that is repetitive in character and requires a minimum of training and decision-making to administer: filing, simple arithmetic, simple bookkeeping, reception, telephone operation, office machine operation, mail department work, "gal/guy Friday" duties, billing, telex operation, and the like.

MIDDLE MANAGEMENT (DECISION MAKERS)

Lower Middle Management

Supervision of clerical workers. Assignment of duties. Monitoring productivity.

Middle Middle Management

Supervision of group of lower middle managers. Salesman, traffic manager, engineer, purchasing agent, personnel manager, and so on.

Upper Middle Management

Management of department, with some autonomous authority.

UPPER MANAGEMENT (TACTICAL AND STRATEGIC PLANNING AND DECISION MAKING)

Management of division or function (marketing, finance, production, legal services, personnel, etc.); corporate officer; director.

RÉSUMÉS INDEX

(Listed by job objective)

Accounting, 233
Administration, nonprofit, 83
Advertising, 243, 247
Banking, 50, 245
Buyer, retail, 298
Career change
    from air force, 191
    from church, 96
    from education, 197
    from navy, 194
    from nursing, 200
Construction, 249
Curator, museum, 93
Data processing, 175, 255
Distribution, transportation, 305
Editor, 70, 72
Engineering, structural, 271
Entry level, 44, 46
Executive
    finance, 268
    industrial, 88
    textiles, 75
Fashion, 265

Health care, 239, 259
Hotel management, 271
Law, 100, 103
Management, senior, general, 54, 67, 79
Marketing, 274, 276
    financial, 279
Merchandise manager, retail, 300
Mergers and acquisitions, 253
Military service, 32
Office administration, 282
Operations, 108
Personnel, 284
Plant management, metal, plastics, 287
Product management, 230
Production, 291
Public administration, 241
Real estate investment, 294
Sales, 62, 303
Sales manager, apparel, 120
Secretary, executive, 237

LETTERS INDEX

Answers to help-wanted advertising,
 173–175
Buyer, 178, 179
Career change, from army, 189
Consultant, 142
Corporation counsel, 146
Covering letter
 general, 165
 solicitation for referrals, 164
Data processing, 154
Executive search, speculative, 144
Financial, 145
Market research, 151

Marketing, 139, 147, 149
 international, 150
Oil exploration, 155
Proposal, job, 162
Public relations, 160
Real estate investment, 152
Research, marketing, economics,
 156
Research and development, 153
Sales, advertising, 148
Senior executive, 136, 143, 158
Television, 190
Third party endorsement, 161

GENERAL INDEX

Abbreviations used are explained at the beginning of the appropriate alphabetic sections.

AMEX, American Stock Exhange
Accomplishment résumé, 107–110
Accomplishments, identify your, 221
Advertising, answering help wanted,
    173–179
Age, influence on employment, 34
American Telephone and Telegraph
    Co., 186
Analytical questionnaire, 113
Art decoration, use in résumés, 20

Basic résumé, 44
Basic steps in writing, 113
Best places to locate a business, 203–
    204
Best Small Companies in America,
    The 200, 220
Boom towns/counties, 203–204
Broadcast letters, 131

Calendar, using the, 168-170
Career changes, 96, 188, 189, 191,
    197, 202–204
Chambers of Commerce, 206, 209
Chronological résumés, 48
  with summary, 53, 120–122
    how to prepare, 57–61
  with variation, 62–64
Classified advertising, help wanted, 6,
    186, 219
College placement offices, 218

Compuserve, 186
Conventions, 218
Corporate personnel departments,
    132, 216
Covering letters, 6, 154, 164
Creating a mailing list, 181—184

D. & B., Dun and Bradstreet
Doctoral degree, 31–32

E.D.P., Electronic Data Processing
Eastlink, 186
Education, influence on lifetime
    earnings, 42–43
Electronic bulletin boards, 186
Elements of a résumé, 25–37
Elite type, 130
Employment agencies, 215
Employment application forms, 214
Employment levels, defined, 328
Equal Opportunity Employment, 34
Executive search, 217

Fax, facsimile machine, 187
Forbes magazine, 220

Gender, 8–9
General Videotext Corp., 186
Getting interviews, 6–7
Getting ready to write your résumé,
    111

333

G.I. Information Services Co., 186
Government hiring, 216
Graphs and charts, 37

Harvard résumé, 87–91
Help-wanted advertising, 7
  classified, 6, 186, 215
  display, 7
  how to read and answer, 173–175
Housing
  affordability, 208
  highest priced markets, 205, 207
  projected best markets, 208

Inflation, 205
Interviewing, 210–213

Job campaigns, 166
  example of results, 167
  record keeping, 171–172
Job competition, 179
Job hunting in the computer/
    telecommunications age,
    185–187
Job responsibilities in major
    employment classifications,
    319
  accounting, 320
  auditing, 321
  data processing, 322
  finance, 322–323
  marketing, 324–325
  personnel, industrial relations,
    manpower development,
    325
  production, 326
  purchasing/materials management,
    326
  retail, 327
Job search
  how to conduct, 181–184
  maxims, 223
  suggestions for, 220
Job sources, 181–184

Letters. See Letters Index
Lists, mailing, 181–184

M.B.A., Master of Business
    Administration
MIS, Management Information
    Systems
Mailing lists, creating your personal,
    181–184
Management consultants, 218
Men and women and résumés, 8–9
Military service, 32, 124

Narrative résumé, examples of, 92
Nature of the résumé, 13
Need for a superior résumé, 14–18

P. & L., profit and loss statement
P.R., public relations
Personal data, 33
Personality conflict, 35
Personnel departments, 215, 216–217
  when to bypass, 132
Photographs, 37
Pica type, 129
Preparation for writing résumé and for
    the job search, 111
Prodigy Service Co., 187
Public libraries, 218

Quality of life, 203–204, 209
Quantum PC-Link, 187
Questionnaire for personal analysis,
    113

R.N., Registered Nurse
References, use of, 27
Relocation, housing, inflation, 203–
    204, 205
Résumé
  creative, 66
  criticisms of, 23, 24
  definition of, 1
  elements of, 25–37
  examples. See Résumés Index
  examples, supplementary, 229
  functional, 3–4, 68
  language, 22
  length, 19–20
  methodology, 57–61

multiplicity of styles of, 39–40
nature of, 13
need for a, 14–18
perfect, 20
professional, 99–106
reading time, 20, 22
reasons for writing a, 11–12, 16
reproduction, 127–130
types of, 4–5
typing, 127–130
usage, 8
what to include, 27–37
what to omit, 25–27
what to write, 123–126
writing your, basic steps, 111, 113, 123
Roget's Thesaurus, 185

S.E.C., Securities and Exchange
    Commission
S.I.C., Standard Industrial
    Classification, 182–186
Sales and broadcast letters, how to
    write and use, 131–167

Self-analysis of questionnaire, 113–121
    guidance in answering, 116–121
Services available to the job seeker,
    68, 72, 74, 213
Speaking skills, 187
Stanhope, Philip Dormer, 15
Stationery, 131
Supplementary résumé examples,
    229
Survey, how to get interviews, 6

Tele-Communications, Inc., 186
Ten Résumé Styles, The, 41–110
    reasons for, 39
Temporary help, 217
Testimonials, 37
Tests, aptitude, 36
Typing, 127–130
Typical executive, 227

Useful words and phrases, 308

Wharton Econometrics, 207